About the author

Don Farr was born and raised in southwest London. He was educated at Emanuel School, Wandsworth, where his lifelong interest in the First World War was kindled. The peripatetic nature of his career in the Diplomatic Service, which took him to most parts of the world over a period of forty years, curbed somewhat his ability to pursue this interest. But since his retirement in 1996 he has been able to make frequent visits to the battlefields of the Western Front, the primary focus of his interest in the Great War. These visits have made a major contribution to the research he has carried out in preparing for the writing of his two books. The first of these, 'The Silent General', a biography of General Sir Henry Horne, was published in 2007.

Don Farr is married with three grown-up children. He and his wife live in Wokingham, Berkshire.

Mons 1914–1918

The Beginning and the End

Mons Town Hall

MONS 1914–1918

The Beginning and the End

Don Farr

Helion & Company Ltd

Helion & Company Limited
26 Willow Road
Solihull
West Midlands
B91 1UE
England
Tel. 0121 705 3393
Fax 0121 711 4075
Email: publishing@helion.co.uk
Website: www.helion.co.uk

Published by Helion & Company 2008
Designed and typeset by Farr out Publications, Wokingham, Berkshire
Cover designed by Farr out Publications
Printed by the Cromwell Press Ltd, Trowbridge, Wiltshire

Cover: 'The 5th Lancers re-enter Mons, November 1918', painting by Richard Caton Woodville (By kind permission of the Queen's Royal Lancers Museum) Back cover: 'The Angel of Mons', painting by Marcel Gillis (Courtesy of the Mons Musée de Guerre 1914/18 et 1940/45); Lt General Sir Arthur Currie (CO1539 Photograph courtesy of The Imperial War Museum, London); Mayor (Bourgmestre) Jean Lescarts (Courtesy of Mons Tourist Office); General Sir Henry Horne (Portrait by Sir Oswald Birley courtesy of Mrs Maive Impey)

ISBN 978-1-906033-28-6

British Library Cataloguing-in-Publication Data.
A catalogue record for this book is available from the British Library.

For details of other military history titles published by Helion & Company Limited contact the above address, or visit our website: http://www.helion.co.uk.

We always welcome receiving book proposals from prospective authors.

This Book is dedicated
with great affection
to my granchildren
in the hope that in due course
it may kindle in them
an interest in the history and lessons
of the Great War.

To:
Elliott Sebastian (Born 23 May 2000)
Joseph Edward (5 June 2001)
Oliver Thomas and Samuel Rupert (both 31 March 2003)
William Frederick (23 July 2003)
Olivia Ann (30 September 2003)
Alec Henry (12 October 2005)
and
Benjamin Charles (14 September 2008)

Contents

List of Illustrations. ix
Maps and Sketches xi
Acknowledgments xiii
Abbreviations. xv
Introduction 1

    I   The Road to Mons. 3
   II   The Town of Mons 10
  III The Battle of Mons, 23 August 1914: 3rd Division, II Corps. . . .13
  IV The Battle of Mons, 23 August 1914: 5th Division, II Corps. . . .27
   V The Start of the Retreat: 24 August 1914 34
  VI The Retreat: GHQ and I Corps. 39
 VII The Retreat: GHQ, II Corps and Le Cateau 49
VIII The Retreat: II Corps:the Aftermath of Le Cateau. 62
  IX 'The Angel of Mons'. 70
   X The Western Front 1914-16 74
  XI Mons Occupied: Part I 87
 XII Mons Occupied: Part II. 103
XIII The Western Front January 1917-July 1918 117
XIV The Campaign of 100 Days: August-November 1918 128
XV The Road Back to Mons: October-November 1918 142
XVI The Liberation of Mons: November 1918 148
XVII Epilogue 159

Appendix A: The Political Road to Mons 169
Appendix B: The Military Build-up to the War. 182
Appendix C: Order of Battle 191

Illustrations 194
Notes. 206
Bibliography 219
Index. 223

List of Illustrations

Front Cover: Detail from 'The 5th Lancers re-enter Mons, November 1918',
painting by Richard Caton Woodville (By kind permission of the
Queen's Royal Lancers Museum)
Frontispiece: Mons Town Hall

1. Field Marshal Sir John French 194
2. General Sir Horace Smith-Dorrien. 194
3. General Alexander von Kluck 195
4. Firm Friends: Generals Ferdinand Foch and Henry Wilson 195
5. Generals Joseph Joffre, Sir Douglas Haig and Ferdinand Foch . . . 196
6. Army Group Commander Crown Prince Rupprecht 196
7. General Sir Henry Horne 197
8. Lt General Sir Arthur Currie 197
9. Mayor (Bourgmestre) Jean Lescarts 198
10. The Mons Garde Civique just prior to Demobilisation, 21.8.14 . . . 198
11. The 4th Bn Royal Fusiliers resting on arrival in Mons, 22.8.14 . . . 199
12. A German Parade in the Grand-Place 199
13. Mayor Jean Lescarts' first Proclamation after the German
    capture of Mons, 24.8.14 200
14. A Typical Poster of the Occupation Years 200
15. 'The Angel of Mons' (painting by Marcel Gillis) 201
16. 'The 5th Lancers re-enter Mons, November 1918'
    (painting by Richard Caton Woodville) 201
17. Two pages from the Mons Golden Book (Livre d'Or), 11.11.18 . . . 202
18. Official Entry of Lt General Sir Arthur Currie into Mons, 11.11.18 . 203
19. General Sir Henry Horne taking the Salute of 7th Canadian
    Infantry Brigade at Mons, 15.11.18 203
20. Saint Symphorien Military Cemetery: 204
    Background: The German Memorial to 4th "Royal" Middlesex Regt
    First and Last Graves:
    Private J. Parr, First British fatality 21.8.14
    Lieut M. Dease, First Victoria Cross winner 23.8.14
    Major W. Abell, First British Officer fatality, 23.8.14
    2nd Lieut H. Holt, First RE Officer fatality 23.8.14
    Private G. Price, Last Canadian fatality, 11.11.18
    Private G. Ellison, Last British fatality, 11.11.18
21. The Memorial to the BEF at Mons 1914 and 1918,
    La Bascule Crossroads 205

Maps and Sketches

Maps

1. Present day Mons town centre 11
2. The Battle of Mons, 23-24 August 1914 14–15
3. The BEF Retirement from Mons, 24 August-5 September 1914 40
4. The Battle of Le Cateau, 26 August 1914 50
5. The Western Front 1915 76
6. The Western Front 1916-1917 .85
7. The German Spring/Summer Offensives 1918 120
8. The Campaign of 100 Days, 8 August-11 November 1918 129
9. The Liberation of Mons, 4-11 November 1918. 149

Sketches

1. The Mons Salient at Obourg and Nimy, 23 August 1914 17
2. The Royal Scots Fusiliers at Lock 1, 23 August 1914 22
3. The Royal Scots Fusiliers at Jemappes, 23 August 1914 22
4. The 1st Northumberland Fusiliers at Mariette, 23 August 1914 24
5. The 1st Royal West Kents - A Coy's action, 23 August 1914 27
6. The 1st East Surreys at Les Herbières, 23 August 1914 30
7. The 1st DCLI at Ville Pommeroeul, 23 August 1914 32
8. The Action at Elouges/Audregnies, 24 August 1914 37
9. The 2nd Royal Munster Fusiliers at Etreux, 27 August 1914 45
10. The Action at Néry, 1 September 1914 66

Acknowledgments

Appropriately I begin my acknowledgments in the town of Mons. On my initial research visit to the town I was taken in hand by the Deputy Manager of the Mons Tourist Office (*la Maison de Tourisme de la Région de Mons*), Michel Vasko, and the Director of the Mons Museum of the First and Second World Wars, Yves Bourdon. Michel put me in touch with local experts on Mons' First World War experiences, identified and supplied copies of unpublished diaries and other documents concerned with the period, garnered me some publicity in the local press, and arranged for me to participate in the commemoration ceremonies held each year on the anniversary of the Battle of Mons. Fortuitously my visit had coincided with the anniversary.

For his part Yves Bourdon gave me the free run of his Museum amd very kindly supplied copies of wartime posters and photographs as well as the evocative depiction of the 'Angel of Mons' by Marcel Gillis, the original of which hangs in the Museum. With Yves' permission I have used all this material as illustrations in the book.

Nearer to home I must record my gratitude to Captain Mick Holtby, the Curator of the Queen's Royal Lancers Museum, for permission to use a detail of Richard Caton Woodville's dramatic painting, 'The 5th Lancers re-enter Mons, November 1918' on the front cover of the book and for the whole painting to appear as one of the book's illustrations.

I should like to thank Loreen Brown, the Contracts Administrator at Hodder Company, for raising no objection to my using the photograph of Generals Foch and Sir Henry Wilson which appeared in the late Robin Neilland's book, *The Old Contemptibles*, published by John Murray (Publishers) in 2005. I must also record my appreciation of the kindness of Mrs Maive Impey in allowing me to use a photograph of her portrait by Sir Oswald Birley of her grandfather, General Lord Horne.

I am once again indebted to Alan Wakefield of the Imperial War Museum's Photo Archive for his help in identifying and providing copies of many of the prints used in this volume. Permission to use these prints was generously given by Yvonne Oliver of the Museum's Photographs Licensing.

Five of the sketches I have used have been copied from Michael Gavaghan's excellent illustrated pocket guide *Mons 1914*, one of his *The Forgotten Battles Series* on First World War battles involving the BEF. I am most grateful to Michael for the readiness with which he gave me permission to use these sketches.

I have once again leaned heavily for support on fellow members of the Thames Valley Branch of the Western Front Association. BarbaraTaylor very readily gave permission for me to use her amazingly clear map of the Le Cateau battlefield as well as producing from scratch at my request an equally clear sketch of the action at Néry. I am most grateful to her. I am equally obliged to Ian Cull and Patrick Moren who have most generously allowed me free access to their detailed research, in the former case into the 1st Royal Berkshires near Maroilles, and in the latter into the 2nd Royal Munsters at Etreux. Maurice Johnson thoughtfully made available to me some sketches of actions during the Battle of, and Retreat from, Mons, of which I have used two.

Finally Mike Lawson, Bridgeen Fox and Vic Sayer have also very kindly loaned me books and maps from their copious collections. Mike has also provided me with some background material, notably on a fellow denizen of Norfolk, Nurse Edith Cavell. At my request Mike also undertook some detailed research into German atrocities in the first weeks of the war. I am grateful to him for allowing me to make free use of his labours.

I must once again record my thanks to my publishers, Helion & Company Ltd, for enabling *Mons 1914-1918* to find its way into print. Demonstrating the triumph of hope over experience, Duncan Rogers accepted with little demur my proposal to write the book. I trust his faith will not prove misplaced. A special word of thanks too, to Claire Hill at Helion who does so much to ensure that the Company's books get into print in such an attractively readable state.

Last but not least I must once again put on record my gratitude to my wife Ann for her vital part in the preparation of this book for publication. She overcame her strong disinclination to be seen within a thousand miles of a World War One battlefield to accompany me to Mons to take notes and photographs. She has also coped with the typesetting, spell-checking, mapmaking, photograph setting, and no doubt other aspects of the black arts involved in dealing with computer hardware and software. I should mention too that she is responsible for the design of the book's front cover. I believe it to be a striking and compelling evocation of the grim realities of warfare.

Abbreviations

ADC(Gen)	Aide de Camp (General)
ANZAC	Australian and New Zealand Army Corps
Bart	Baronet
BEF	British Expeditionary Force
Bn	Battalion
Bt	Baronet
CB	Companion, Order of the Bath
CID	Committee of Imperial Defence
CIGS	Chief of the Imperial General Staff
C-in-C	Commander-in-Chief
Coy	Company
CRB	Commission for the Relief of Belgium
CSM	Company Sergeant Major
CVO	Companion, Royal Victorian Order
DCLI	Duke of Cornwall's Light Infantry
DMO	Director of Military Operations
DSO	Distinguished Service Order
DWR	Duke of Wellington's Regiment
FB	*Franc Belge* (Belgian Franc)
FM	Field Marshal
GAF	Group of Armies in Flanders
GCB	Knight Grand Cross, Order of the Bath
GCVO	Knight Grand Cross, Royal Victorian Order
GHQ	General Headquarters
GOC	General Officer Commanding
GOC-in-C	General Officer Commanding-in-Chief
GQG	*Grand Quartier Général* (French Supreme Headquarters)
GSO	General Staff Officer
HE	High Explosive
HLI	Highland Light Infantry (Glasgow Regt)
HMS	His Majesty's Ship
HQ	Headquarters
IRA	Irish Republican Army
IWM	Imperial War Museum
KCB	Knight Commander, Order of the Bath
KCIE	Knight Commander, Order of the Indian Empire
KCMG	Knight Commander, Order of St Michael and St George
KCVO	Knight Commander, Royal Victorian Order
Km(s)	Kilometre(s)
KOSB	King's Own Scottish Borderers
KOYLI	King's Own Yorkshire Light Infantry
KRRC	King's Royal Rifle Corps
MBE	Member, Order of the British Empire

MC	Military Cross
NATO	North Atlantic Treaty Organisation
MVO	Member, Royal Victorian Order
NCO	Non Commissioned Officer
OH	Official History of the Great War
OHL	*Oberste Heeresleitung* (German Supreme Headquarters)
POW(s)	Prisoner(s) of War
PPCLI	Princess Patricia's Canadian Light Infantry
QMG	Quartermaster General
RA	Royal (Regiment of) Artillery
RCR	Royal Canadian Rifles
RE	Royal Engineers
RFA	Royal Field Artillery
RFC	Royal Flying Corps
RGA	Royal Garrison Artillery
RHA	Royal Horse Artillery
RQMS	Regimental Quartermaster Sergeant
RWF	Royal Welsh Fusiliers
SHAPE	Supreme Headquarters Allied Powers Europe
SLI	Somerset Light Infantry
SWB	South Wales Borderers
VC	Victoria Cross
WFA	Western Front Association

Introduction

Early on the morning of 22 August 1914 a squadron of British cavalry gave chase, from their positions about two miles northeast of Mons, to a detachment of German Lancers. It is believed that, during this pursuit, the first British shot in anger of the First World War was fired. On 11 November 1918 some of the last shots of the Great War were exchanged in the same area.

In the four years two months and three weeks between these dates the quest for victory in northwest Europe had been largely fought out many miles away from Mons. After the day-long battle of 23 August 1914 in which the British Expeditionary Force successfully resisted the German attempts to achieve a breakthrough around Mons, they were obliged to retire to avoid being outflanked and possibly surrounded by the enemy. Thus began the Retreat from Mons which was to last 12 days, only ending when the BEF and their French allies turned and began the offensive which drove the Germans back to the River Aisne.

The stalemate which then ensued led to the formation of an unbroken line of trenches from the Channel to the Swiss frontier. This line was to become known as the Western Front. It trapped Mons and many other Belgian and French cities, towns and villages well behind the front lines and under an oppressive German occupation. It was more than four long years before Mons was to find itself once again within reach of the advancing allied armies. This culminated in the recapture and liberation of the town on the very last night of the war before the Armistice came into effect at 11h00 on 11 November 1918.

The liberation of Mons by the BEF First Army's Canadian Corps was to give particular pleasure to the officers and other ranks of the British Army, especially that handful still alive and on active service who had been present at the Battle of Mons over four years earlier. There it had all begun for the BEF and fittingly there it had finished. The commander of the liberating troops, General Sir Henry Horne, expressed the general satisfaction in his letter home on Armistice Day.

At 11h00 today hostilities ceased!.........We took Mons. We were well round it last night and early this morning we disposed of the Germans who made an attempt to hold it, and occupied the town. I am so pleased. I began at Mons and I end the fighting at Mons! The C-in-C was very pleased. I saw him today and told him.

How was it that an unpretentious Belgian town came to loom so large in the British national psyche, perhaps second only to the position occupied by Ypres? What accumulation of historical and military circumstances led to a British Expeditionary Force finding itself in Mons in 1914 and made it so special that its liberation should take place before the Armistice intervened? How did legends of divine intervention attach themselves so readily to the fighting around Mons? What did the inhabitants of Mons make of their town becoming the scene of heavy fighting at either end of the war? How did they cope with German occupation and what must have seemed little prospect for much of the time that

1

it would ever end? How was the liberation of the town accomplished? And, once accomplished, to what sort of future could the people of Mons look forward?

A simple recollection of their nation's and region's history would have suggested to the citizen of Mons in that fateful month of August 1914 that there was very little hope that they would avoid being fought over in a European conflagration such as the one that had been unleashed by the German invasion. Not for nothing had Belgium become known as the Cockpit of Europe. It had acquired that doleful reputation as a consequence of the number of military campaigns conducted, and pitched battles fought, on its soil, in total numbers far in excess of those conducted and fought in any other part of the Continent. As well as being a prominent part of the Cockpit, Mons was also seated firmly in the centre of what Charles de Gaulle termed 'the fatal avenue', that stretch of territory north and east of Paris running through Belgium and northern France, from the Moselle valley in the east to the Channel coast north from the River Somme estuary. It is over this area that, stretching back to mediaeval times, and even further, national rivalries involving the French, Germans, Spanish, Austrians, English and Dutch have been bloodily played out, finally ending, it must be hoped, with the Second World War.

The pages that follow are an attempt to offer answers to the questions posed above as the 90th anniversary of the end of the conflict which brought Mons to such international prominence is being observed.

Chapter I

The Road to Mons

On 4 August 1914 Great Britain declared war on Germany. Less than three weeks later, on the 22nd, British and German cavalry units exchanged shots which ushered in more than four years of bloody confrontation in northern France and Belgium. It began, and would end, close to the small Belgian town of Mons.

The political and military circumstances and events which led to a British Expeditionary Force finding itself at Mons in August 1914 are outlined in detail in the Appendices to this book. Suffice it to say here that war with Germany had long been expected and planned for by the Military Operations staff at the War Office in London, if less so by their political masters, the Liberal government of Prime Minister Herbert Asquith. Judging from two meetings hastily convened and chaired by the Prime Minister on the first two full days of the war (which were attended by all the relevant senior political, military and naval figures) the Government had no clear strategy for war worked out. It was largely in the absence of this that the meetings fell back on the plan (he would have said commitment) masterminded by Brigadier General Henry Wilson, the War Office's Director of Military Operations, to send an expeditionary force of six infantry divisions and five cavalry brigades to take up positions in the Maubeuge area on the left of the French armies.

The newly appointed Secretary of State for War, Field Marshal Lord Kitchener, was deeply concerned to learn that the British Expeditionary Force (BEF) was to be deployed in conformity with the role implied for it by the infamous Plan XVII[1], the French General Staff's blueprint for the conduct of war with Germany. The notorious shortcomings of this Plan are fully described in Appendix B. It could hardly have been better designed to play into the hands of the Germans seeking to implement the Schlieffen Plan[2], their own blueprint for victory in a two front war. Kitchener, instinctively suspecting what the Germans were up to, foresaw potential tragedy for the BEF, required to assemble dangerously close to the Belgian border and with little between it and the Channel, nearly 100 miles away, to cover the area through which the right wing of the German army was scheduled to advance.

Kitchener's advent was too late and his arguments insufficiently backed with persuasive evidence to force a change in the War Office's plans. But, to the intense annoyance of Wilson, who feared the effect it would have on the French, already disillusioned by British failure to honour Wilson's promise that the two countries' mobilisations would be synchronised, Kitchener was able to scale down the initial size of the BEF to four infantry and one enlarged cavalry divisions, leaving the only other two regular army infantry divisions at home on the implausible pretext that they might be needed to meet the threat of a possible German invasion.[3]

Whatever criticisms could be directed at the choice of area for the BEF's assembly, few could be levelled at the mechanics of the operation to get them there. The recall of the nearly 70,000 reservists needed to bring the BEF's units up to wartime establishment was set in motion on the day war was declared and mobilisation decreed. Kitting them out was more of a problem with local shortages of boots and items of uniform and equipment being reported. There was clearly no time for those recalled to the colours to be properly reintegrated or physically hardened before the great embarkation of men, equipment and horses destined for the French ports of Le Havre, Rouen and Boulogne began on 12 August. By the 17th the cross-Channel operation was virtually complete.

Under the overall command of Field Marshal Sir John French the BEF was made up of I Corps (1st and 2nd Divisions) commanded by Lt General Sir Douglas Haig, II Corps (3rd and 5th Divisions) commanded by Lt General Sir James Grierson and the Cavalry Division commanded by Major General Edmund Allenby. Sadly, General Grierson died of a heart attack on 17 August when on his way to the front. Lord Kitchener decided to replace him by General Sir Horace Smith-Dorrien, to the dismay of Sir John French, whose long-standing detestation of Smith-Dorrien was warmly reciprocated.

The choice of Sir John French to command the BEF was not to prove a happy one. As the senior serving soldier in the British Army (if you discount his brief period on the sidelines after he was forced to resign as Chief of the Imperial General Staff as a consequence of the 'Curragh Mutiny'[4]) no one could dispute his right to the position. But there were some, notably Kitchener and Haig, who doubted his suitability for it. French's reputation for dash and leadership had been established in the South African War where he had commanded the Cavalry Division and emerged with an enhanced reputation from a war which had destroyed those of many of his peers. But brilliance as a cavalry commander does not necessarily translate into brilliance, or even competence, as the commander of an army of all arms. This was to prove to be the case with Sir John. He was not helped by the ambivalent instructions he received from Lord Kitchener on taking over his new responsibilities. These told him to make 'every effort...to coincide most sympathetically with the plans and wishes of our Ally' while at the same time emphasising that his command was an entirely independent one and that he would in no case come under the orders of any Allied General.[5] In drafting these instructions Kitchener was understandably trying to prevent the BEF being sucked into some harebrained French offensive called for under Plan XVII, of which his opinion has already been recorded. But carrying out such instructions satisfactorily would have taxed minds a great deal more subtle than Sir John's.[6]

By 20 August the BEF was fully assembled near Maubeuge. Perhaps fortunately, given the hot weather and the new boots many of the reservist troops were wearing, their journeys from the arrival ports to the assembly areas had been made largely by train, the other ranks in the French railway wagons designed for 40 men or 8 horses, the officers in passenger carriages. But the discomforts of the travelling accommodation were more than offset by the rapturous welcome the British troops received from the local population at every one of their many stops.

The BEF's assembly area stretched from Maubeuge southwest towards Le Cateau, a distance of roughly 25 miles. Haig's I Corps were closest to Maubeuge with Smith-Dorrien's II Corps on their left and the Cavalry Division nearest to Le Cateau. The plan now envisaged for the French Fifth Army of General Charles Lanrezac and the BEF on their left was an advance into Belgium to take the offensive and sweep aside, or outflank, the supposedly weak right wing of the German Army. Despite the misgivings Sir John French had heard expressed by none other than Kitchener on the assumptions made by Plan XVII about the strength of the German right wing, he allowed himself to be convinced by the newly promoted Major General Henry Wilson, now his Deputy Chief of Staff at GHQ, that the French plan's assessments were sound. Ironically Sir John's confidence in Plan XVII was no longer, if it ever had been, shared by General Lanrezac whose Intelligence was already providing indications of the true strength of the German dispositions in front of him and their potentially baneful consequences for the allied left wing.

Whatever situation the two allied armies might find as they advanced into Belgium, the effectiveness of their response to it would have been greatly aided by close liaison between the respective Army Commanders and their staffs. Regrettably this was not to be the case. The British C-in-C's relationship with General Lanrezac was in marked contrast to that between him and the French Commander-in-Chief, General Joffre, which, despite their lack of a common language, was cordial, being based, at least initially, on mutual respect and Joffre's sensitive handling of the inter-allied relationship. The lack of a common language was also a handicap in the Lanrezac-French relationship but in this case it could not conceal from the British C-in-C the contempt in which the BEF in general and he in particular were held by the Frenchman, manifested as it was in heavy sarcasm at his expense which would have been unmistakable in whatever language it was expressed.[7] The consequent lack of consultation and communication between the two headquarters was to have potentially disastrous consequences and lead to a further deepening of the mutual mistrust.

The growing divergence between the French Fifth Army Intelligence's assessment of the strength and direction of advance of the German right wing and that of the Grand Quartier Général (GQG), the French Supreme Headquarters, was finally having an effect on the complacency of the latter. Fifth Army had learned that large numbers of cavalry belonging to the German Second Army had crossed the River Meuse from the south to the north bank at Huy, midway between Liège and Namur, which could only indicate that a significant wide flanking movement was underway. (Unbeknownst to Lanrezac or to the BEF, north of the Second German Army was the even larger First Army making its wider sweep which would bring it into collision with the BEF when it turned south.) In the light of what was now known to Lanrezac and reluctantly accepted by GQG, he was given permission to change the direction of his advance into Belgium from northeast to north. Regrettably he failed to convey his concerns at what might be developing to the BEF.

Lanrezac began his deployment into Belgium. Leaving one corps to cover the Meuse river crossings between Dinant and Givet on his right flank, the rest of his army took up positions along the line of the River Sambre between Namur and Charleroi. From here, he confirmed to GQG, he would be ready to counterattack any German attempt to advance between Namur and Charleroi to attack the French Fourth Army's left flank. That he did not set much store on

GQG's assessment of the situation, which foresaw this possibility, is evidenced by the fact that he also raised the prospect of a retirement by his own army becoming necessary if his estimate of the size of the German right wing proved more realistic than GQG's. Perhaps even worse than his neglect to convey his growing concerns to the BEF was his failure to confront Joffre with them. Not that the latter was at this stage prepared to accept any evidence of German deployments which would imply that Plan XVII was proving to be almost criminally guilty of having made assumptions of enemy intentions which were hopelessly wide of the mark. Ironically, but not uniquely in military annals, Lanrezac would soon pay the price for sounding alarmist and then being proved right, by losing his command.[8]

The BEF too began its deployment into Belgium in accordance with orders issued by GHQ on 20 August. These foresaw a three-day march beginning the following day to take up a line facing northeast between Lens (about 8 miles north of Mons) and Binche. It was intended to bring the BEF up into line with the French Fifth Army, also facing north east in conformity with Plan XVII. But as was by now known, even at GHQ, Lanrezac's army had changed its deployment to a line facing north. This seems to have been glossed over by a GHQ still almost totally unaware that the BEF was being set on a collision course with the hugely powerful German First Army.[9]

The BEF's march into Belgium was led by the Cavalry Division. They were followed by II Corps with I Corps bringing up the rear. The march, begun on 21 August, continued the following day with the aim of coming into alignment with the French Fifth Army so that a joint offensive could be launched on the 24th. But it was on the 22nd that the mounting evidence of massive German troop movements in front of the two allied armies reached a point where any plans for further advances, still less for offensive action, had to be replaced by plans for survival and extrication. To some extent these latter would be helped by tensions in the German High Command. General Alexander von Kluck, Commander of the German First Army which was on the right of the German advance, was concerned over the whereabouts of the BEF and wanted to advance down the Belgian and northern French coast in order to neutralise it. Had he been allowed to follow this strategy there is little doubt that the BEF would have been enveloped and destroyed. As it was, he was ordered to turn south prematurely by the Second Army Commander, General Karl Bülow, to close the gap opening up between the two German armies. This brought von Kluck's Army onto a southerly route which would lead straight to Mons.

With GQG intelligence assessments still minimising the size of the German right wing, and communications with Lanrezac's Army tenuous at best, the BEF was to a large extent thrown back on its own resources to establish the true situation. But Sir John French was to get some valuable information indirectly from the French Fifth Army. His Deputy Chief of Staff, Henry Wilson, had, in the absence of his superiors, received a visit from Lieutenant Edward Spears, the British Army liaison officer at Fifth Army HQ. Spears had expressed his concern that Lanrezac did not appear ready to sacrifice what he deemed to be very favourable defensive positions along the south bank of the Sambre for the sake of implementing the joint offensive with the BEF. Characteristically Wilson was ready to dismiss this alarmist (but entirely accurate) report but did agree to recommend that Sir John should visit Lanrezac as soon as possible to bring himself up to date on the latter's plans. Consequently, early on 22 August, Sir John set off for Fifth Army HQ at Chimay not knowing that Lanrezac was now at the HQ of his X Corps at Mettet. On his way French quite fortuitously bumped into Lieutenant Spears. The latter told him that, as a result of heavy fighting involving the Fifth Army's III and X Corps, in which they had come off much the worse, Lanrezac was no longer in a position to undertake the proposed joint offensive with the BEF. For good measure Spears passed on a warning he had picked up from Lanrezac's Intelligence that a grave threat to the BEF was building up on its left flank. Spears wanted Sir John to hear all this at first hand from Lanrezac, but the British C-in-C did not feel able to travel all the way to Mettet.[10]

For the moment Sir John did nothing to change his orders to the BEF. He was still in thrall to GQG, and its proponent Henry Wilson, and his earlier bruising encounter with Lanrezac had not left him inclined to set much store on anything gleaned from that source. His own BEF intelligence staff, efficiently and competently led by Colonel George Macdonogh, had also been finding it an uphill struggle to persuade GHQ of the accuracy and immediate relevance of their information, which had detected and reported signs of the size of the German threat well prior to the fateful day of 22 August. On this day Colonel Macdonogh was able to include in his reports not only Spears' information, but also intelligence gleaned from two other sources, air reconnaissance and the first encounters of the BEF's cavalry screen with their German opposite numbers.

Air reconnaissance was a new element in warfare. 1914 was only 10 years on from the first recorded powered flight in history but its potential had already been demonstrated to one of the main figures in the BEF, Sir Douglas Haig, who had been humiliated at the British Army's summer manoeuvres in 1912 by his opponent General Grierson's effective use of the fledgling air arm to outmanoeuvre him.[11] Haig had certainly taken aboard the implications for future military operations of his defeat, but Sir John French was still showing reluctance to set much store on the new resource. The Royal Flying Corps (RFC) was established in 1912 and by the outbreak of war was able to provide 4 squadrons to accompany the BEF to France. From 18 August they were based at Maubeuge from where, in their primitive aircraft and with a sketchy grasp of navigation, they launched their reconnaissance sorties. On the 22nd one of these reported that a massive body of German troops marching west from Brussels had wheeled southwest and was now heading in the general direction of Mons, but on a course which might well enable them to outflank the BEF. Other reports stated that a large German column had been observed near the town of Nivelles, halfway between Brussels and Mons. It seemed to be heading straight towards the advancing British.[12]

Collateral for these reports was now coming in from the British cavalry which had been in visual contact with the enemy but at too great a distance to bring on an engagement. Their observations were however adequate enough to indicate that a German column was approaching Mons from Brussels. (When this report was seen by Henry Wilson it was disparaged as exaggerated by an officer still unwilling to contemplate the possibility that Plan XVII had got things terribly wrong. A similar attitude was taken to the RFC's reconnaissance reports.)[13]

Early on 22 August saw the first engagement involving exchanges of fire. It involved British and German cavalry units. C Squadron of the 4th Royal Irish Dragoon Guards, commanded by Major Tom Bridges, had bivouacked overnight in a wood beside the Mons-Brussels road about two miles northeast of Mons. As they moved off in the direction of the village of Casteaux they spotted 4 German cuirassiers (lancers) heading cautiously towards them. Possibly sensing they may have been seen the German patrol turned around and began trotting back towards the town of Soignies. One of Bridges' troop commanders, Captain C B Hornby requested, and was given, permission to set off in pursuit with two troops. At an early stage in the pursuit one Corporal E Thomas dismounted briefly and fired off a round which has become accepted as the first British shot in anger of the Great War. Corporal Thomas claimed a hit and the Germans were soon to suffer more casualties as, even though they had been reinforced by two troops of Hussars, they took the full force of a British charge which put them to flight, but not before they had lost several dead and had others taken prisoner. In pursuit once again Captain Hornby dismounted his men when they were confronted by a troop of German cyclists in good defensive positions at the top of a crest in the road. The Germans were then treated to a demonstration of the British cavalry's musketry skills as, armed with and practised in their Lee Enfield SMLE rifles, they comprehensively outgunned their opponents. Once again the Germans broke off the engagement and retired precipitately, this time not pursued by Captain Hornby and his men, who triumphantly rejoined Major Bridges and the rest of the Squadron complete with their prisoners and a number of discarded German lances. Captain Hornby's was not the only cavalry clash of the day. Two squadrons of the Scots Greys and a troop of the 16th Lancers also had encounters in which they convincingly bested their opponents.[14]

These were first revelations for the Germans that the British cavalry was more than a match for theirs. The experience was to be repeated on several future occasions before cavalry became sidelined with the onset of trench warfare. It was severely to dampen the aggressive ardour of the German cavalry and their consequent usefulness as the eyes of the German field commanders. In the immediate context of Mons General von Kluck's cavalry had been denied any opportunity to provide him with details of the exact whereabouts of the BEF. This ignorance was to inhibit his freedom of manoeuvre when battle was joined.[15]

It is ironic that Sir John French's detestation of General Sir Horace Smith-Dorrien, which was to do so much harm to the smooth operation of the BEF in the early period of the war and ultimately to both their careers, was largely caused when Sir Horace succeeded Sir John as C-in-C Aldershot Command in 1907. Sir Horace soon established that his predecessor's period in command had been characterised by stagnation except in the training of French's beloved cavalry. Even that had focused on perfecting the cavalry charge with sword and lance and had paid little attention to the less glamorous but potentially more valuable skills of musketry and fighting dismounted. Sir Horace quickly established rigorous training regimes for all the officers and men in his command, focusing on musketry marksmanship and the employment of machine guns. The cavalry, who were deficient in these basic skills to a marked degree, were re-equipped with the same rifle as the infantry and their proficiency with it rapidly improved.

Sir John saw in this a demeaning of the cavalry role even though he was not so foolish as to deny the importance of the cavalry acquiring the skills needed to fight dismounted if the necessity arose. Had it not been for these new found skills it is safe to say that the British cavalry would not have dominated their German opposite numbers in the way that they did in the early months of the war.[16]

The disclosures of the prisoners captured by the Royal Irish Dragoon Guards and the reports of the cavalry commanders involved in these early clashes, were added to the accumulating evidence that major enemy forces were approaching the BEF from the north. But still GHQ remained unconvinced. It was to take information brought from Lanrezac's HQ by the doggedly persistent Lieutenant Spears to lift the scales from GHQ's eyes. Following his previous meeting with Sir John French, Spears had returned to Fifth Army HQ where he learned that Lanrezac's command was being forced back by strong pressure from the German Second Army. A new development was the build up of a threat to the French Army's right flank with the arrival on the Meuse near Dinant of XII Saxon Corps of the German Third Army. Even though two of Lanrezac's corps were still intact and had plenty of fight left in them he determined that his army should continue to retreat and had notified Joffre, but not the British C-in-C, accordingly.

Spears saw immediately that such a retreat would place the BEF in danger of being outflanked not only to their left (a danger which, despite clear warnings, GHQ continued to disregard), but also now to their right by a German exploitation of the gap which would inevitably become apparent between the BEF's right flank and the departing French. The nightmare scenario of a complete envelopment of the BEF lent urgency to Spears' precipitate return to BEF HQ at Le Cateau. There he reported his findings to Colonel Macdonogh who needed no urging to confront the C-in-C and his senior staff with them. This time there could be no brushing aside of the unpalatable. After only brief reflection and consultation Sir John notified all senior officers present at GHQ, with very little elaboration or explanation, that there would be no general BEF advance on the morrow. There must have been some understandably bewildered officers among those who, only minutes previously, had been finalising the detailed plans for the advance.[17]

The scene was set for the Battle of Mons.

Chapter II
The Town of Mons

In just a few days in late August 1914 the small Belgian town of Mons was thrust into the forefront of the consciousness of the British people where it was to remain for a long time. It is safe to say that until the Battle of Mons was fought, there could have been very few British who had even heard of the town. Not surprisingly, as even by Belgian standards it hardly rates as of major importance compared with the likes of Brussels, Antwerp, Ghent, Liège or Charleroi. Nevertheless, it has an ancient and, at times, colourful history.

There is clear evidence that, as long ago as Neolithic times, around 2,000 BC, flints were being mined at Spiennes, just south of present day Mons. The flints were converted in significant numbers into semi-finished tools which were marketed throughout the region. A thousand years later bronze was being cast in Spiennes reinforcing the area's importance as a mining and metal and stone-working centre and regional communication crossroads.

The site of present day Mons offered obvious security attractions with its central and nearby hills in a relatively flat region. The Romans recognised this when they set up a camp on the main hill which was initially called *Castri Locus* and later *Montes*. Under Roman control the surrounding region developed as a cereal producing area supplying Roman garrisons in the Rhineland.

The development of Mons as a town and regional capital can be dated from the seventh century. A noblewoman, Waudru, decided to give up husband and children in favour of devoting her life to God. She retired to an oratory which she had built on the present day Mons hill around 650 AD. Through the succeeding centuries the oratory grew in importance and wealth, becoming an abbey then a monastery before becoming a secular chapter and collegiate church which the current building, constructed between 1450 and 1686, remains.

Further impetus to the growth of Mons was given by the decision of the Count of Hainaut in the ninth century to build a fortress surrounded by a wooden palisade on the top of the central hill. The palisade was replaced by a stone wall two hundred years later. In the middle of the twelfth century a further stone wall was built enclosing all the buildings on the hill. In 1290 work began to fortify the outer wall and create the fortified town which Mons would remain until the dismantling of the fortifications in 1861.

Over the years Mons developed as a regional crossroads and commercial centre. A population of fewer than 5,000 at the end of the thirteenth century had risen to more than 20,000 when the walls came down and allowed the town to spread outwards and the population to grow even more.

Mons' geographic position and commercial importance meant that it would inevitably become embroiled in the turmoil seemingly endemic in the so-called 'Cockpit of Europe'. In the late Middle Ages Mons was under the suzerainty of the House of Burgundy. From 1477 it was ruled by the Hapsburgs and became part of the Spanish Netherlands. In 1572 the town was captured by Louis de

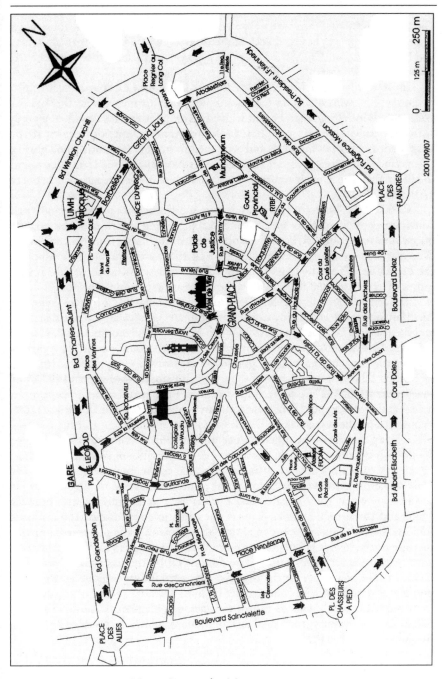

Map 1: Present day Mons town centre
(Map courtesy of Mons Tourist Office)

Nassau, a German Protestant nobleman allied to the Dutch in their struggle against Spain. It was besieged and retaken the same year by the Spanish Regent and Commander-in-Chief, the Duke of Alba, with predictably dire consequences for the town's Protestants.

In 1691 Mons was once again besieged, this time by the French armies of Louis XIV, who had long harboured ambitions to incorporate the Spanish Netherlands into France (ambitions which had brought him into conflict not only with the Spanish but also with England). The French captured the town after a siege lasting less than a month and remained in occupation until 1697. During this period Louis' great military engineer, Marshal Vauban, reinforced the town's fortifications. The French returned for a further period of occupation between 1701 and 1709.

In 1715 the Spanish Netherlands became the Austrian Netherlands as a consequence of the Treaty of Utrecht, which brought the War of the Spanish Succession to an end. Renewed hostilities between France and Austria, in the War of the Austrian Succession, led to a further successful siege of Mons by the French in 1746. The latter dismantled the town's fortifications, which were promptly reconstructed in 1750 after the Austrians regained possession.

The French Revolution of 1789 brought on war with Austria. Following Austrian defeats at the hands of the revolutionary armies at Jemappes in 1792 and Fleurus in 1794 the French reoccupied Mons. They incorporated the former Austrian Netherlands into metropolitan France and Mons became the capital of the *Département de Jemappes*. The political events surrounding the reconstruction of Europe following the defeat of Napoleon Bonaparte and the creation of an independent Belgium are more fully described in Appendix A. Suffice it to say here that the citizenry of Mons were active in their opposition to Dutch suzerainty manifested by the presence of a Dutch garrison in the town.

During the rest of the nineteenth century and up to the outbreak of the First World War the town of Mons, now capital of the Province of Hainaut, continued its role as a communications hub and commercial centre. But a further dimension to its economic activities was added by the growth of the coal mining industry in the area known as the *Borinage*. This word is used to describe the area between Mons and the French frontier. It does not apply to Mons itself.[1] The increased importance of Mons and the demolition of the town's walls prompted a further increase in the town's population to more than 28,000 in 1914. While the town itself, with its impressive main square dominated by the imposing Town Hall, had a certain charm and attractiveness, the surrounding region certainly had not. It was described with some feeling by John Terraine as 'one of the dreariest in Western Europe'[2], with its mines and factories, slag-heaps and drab mining villages on either side of the Canal de Condé along which the battle of 23 August would be largely fought.

Chapter III

The Battle of Mons, 23 August 1914: 3rd Division, II Corps

GHQ's new orders called for the BEF's units to remain broadly in the positions they had reached at the end of their march on 22 August. Only small adjustments were made, the main one being that the Cavalry Division were ordered to the area of Thulin and Elouges to protect II Corps' left flank. In effect the new orders meant that II Corps' planned swing round the west of Mons to take up positions on the northern sector of the line Lens-Binche was halted on a sector of the Canal du Centre known as the Canal de Condé (the Mons-Condé Canal), which ran west-east between the towns of Condé and Mons. On reaching Mons it reverted to the name Canal du Centre as it described a wide sweep to the north and east before resuming a broadly easterly course.[1] It was along its course that the Battle of Mons would largely be fought. It meant that almost the full force of the German attacks would fall on Sir Horace Smith-Dorrien's Corps. Sir Douglas Haig's I Corps had virtually completed its planned northeast wheel southeast of Mons to positions where it was not to come under direct assault on 23 August.

Sir John French convened a meeting of his Corps and Cavalry Division commanders for 05h30 on 23 August at General Smith-Dorrien's HQ in the Château de la Haie (sometimes called the Château de la Roche) near the village of Sars-la-Bruyère, about 12 kilometres southwest of Mons. If the purpose of the meeting was to enable the C-in-C to lay down clear instructions to his subordinates and provide them with accurate estimates of enemy strength, it fell short on both counts. According to Smith-Dorrien, Sir John told his commanders to 'be prepared to move forward, or to fight where we were, but to get ready for the latter by strengthening our outposts and by preparing the bridges over the Canal for demolition.' Smith-Dorrien, who had assumed command of II Corps less than 48 hours earlier, told Sir John that he did not regard the canal as by any means an ideal defensive line. He had already reconnoitred a shorter line a couple of miles south of it which he thought much more suitable for a prolonged defence. Orders were being prepared for his forward troops to retire to this line if and when their positions on the canal line became untenable. Sir John did not seem to dissent from these arrangements.[2]

Smith-Dorrien's dissatisfaction with the Canal du Centre as a defensive line was soundly based. The area through which it ran offered every advantage to the attacker and virtually none to the defender. The canal itself was insufficiently wide or deep to constitute a serious obstacle especially if the attackers managed to capture some of its 24 crossings intact. For almost the full length of its 16 miles between Condé and Mons it ran through an industrialised area characterised by the dense housing, mine-heads, slag-heaps and factories traditionally associated with coal mining areas. From the military point of view their effect was to

13

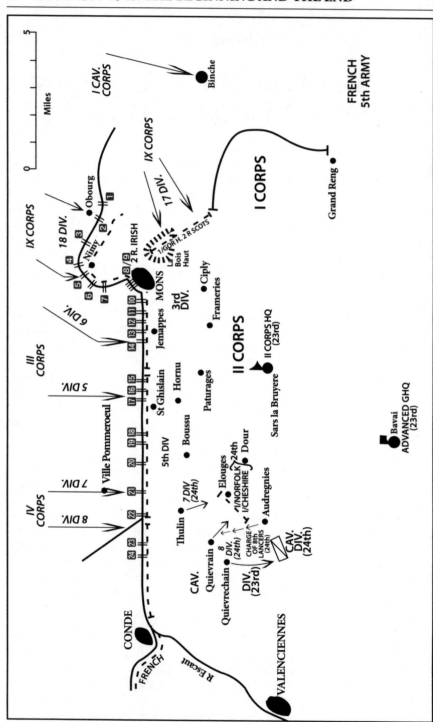

Map 2: The Battle of Mons

Map 2: Legend

CROSSING Canal du Centre	DEFENDED BY
1. Lock No 4	
2. Obourg Road Bridge	4th Middlesex
3. Lock No 5	
4. Rue des Bragnons Bridge	
5. Nimy Road Swing Bridge	
6. Nimy Railway Bridge	4th Royal Fusiliers
7. Lock No 6	
8/9. Ghlin Road/Railway Bridge	
Mons/Condé Canal (Canal de Condé)	
10. Lock No 1	
11. Ghlin/Jemappes Lifting Road Bridge (Gas Poste)	1st Royal Scots Fusiliers
12. Lock No 2	
13. Pont Richebe	
14. Mariette Bridge	
15. Iron Railway Bridge	
16. Lock No 3 Lifting Bridge	1st Royal West Kents
17. St Ghislain Tertre Road Lifting Bridge	
18. Iron Road Bridge, Lock No 4	2nd KoSB
19. Les Herbières Railway Bridge	1st East Surreys
20. Pont d'Hautrage	
21. Thulin-Pommeroeul Lifting Road Bridge	1st DCLI
22. Lock No 5	
23/24. St Aybert Bridges	19th Brigade

afford the defenders very limited fields of fire while offering perfect cover and concealment to the attackers. They also offered serious difficulty to the batteries of the Royal Field Artillery in their search for suitable sites from which to offer supporting fire to the infantry. The inevitably complex drainage systems endemic to the region provided a further source of difficulty for the defenders by limiting their scope for manoeuvre.[3]

It is not clear whether Sir John mentioned to his subordinates the strange request he had received late the previous night from General Lanrezac. The latter had asked him to attack the right flank of the German Second Army from which his own army was under assault. Understandably, in the rapidly developing circumstances, Sir John had rejected this request but, with remarkable forbearance considering the way Lanrezac was behaving towards the BEF, had undertaken that his army would maintain their positions for 24 hours.[4]

Sir John must have surprised his colleagues with an upbeat assessment of the strength of the enemy, distinctly at odds with the intelligence which had been provided by his cavalry and airmen and the revelations of the previous night. Sir John reckoned that the BEF were facing little more than one, or at most two, corps and perhaps a cavalry division. (By the afternoon they were in fact to be facing three corps with a fourth closing fast.)[5]

Leaving aside his clearly inaccurate interpretation of the intelligence available to him, other aspects of the Field Marshal's idiosyncratic leadership style were to surface during the course of the battle. The first was his immediate departure, after the meeting broke up, for Valenciennes where the routine duties he undertook, which could well have been postponed or cancelled, took him away from anywhere where he might have been able to exercise some control of events. When he returned to his headquarters during the afternoon, he still made no effort to assert his authority. In effect he seemed to leave it to his corps and divisional commanders to conduct the battle. This apparently cavalier approach to the responsibilities of command is not however quite what it seems. Sir John's conduct stemmed from his belief that there would be no developments of significance during the course of 23 August, that the Germans would spend it just trying to get a feel for the BEF's positions and strength. The blame for Sir John's misguided assessment of the true situation can almost certainly be laid at the door of Henry Wilson, whose persistence in discounting any intelligence which did not fit his preconceptions was quite remarkable.[6]

If Sir John was inclined to downplay the evidence that had accrued with his Intelligence Section of German strength and dispositions, his principal opponent in the forthcoming battle, the German First Army Commander, General von Kluck was even more guilty of lax interpretation of the scraps of intelligence he had available to him. He still had no concrete information on the precise whereabouts of the BEF but chose to believe that all that was between his army and its route southwest were some British cavalry units. As a result his army was advancing towards the Mons area in echelon, less intent on bringing their full force to bear on the BEF than in continuing the wide sweeping movement called for by the Schlieffen Plan. This meant that, as the extent of the opposition became more apparent, he was to feed his corps piecemeal into the battle as they became available. By so doing he lost the near certainty of complete victory that a concentration of his forces would have brought.[7]

In these circumstances it was inevitable that the first contact with the British by a major unit was by von Kluck's IX Corps which was on the inside, or the left, of the German First Army's manoeuvre. To their right was III Corps, then IV Corps. On von Kluck's right wing II Corps would find themselves a day's march away from any hope of intervening in the fighting of the 23rd.

The Order of Battle of the BEF is shown at Appendix C. As far as the events of 23 August are concerned it is only the dispositions of II Corps which have any real bearing, as the brunt of the fighting fell almost entirely on them. The various units of the Corps had reached their planned positions by late on the 22nd. At that point they were expecting to resume their advance the following day. They nevertheless did their best in the rather unhelpful terrain to entrench and create defensible positions. Occupying the right of the Corps' line were Major General Hubert Hamilton's Third Division. On their left were Major General Sir Charles Fergusson's Fifth Division. The line was completed from Thulin to St Aybert by the independent 19th Infantry Brigade which had only been formed on the 22nd at Valenciennes and had immediately moved up to join the BEF.[8]

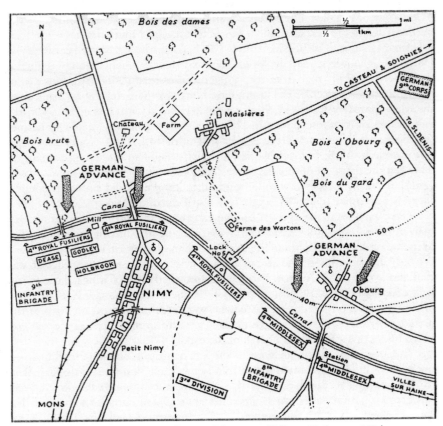

Sketch 1: The Mons Salient at Obourg and Nimy, 23 August 1914

The weather at daybreak on Sunday 23 August was misty and damp but with the promise that once the sun had got to work the mist and damp would give way to a fine sunny day. To the wonderment of the British troops the great majority of the local population seemed to regard the 23rd as a typical Sunday. This despite the fact that many of these same people had spent the previous day helping the newly arrived British dig trenches and build up their defences. The bells of the churches pealed out to summon the faithful who, dressed in their Sunday best, responded. For many others, more intent on pleasure than prayer, it was the day for taking trains into Mons to visit the markets or just enjoy a relaxing day. (The trains and municipal trams were to run as if 23 August was just another summer Sunday.)[9] This was not bravado on the part of the locals. There must have been a great deal of ignorance about the close proximity of the German army. Even though a major source of allied intelligence on German movements was provided by local peasantry, almost certainly it had not percolated through to much of the population that Brussels was in German hands and that the much vaunted fortress cities of Liège and Namur, designed to stop an invader in his tracks, had in the former case fallen and in the latter, was about to follow suit.

The 4th Bn Middlesex Regiment and 2nd Bn Royal Irish Regiment, two of the four battalions of the Third Division's 8th Infantry Brigade, which was located on the right of II Corps' line, found themselves occupying a salient formed by the northern swing of the Canal du Centre before it edged south and then resumed its easterly course. The Brigade's other two battalions, 2nd Royal Scots and 1st Gordon Highlanders, were deployed facing north east roughly along the line of the present-day N40 road from the La Bascule crossroads, about two kms east of Mons, towards the village of Harmignies. North of them, on the eastern side of the salient proper, were 4th Middlesex, with 2nd Royal Irish close up behind them and theoretically in reserve. Smith-Dorrien saw the salient as, by its very nature, the most vulnerable part of the line he had to defend. The German IX Corps' line of march would bring their leading units straight to it and consequently it had been the first part of the line to see action; on the afternoon of the 22nd 4th Middlesex exchanged shots with some probing German cavalry thereby becoming the first BEF infantry unit to fire shots in anger during the war.[10]

But even prior to this the war had begun in earnest for 4th Middlesex. One of their number is generally accepted to have been the first British infantry fatality of the war from enemy action. There is more than one version of how, and when, Private John Parr met his death but there is now general agreement that he was shot and killed on 21 August, two days before the Battle of Mons and one day before his Battalion took up their positions in the Mons salient. Private Parr was one of two of the Battalion's cyclists who were ordered to seek out signs of the presence of German cavalry north of the Canal du Centre. He was spotted and killed by his quarry while still north of the canal.[11]

Responsibility for the defence of the left hand side of the salient devolved upon the right hand battalion of 9th Infantry Brigade, 4th Royal Fusiliers. Next to them along the canal running due west from Mons were 1st Royal Scots Fusiliers with, on their left, two companies of 1st Northumberland Fusiliers. The 1st Lincolns formed Brigade reserve. The 7th Infantry Brigade was in Divisional reserve.[12]

Insofar as the BEF had an overall strategy for the battle about to be joined it was to deny the Germans the use of the crossings over the Canal du Centre. The 4th Middlesex had three of these to contend with; the road bridge on the Obourg-Mons road and the crossings at Locks 4 and 5. In addition they shared responsibility with 4th Royal Fusiliers for the Rue des Bragnons bridge, at the apex of the salient. Lock 4 was about 500 metres east of the Obourg-Mons road bridge and Lock 5 about two kilometres to the west. The Rue des Bragnons bridge was a further kilometre on from Lock 5. Slightly to the south and east of the road bridge was the main building of Obourg railway station. The Middlesex had spent the limited time available to them since their arrival strengthening it for defence.

The Battalion's two main problems were the length of line they had to defend, which left them very thinly stretched, and the unavoidable problem attached to salients, that they were vulnerable to fire from three sides. In the case of their present situation they were also overlooked from the high ground to their north which offered the German artillery complete observation over their positions. As soon as there was sufficient light the German guns began to search out the British positions in the salient. At around 08h00 the first small arms fire was exchanged across the canal with German infantry of the 18th Division, some of whom took advantage of the shelter of houses in the village of Obourg. Their main target was part of D Company of the Middlesex who were well concealed in the Obourg station building.

The 4th Royal Fusiliers, the Middlesex's fellow defenders of the salient, were also targeted by the German artillery as they held the line stretching from their junction with the Middlesex at the Rue des Bragnons bridge, at almost the apex of the salient, in a southerly direction to the western outskirts of Mons itself. In addition to the shared responsibility for the Rue des Bragnons bridge the Fusiliers had five other bridges to look after. The most important of these were the Nimy road and railway bridges, about 200 metres apart, but there were also the bridge at Lock No 6 and the Ghlin road and railway bridges, within a few yards of each other. The Battalion's supporting artillery, the four 18 pounders of 107 Battery RFA, had positioned themselves close to Mons railway station from where they hoped to offer the forward infantry companies some support. But despite their best efforts their positions did not enable them to do so.[13]

The two British battalions holding the salient were at this stage of the war at their full wartime establishment of about 1,000 officers and men. Their positions were to come under attack from the equivalent of six infantry battalions of the 18th Division of the German IX Corps, a total of roughly 6,000 men. These odds of roughly three to one were typical of those that faced II Corps all along the line.

An important aspect of the denial of the canal crossings to the Germans would be their demolition once it was clear that no other recourse was left. The technical responsibility for this rested with II Corps' Royal Engineers. Unfortunately, despite the great bravery of the Sappers, many of the crossings remained unblown and were seized intact by the Germans. There were a number of reasons for this failure. There was the usual dilemma about when the demolitions should take place. Third Division HQ had ordered that the crossings should be prepared for demolition but that nothing should be destroyed until the Division's retirement was unavoidable. Preparations were hampered by a shortage of suitable explosives and an even more serious lack of fuses. Finally the Sappers had often been diverted from carrying out the preparation involved by equally pressing needs for their services to prepare strong-points near the canal and assist in the preparation of Smith-Dorrien's second line. The result was that by the time the Sappers needed to blow the crossings the Germans often had them under such a concentrated fire that approaching them was impossible.

It was D Company of 4th Middlesex who were the recipients of the first infantry assaults of the battle. As with the previous exchange of small arms fire the main target of the German assault was the Obourg station building which protected the Obourg road bridge. The defenders were amazed at the crudity of the German tactics. They came on in densely packed formations, firing their rifles from the hip, apparently intent on overwhelming the defenders with sheer force of numbers. The defenders' skilled musketry and machine guns ensured that they paid a very heavy price before the assault wavered and pulled back. After about 30 minutes the attack was renewed with the Germans now advancing in open order, which diminished the effectiveness of the British fire. This time the weight of numbers paid off and by 10h30 the Germans had succeeded in seizing and crossing the bridge which the Sappers, escorted by two platoons of 2nd Royal Irish Regiment, had been unable to reach and demolish because of the proximity of the attackers and the intensity of their fire. The same was true of the other bridges on the Middlesex front. At the Rue des Bragnons bridge, the RE team had been rushed by the Germans as they attempted to lay their charges. Second Lieutenant H.W. Holt had been killed, the first RE officer fatality of the war.[14]

With the Germans across the canal the pressure on the Middlesex soldiers at Obourg station increased as did the threat of their being surrounded and cut off. Almost all the defenders had been either killed, or wounded too seriously to move. Those who were physically able to, withdrew southwards to the shelter of the Bois d'Havré leaving one of their number who was wounded but still capable of firing his rifle, to cover their escape. The name of this hero, who was finally killed at his post, remains unknown to this day.

With B Company of the Middlesex also being pushed back from the canal, initially to the line of the railway, the Battalion were becoming engaged in a fighting withdrawal to avoid being cut off by the ever increasing number of Germans on the south side of the canal. Despite the pressure the Middlesex were managing to keep their line intact as they fell back on the Communal cemetery and the adjacent convent and psychiatric hospital. The latter building had been set alight by artillery fire and its terrified patients were fleeing in panic. Some were killed in the crossfire.

By now all four Middlesex companies were fully engaged and taking casualties. The 2nd Royal Irish Regt were called forward to protect the Middlesex's left flank, in danger of being turned through the gap which had opened up between them and 4th Royal Fusiliers. Both battalions suffered heavily from German artillery and machine gun fire, which put most of their own machine guns out of action. The Irish were gradually to take over from the Middlesex as the latter sought to withdraw from the battle by making for their positions on the Second Line at

Nouvelles, by way of Bois la Haut. They were to take a further 60 casualties in fighting their way through the village of Hyon, which the Germans had already occupied, before reaching their destination.

The 2nd Irish Regt were in their turn retiring but found the road south blocked by the Germans, near Bois la Haut. D Company became separated from the rest of the Battalion and fell back. RQMS T.W. Fitzpatrick, observing this, collected together about 40 cooks, storemen, drivers and batmen and dug in on the right south side of the La Bascule crossroads. There they put up a spirited and stubborn rearguard action which covered the retirement of the remnants of the two battalions. It lasted until they were ordered to withdraw and rejoin their Battalion at 23h00. RQMS Fitzpatrick had placed his group under the command of 1st Gordons, whose left flank Company were also at the crossroads. The Gordons, 1st Royal Scots and two companies of 2nd Royal Irish Rifles of 7th Brigade had the task, from their positions along the road from the La Bascule crossroads towards the village of Harmignies, of preventing a German breakthrough from the east. The Germans appeared determined to achieve this before nightfall and even reverted to their tactic of earlier in the day of advancing in dense formations firing from the hip to overwhelm their opposition with sheer weight of numbers. Once again their assault ended in bloody failure as the British musketry and the fire from three RFA batteries took their toll.[15]

At 21h00 the order was given for the Brigade to withdraw to positions on the Second Line at Nouvelles. The acting CO of 2nd Royal Irish Regiment was ordered to withdraw the remnants of his Battalion south east to the La Bascule-Harmignies road. There they met up with their own D Company, the 18 survivors of RQMS Fitzpatrick's group and the Gordons. By 23h00 8th Brigade had disengaged and were on their way to Nouvelles.

The German First Army's line of march meant that their first contact with II Corps was at the easternmost point of the latter's line and then gradually extended to the west during the course of 23 August. Very soon after 4th Middlesex came under infantry assault therefore, it was the turn of their immediate neighbours, 4th Royal Fusiliers. The London regiment had had a busy and tiring night digging in and preparing their defences. The assault by the 84th Infantry Regiment of IX Corps began at roughly 10h00. Their main objectives were the road and rail bridges at Nimy. The road bridge was a swing bridge which had been swung back by the defenders to prevent its use.

The German assault was notable yet again for its seeming disregard for casualties as they advanced in dense formation without attempt at concealment, misguidedly relying for protection on an artillery barrage. They were cut down in swathes. But the pressure was maintained and the defenders were suffering serious casualties, mainly from the German artillery. A German soldier, Musketeer Oscar Niemeyer, swam across the canal and under heavy British fire managed to operate the machinery to swing the bridge back into place before he was killed. This made a successful German crossing of the bridge just a matter of time.

The railway bridge was defended mainly by two machine guns under the command of the Battalion's machine gun officer, Lieutenant Maurice Dease. They inflicted serious casualties on the attackers who were trying to cross this bridge while the road bridge was swung back and impassable. As Lt Dease

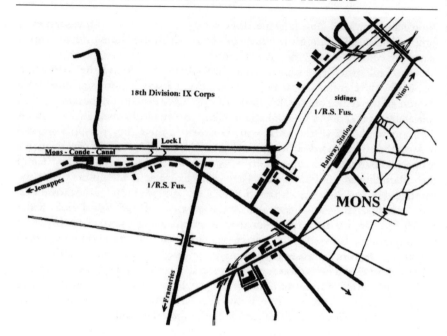

Sketch 2: The Royal Scots Fusiliers at Lock 1, 23 August 1914
(Sketch courtesy of Michael Gavaghan)

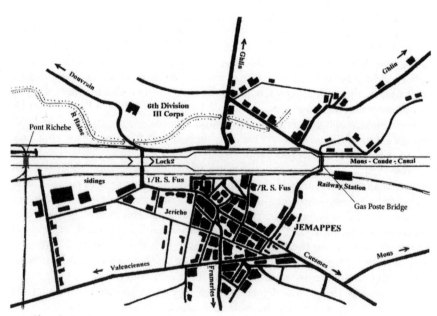

Sketch 3: The Royal Scots Fusiliers at Jemappes, 23 August 1914
(Sketch courtesy of Michael Gavaghan)

shuttled between his guns and the ammunition stockpile he was wounded three times, the last time fatally. The machine guns fell silent as their crews became casualties, usually fatal. Only one of the guns remained serviceable and Private Sidney Frank Godley, who had already been wounded, volunteered to man it and keep it firing as the remaining survivors withdrew. He kept this up until the gun failed whereupon he broke it up and threw the parts into the canal. He was subsequently taken prisoner. For their bravery in this action Lt Dease and Pte Godley were awarded the first two Victoria Crosses of the war. The attempt to blow the rail bridge failed when the officer seeking to destroy it, Lt. A.F. Day RE, was wounded and taken prisoner.[16]

The Company given responsibility for defending the other three crossings in 4th Royal Fusilier's sector had originally taken up positions well to the west of the canal. They were recalled from these late on the night of the 22nd when it had become apparent that the following morning would bring a defensive battle rather than a continuation of the advance. But Captain Byng, the Company Commander, maintained some positions just to the west of the canal. In the event the Germans focused their attentions on the two Nimy crossings and it was only in the last 45 minutes before the Battalion began its withdrawal that Byng's Company came under serious attack. The bridges had been primed for destruction and as soon as the last Fusilier crossed back to the eastern side, Corporal Payne RE detonated the charges, apparently successfully.

The order for the Battalion to retire came at around 13h40 by which time the German infantry had succeeded in crossing the canal using the two Nimy bridges. Despite the continuing close attentions of the German artillery the retirement was achieved in textbook fashion with the Battalion's supporting companies covering the advanced companies as they fell back. The route of the retirement was south through Mons to their Second Line positions at Ciply, a small village about two miles south of the town.[17] The Germans did not pursue the Fusiliers with any great ardour but when they did they came up against 1st Lincolns of the 9th Brigade who were defending the routes south from Mons from positions just inside the town's boundary. During their progress through Nimy and Mons the Germans had taken hostages whom they drove before them as a human shield. The 4th Royal Fusiliers rearguard were the first to experience this disregard for the rules of war. When the Germans reached the Town Hall they added the Town's Mayor (Bourgmestre), Jean Lescarts, to their hostages. In the ensuing clash with the Lincolns, five of the hostages were killed in the crossfire with several others wounded. The rest, including Mayor Lescarts, made good their escape in the confusion. (The five unfortunate victims were not the first civilians to suffer at the hands of the Germans that day. The troops assaulting the Nimy bridges had already destroyed houses in Nimy village and shot a number of Belgian civilians.[18]) Notwithstanding their use of a human shield the Germans were sufficiently discouraged by the reception accorded them by the Lincolns to abandon their attempts to break through. They moved off to the west which enabled the Lincolns to make an untroubled retirement to Nouvelles by way of the village of Mesvin.[19]

To the left of 4th Royal Fusiliers at the start of the day were 1st Royal Scots Fusiliers. Like their London neighbours they had not stopped at the canal during

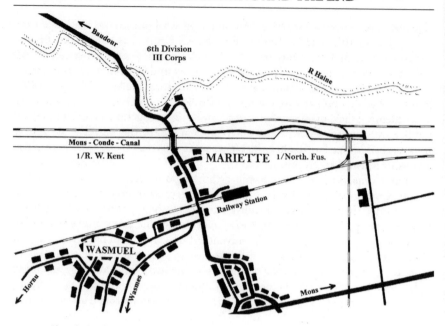

Sketch 4: The 1st Northumberland Fusiliers at Mariette, 23 August 1914
(Sketch courtesy of Michael Gavaghan)

their advance of the previous day. They had crossed it at Jemappes and marched on a further two miles to Ghlin, their planned jumping-off point for the next day's advance. They had however been recalled and ordered to prepare defences covering a 2,000 yard stretch of the canal and four crossing points. These were, from right to left, Lock No 1, the Ghlin-Jemappes lifting road bridge (Gas Poste), Lock No 2 and the Pont Richebe at Jemappes. The bulk of the Battalion withdrew to the southern side of the canal but outposts were left on the northern side to cover the approaches to each bridge.

On the 23rd there was an early brush with a German cavalry patrol from IX Corps after which there was a long hiatus.[20] It was broken at 10h30 when German artillery began shelling the Scots. This was soon followed by the massed columns of the German 6th Infantry Division which, unlike most other German units that day, quickly abandoned such suicidal tactics in favour of more orthodox methods. Nevertheless they only succeeded in getting to within 200 yards of the Pont Richebe before the Scottish rifle and machine gun fire stopped them.

The Scots had already withdrawn their outposts and attention now turned to the need to destroy the crossings, once permission was given, before the Germans could make use of them. The Scottish CO knew by early afternoon that the Germans had successfully crossed the canal to the east of his Battalion's positions and that it was only a matter of time before an order to withdraw was received. This duly came at 14h30 and was the signal for the bridges to be destroyed. In the event only the Gas Poste and Lock No 2 bridges were successfully blown; the other two remained intact. Responsibility for destroying the Lock 2 crossing had been given to Lance Corporal Charles Jarvis RE who won the Victoria Cross for his courage in setting 22 charges while under fire for 90 minutes.

The Germans were none too quick to take advantage of the availability of Pont Richebe, but they began to move across at 15h15. Their intrusion greatly complicated the efforts of the Scots to extricate themselves in what became a fighting street-by-street withdrawal with significant casualties on both sides. The Scots were greatly helped when the two reserve companies of 1st Northumberland Fusiliers, who were making a rather tardy withdrawal themselves, were able to attack the Germans in flank and take some of the pressure off the Scots. The Scottish survivors finally got back to the relative haven of Frameries, three miles south of the canal.

Two companies of 1st Northumberland Fusiliers completed the front line presence of 9th Infantry Brigade and 3rd Division. The Battalion's other two companies and 1st Lincolns formed the Brigade reserve. The two forward companies were ordered to defend the crossing at Mariette, about a kilometre to the west of the Pont Richebe. The Mariette crossing was in effect two bridges as the canal at this point consisted of two channels. The southern bridge, about 20 feet long, crossed a narrow but deep drainage canal. The much longer northern lifting bridge crossed the 60 feet wide canal proper. The dry land between the two bridges was about 40 feet wide.

The Northumberlands appear to have realised earlier than most that there would be no question of their advancing on the 23rd, and that almost certainly the day would see them fighting a defensive action. Their preparations were accordingly thorough. One company was assigned to the defence of the bridges; the other to cover the canal between the Mariette bridge and the Battalion's junction with the Scots. The lock keeper's house on the north bank was fortified and garrisoned. Barbed wire was used to barricade the gaps between houses on the north bank Other obstacles were created by jamming shut the level crossing gates on the railway, which ran close to and parallel with the north bank, and by the use of scavenged iron railings. All the buildings on the dry land between the two bridges were demolished, but the ruins were used to conceal troops to provide support for those on the northern bank. Houses lining the south bank were loop-holed and manned by the second company.

It was not until until 10h30 that German artillery began to target the Mariette bridge. Half an hour later a column of infantry came marching down the road leading to the bridges as if unaware of the British presence. They were engaged and forced to retire after suffering heavy casualties. Unlike the infantry, the German artillery, which had managed to bring up two field guns to within about half a mile of the canal, did take a small toll of the defenders. But it was beginning to look as if the Northumberlands had the situation well in hand when a number of little Belgian girls came walking down the road in all innocence. The defenders naturally ceased fire and the German infantry took advantage of this to move up to positions only 200 yards or so from the crossings. From there they could direct oblique fire at the garrison in the lock keeper's house. The garrison promptly withdrew in good order but the Germans quickly discovered that they were no more able to reach the crossings than they had been before, so well covered were they by the fire of the Northumberlands. [21]

For the next three hours or so a relative quiet descended on 1st Northumberland's front. The order for units of 9th Brigade to withdraw from the canal was issued at 14h30 but was not received by the company defending the crossings. They were in any case determined to stay in position to offer as much cover as they could to the two Sappers, Captain T. Wright and Sergeant Smith, who arrived at the bridges to blow them at around 15h00. Despite prolonged and heroic efforts under fire, for which Captain Wright would receive the VC, it proved impossible to complete this task.[22] Once the Sappers had accepted defeat and departed, at about 17h00, the two companies began their withdrawal towards Frameries. Following a slightly circuitous route to avoid running into the Germans who had crossed the Pont Richebe, they reached their destination after dark.

By and large and by late at night the various units of 8th and 9th Brigades of 3rd Division had extricated themselves from the Mons salient and the canal line and made it back to the prepared second line. Inevitably small bodies of men and some individuals had been overrun by the fighting and would only rejoin their units over the next few days.

Chapter IV

The Battle of Mons, 23 August 1914: 5th Division, II Corps

The II Corps' 5th Division were responsible for guarding the Canal de Condé line from halfway between the Mariette bridges and the iron railway bridge near St Ghislain village, westward to Pommeroeul road bridge, a distance of approximately five and a half miles. The Division's 13th Infantry Brigade covered the eastern three miles and 14th Brigade on their left the rest. The divisional right wing Battalion were 1st Royal West Kents. They had been the first unit of the Division to arrive during the morning of the 22nd and had been ordered to defend the three bridges near St Ghislain. The easternmost of these, a little less than 2,000 yards west of the Mariette bridges, was the iron railway bridge. Close by was the lifting bridge at Lock No 3. A further 1,000 yards to the west was another, larger, lifting bridge carrying the road between St Ghislain and Tertre. The Battalion front totalled 3,000 yards. D Company were given responsibility for the railway bridge and C Company for the other two. A and B Companies were in reserve at Hornu, a couple of miles south.

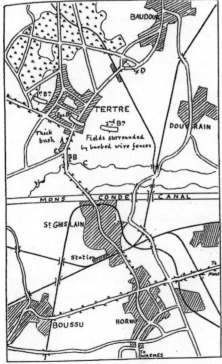

represents a Battalion of the 12th Brandenberg Grenadier Regiment

Sketch 5: The 1st Royal West Kents – A Coy's Action, 23 August 1914

The two forward companies spent the rest of the 22nd following their arrival fortifying the buildings close to the canal, loop-holing walls, setting up barbed wire barricades and digging trenches on the north bank. C Coy took up positions north of the canal to overcome the problem presented by buildings on the north bank obstructing their field of vision from the south side. They occupied a glass factory from where they could inflict great execution on an advancing enemy without loss to themselves. Although much of the ground in the Battalion area was water meadow and unsuitable for the deployment of artillery, four 18-pr guns of 120 Battery RFA found suitable positions on the canal's southern embankment from where they were to add significantly to the enemy's misery.

At first light on the 23rd work was resumed on strengthening the battalion's defences. A Coy, in reserve, commanded by Captain G.D. Lister, were ordered northwards to the left hand bridge across the canal to rendezvous with and support the divisional Cyclist Coy and mounted troops (A Squadron, 19th Hussars) who would be reconnoitring north of the canal. The rendezvous took place at around 08h15 and the troops crossed the canal and advanced northwards. Captain Lister stopped his unit at a crossroads south of Tertre, where, if necessary, they could cover the retirement of the mounted troops, who continued to press further forward.[1]

Captain Lister deployed his platoons around the crossroads, one northwest, one southeast and one east. The fourth platoon was left in reserve further to the southeast. Lister prepared lines of retreat to the canal which entailed cutting a fair amount of agricultural barbed wire. There was little he could do about a number of deep dykes which would have to be crossed. As far as possible he sought to avoid the lines of retreat masking the fire of the Battalion's main body in position along the canal.[2]

Hardly had he completed his preparations when an officer and four cyclists came racing down the road from Tertre. The officer told him that the rest of his detachment had been blown to pieces by enemy artillery. A cyclist was ordered back to the canal with this information. Within a matter of minutes enemy infantry of the 12th Brandenburg Grenadiers, part of 5th Division of III Corps, were observed debouching from Tertre in large numbers. Lister counted 4 to 500 on the east side of the road. They were immediately engaged with rifle fire which inflicted heavy casualties. Recovering from their initial shock the enemy began to return a heavy fire. A battery of enemy artillery located just south of Baudour, and an enemy machine gun company were brought into action.

Very shortly after these initial exchanges Capt Lister received by cyclist a request from the Commander of the divisional mounted troops to cover their retirement. Lister thought he could best do this by maintaining his Company's present positions as he had no idea of where the mounted troops were. Enemy infantry were also deploying east and west of the Tertre-St Ghislain road. Lister reacted by sending half his reserve Platoon to reinforce his northwestern Platoon which was looking rather exposed. He sent a further report back to the canal and asked if there was any news of the whereabouts of the Divisional Cavalry. The response was negative; the same response authorised him to begin to withdraw if things were getting too hot.

This was indeed the case and Lister ordered his northwestern Platoon to begin the retirement. At this point he became aware that, owing to a misunderstanding, his eastern Platoon had begun to retire from its positions, in good order despite the fact that it had evidently suffered some losses. It was impossible to get an order through to the Platoon to stop their retreat, so Lister instructed his last half platoon in reserve to line a deep and boggy dyke to plug the gap that had opened up.

Meanwhile the first Platoon had successfully disengaged and got away. The next stage would be for the platoon southeast of the crossroads to retire. When organising cover for this Lister showed too much of himself to the enemy and fell wounded. He soon became unconscious and woke up to find himself a prisoner of war.

Only about 90 of the original 200 men got back safely to the Battalion's main positions south of the canal. But Lister's men had inflicted heavy losses on 3 battalions of the Brandenburg Grenadiers and their artillery battery and machine gun company.[3] A company commander in one of the Brandenburg battalions, Capt Walter Bloem, was to write, 'A bad defeat, there could be no gainsaying it; in our first battle we had been badly beaten, and by the English - by the English we had so laughed at a few hours before'.[4]

The depleted A Coy was relieved by B Coy which took up position on the canal. For the rest of the day until nightfall the West Kents continued to defy everything the Brandenburgers could throw at them. Late at night they disengaged and withdrew to Wasmes. They had to leave behind two of 120 Battery's guns which could not be moved from their exposed positions on the canal. Once the infantry were clear the Sappers of 17th Field Company successfully blew the road and rail bridges in the West Kent sector.

To the West Kent's left and forming 13th Brigade's left flank were 2nd King's Own Scottish Borderers (KOSB). The battalion's task was to defend the iron road bridge at Lock No 4 at the village of Les Herbières and the more than 1,000 yards of canal bank between the crossing and the West Kent's positions. The two remaining battalions of the Brigade, 2nd Duke of Wellington's Regt and 2nd King's Own Yorkshire Light Infantry (KOYLI) were in reserve in St Ghislain.

The KOSB made careful preparations for the defensive battle they knew was coming. Two companies prepared trenches on the canal bank before one of them took up positions half a mile north of the Lock 4 crossing to cover the approaches to it. The other company were given responsibility for defence of the bridge and the canal bank. Houses were knocked down to improve fields of fire and one house on the south bank was fortified and turned into a machine gun post.

The rifles of 2nd KOSB and the 2nd KOYLI machine guns, which had been sent forward in support, materially assisted the West Kents in keeping the enemy away from the St Ghislain-Tertre road bridge. As the enemy attack moved further to the west the Les Herbières bridge came under threat at around 13h00 from 52nd Infantry Regiment of the German III Corps. Using rather more sophisticated infantry tactics than their neighbours the Brandenburgers, they seemed to pose a sufficient threat for reinforcements from 13th Brigade's reserve battalions to be sent forward at around 14h00 to provide close support for the KOSB. But by the time they arrived the German attack had already been brought to a standstill and they were not needed.

At 15h00 the advanced company of the KOSB were withdrawn to the canal. In the evening, with all the infantry on the south side, the Sappers were finally given the go ahead to destroy the bridge. But by this time the Germans were virtually on top of it. When the charges misfired there was little that could be done about it despite the Sappers' best efforts. But even though the bridge fell into enemy hands intact, there was little inclination on their part to attempt to cross in the gathering darkness. The 2nd KOSB were thus able to retire when the order came for them to do so. The 2nd KOYLI were sent forward to cover their retirement. By dark they were the sole remaining forward unit of 13th Brigade. Their order to retire came just before midnight. It was accomplished without undue difficulty.[5]

The easternmost battalion of the 5th Division's 14th Brigade was 1st East Surrey Regt. On their left were 1st Duke of Cornwall's Light Infantry (DCLI). In reserve were 2nd Suffolks and 2nd Manchesters. The East Surreys had the task of defending a lifting road bridge, the Pont d'Hautrage, and the railway bridge at Les Herbières, almost a mile to the right. The main railway bridge was a fixed structure, but that carrying the railway over the deep drainage canal parallel with the main canal was a lifting bridge. The East Surreys were in touch with the KOSB on their right and the DCLI on their left and had agreed with both of their neighbours that none of them would retire before dark or without informing the others.

With their good fields of fire, the East Surreys were in positions which were more suited for defence than those available to the other battalions defending the

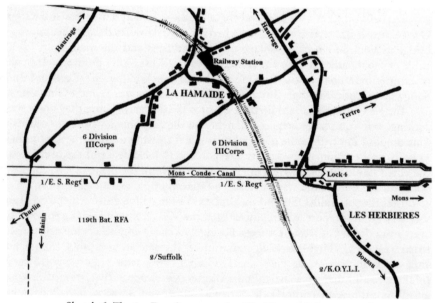

Sketch 6: The 1st East Surreys at Les Herbières, 23 August 1914
(Sketch courtesy of Michael Gavaghan)

line of the canal. A feature was a 500 yard long railway embankment running from north of the railway bridge towards Hautrage station nearly 2,000 yards away. One company of the Surreys and the Battalion machine guns were placed on either side of this embankment. Part of another company, which was defending the road bridge from its southern end, were also placed just north of the canal covering a fork in the road. A third company were spread along the southern bank of the canal between the two bridges. The fourth were in reserve.[6]

It was not until 13h00 that the Surreys came under fire, the first recipients being the Company at the railway embankment. The German machine guns inflicted casualties but when their infantry tried to cross the railway embankment they suffered severe losses in their turn from the Surrey's machine guns. A bayonet charge evicted the enemy from some Surrey trenches they had occupied. At 18h00 the Company and machine guns were ordered back to the southern bank of the canal. The platoons on the west of the embankment did not receive the order and stayed put. They were soon under severe pressure from the enemy, no longer hindered by the Surrey machine guns from climbing the embankment. Only a very few succeeded in breaking out and getting back across the canal. The remainder were killed, or wounded and made prisoner.

With all those back who were going to get back the Sappers of 59 Field Coy blew the bridges in the Surrey sector. The Pont d'Hautrage and the lifting railway bridge were destroyed but the main railway bridge was only partially damaged and remained passable. But the Germans were to stay on the north side of the canal until the following day. The East Surreys began their retirement from the canal shortly before midnight and made their way back to Dour by way of Boussu. Their losses had been heavy, 221 killed, wounded or missing. The 2nd Suffolks had also suffered some casualties in the company which had been sent forward to support the Surreys at the railway embankment. They withdrew slightly ahead of the Surreys and the whole Battalion also made their way to Dour.[7]

The 1st DCLI were responsible for the canal line from west of the Pont d'Hautrage to the crossing at Lock No 5 a distance of about 3,000 yards. About midway along this stretch of canal was a lifting road bridge linking Thulin to the south with Pommeroeul to the north. This was likely to be the axis of any assault by the Germans. The CO of the DCLI was concerned at the vulnerability of what he perceived as his open left flank although it was in fact being protected by the Cavalry Division. The remaining two crossings before the canal reached Condé, bridges at St Aybert, were being guarded by 6th Dragoon Guards (Carabiniers) of 4th Cavalry Brigade pending the arrival of 19th Independent Infantry Brigade later in the day. Presumably the DCLI's CO would have felt more comfortable with an infantry unit on his left. He was also worried by the obstacle to his line of retreat presented by the narrow but deep River Haine a mile south of the canal. This was partially resolved by the construction of a bridge over the river by the same Sappers who had prepared the Thulin-Pommeroeul bridge for demolition during the afternoon.

The DCLI opted to defend the bridge by deploying many of their troops north of the canal. Apart from a couple of early morning brushes with German cavalry, seemingly unaware of the British presence, it was not until 16h45 that the Germans launched their attack down the Pommeroeul road, four abreast as if on

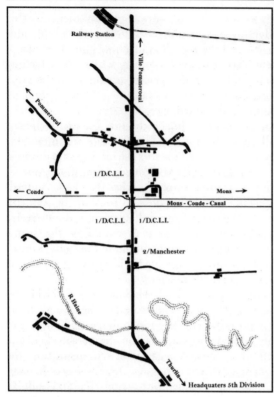

Sketch 7: The 1st DCLI at Ville
Pommeroeul, 23 August 1914
(Sketch courtesy of
Michael Gavaghan)

parade Even though the DCLI machine guns had been withdrawn south of the canal the Germans were mown down by the fast and accurate rifle fire. Having very effectively discouraged any further enterprise by the enemy the DCLI withdrew to the southern side of the canal. The road bridge was then successfully blown by the Sappers. At 18h00 the Cornishmen left the canal and took up new defensive positions on the River Haine.[8]

In a final flourish, the machine guns of the reserve Battalion, 2nd Manchesters, punished the Germans severely when, assuming correctly that the blowing of the road bridge meant that the British had retired, they showed too much of themselves as they approached the wrecked bridge.[9]

The 1st DCLI's CO's concern about his, and the BEF's left flank, was alleviated by the timely arrival of the leading elements of the 19th Independent Infantry Brigade on the canal. It was to inspect this newly constituted Brigade that had taken Sir John French to Valenciennes that morning immediately following his meeting with his senior Commanders at Sars-la-Bruyère. The leading battalions of the Brigade reached the canal and had relieved the cavalry by 15h00. The 1st Middlesex were on the right and 1st Cameronians (Scottish Rifles) on their left. The Brigade's other two battalions, 2nd Argyll and Sutherland Highlanders and 2nd Royal Welch Fusiliers, were some distance back in support.

The 1st Middlesex assumed responsibility for the crossing at Lock No 5. Shortly after 17h00 the enemy attacked. They managed to mount a machine gun in a position which commanded the buildings being used by the British battalion. Although they had to evacuate the buildings the Middlesex had no difficulty in holding off the enemy assisted by the successful blowing of the bridge by 1st Field Squadron RE. The remaining two crossings in the Brigade's sector were also successfully blown in the early hours of the 24th, once the cavalry patrols had all returned to the south side of the canal.[10]

The 1st Middlesex were to withstand a further attack in the early hours of the 24th before they conformed to the orders the Brigade had received to withdraw to Elouges, about 6 miles to the southeast. They began their march at 02h00 by way of Hensies and Quiévrain.

By dawn on Monday 24 August the bulk of II Corps were on their planned positions on the prepared Second Line. The retirements from the salient and the canal line had taken place at different times during the previous night and the early morning, but had largely been effected without serious disturbance from the enemy who had been badly shaken by their first encounters with the British and were in no mood to close with them in the darkness even where the opportunity offered.

General Haig's I Corps had hardly been involved in the events of the day. From their positions southeast of Mons they were in tenuous contact with the French Fifth Army on their right, although there was a significant gap between the two, and II Corps on their left. There were some minor artillery exchanges with the enemy but, as far as the infantry were concerned the Corps' participation was limited to two battalions of the Guards Brigade taking over some ground from II Corps' 8th Infantry Brigade to help that sorely pressed unit. In addition, at General Smith-Dorrien's request, Haig sent 3 battalions of his 5th Brigade to cover a two mile gap from Frameries to Paturages which had opened up between the 3rd and 5th Divisions as a result of the varied timings of the retirement of their battalions to their Second Line positions.[11]

Both the senior commanders and the troops engaged could look back with some satisfaction on the outcome of the day. Despite a marked inferiority in numbers they had given such a good account of themselves that the enemy had largely failed to drive them out of positions not of their choosing. They had inflicted serious casualties and induced a healthy respect for their professionalism in their opponents, whose reputation for invincibility had been severely dented. Even though the Germans would claim the Battle of Mons as a victory, it was in no real sense a defeat for the British. They had imposed a 24 hour delay on the timetable of the German advance, one of a handful of such setbacks which would ultimately ensure the failure of the Schlieffen Plan and make possible the Battle of the Marne.

Chapter V

The Start of the Retreat: 24 August 1914

Of itself, the situation of the BEF in the early hours of 24th August was not of huge concern to the senior commanders. What was of concern however was the situation of the French Fifth Army and how this might effect Sir John French's command. Even with their overnight withdrawal from the Mons salient and the canal line, the BEF were still well in advance of the French army and there was a worrying gap between the two. Sir John's undertaking to General Lanrezac late on 22 August that his army would maintain its positions for 24 hours had been honoured and had the French army been in a position to conduct an advance or at least stay firmly put, there would have been no discernible reason for the BEF to contemplate retreat. (At this stage GHQ were unaware of the growing threat represented by an advance of divisional strength by the Germans which would take them well to the west of the westernmost positions of the BEF.) As late as 20h40 on the 23rd Sir John was of the view that the next day the enemy would renew their attack on II Corps from the north and that, having strengthened their physical defences overnight, General Smith-Dorrien's Corps should stand and fight.[1]

During the night however it became apparent that the French Fifth Army's next move was going to be a retirement. The French Fourth Army, on the Fifth Army's right, had been forced to order a retirement for the 24th which would further expose the Fifth Army's right flank, the vulnerability of which had already been demonstrated by an attack on its rear by the German Third Army advancing from the east. General Lanrezac, whose army was also wilting under a strong German Second Army attack from the north on its frontage near Charleroi, in turn ordered a general retirement of his army to begin before daybreak on the 24th. On hearing of Lanrezac's order, the Commander of two French reserve divisions which had been heading northwards to plug the gap between the Allies decided not to advance beyond his command's assembly area 10 miles east of Maubeuge. These two decisions would have the effect of widening even further the gap between Lanrezac's army and the BEF. His failure to forewarn Sir John French of his intentions, was the final straw as far as the latter was concerned.

Sir John became privy to Lanrezac's plan when Lieutenant Spears arrived at GHQ in Le Cateau from Fifth Army HQ at Mettet at around 23h00 on the 23rd. When his information on French intentions had been digested, Spears was sent back with a terse message for Lanrezac to the effect that the BEF were no longer under any obligation to remain where they were and would act as circumstances dictated.[2] At around 01h00 on the 24th the Chiefs of Staff of I and II Corps, who had already been summoned to GHQ, were instructed to prepare to make a general retreat southwards of about 8 miles to an east-west line running from the village of La Longueville, about five miles west of Maubeuge, to the hamlet of La Boiserette, by way of Bavai, a total length of about 7 miles. The detailed arrangements were left to the Corps Commanders to settle between them.[3] Both Corps were enjoined to avoid at all costs being sucked into Maubeuge. To this end they would be denied use of the roads running through the city. The fear of being trapped in a fortress city was a prevalent one. If the fate of Sedan and Metz in the Franco-Prussian War were not sufficient warning, the more recent fate of Liège was.[4]

As on the 23rd the experience of the two Corps was to differ markedly. Once more the brunt of the fighting would fall on parts of II Corps, while I Corps would be left relatively unmolested. The inference of this, that the Germans were concentrating on making a decisive effort further to the west, was confirmed by aerial reconnaissance reports which began to come in not long after daylight. By this time both 1st and 2nd Divisions of Haig's Corps had disengaged without trouble and were on the road south. Even the rearguard, which had been established under the command of Brigadier General Henry Horne, came under no real pressure. The components of the Corps reached their destinations by 22h00, having suffered more from fatigue and heat exhaustion than from the attentions of the enemy.[5]

Before dawn, the Germans had already made clear their intentions with regard to II Corps, when they opened a heavy artillery bombardment on the Corps' right flank which rapidly spread along the whole length of the Corps' line. By 05h15 it was clear that a major infantry assault was developing, making the task of disengagement that much more difficult for Smith-Dorrien's divisions. The 8th Brigade, which had been so heavily engaged the day before, was the first to receive the order to retire and was able to do so quite comfortably in the absence of any significant enemy infantry presence opposite them. The other two brigades of 3rd Division were less fortunate when it became their turn to follow suit. They both came under heavy infantry attack when they began their moves back. The 1st Lincolns, who were the rearguard battalion of 9th Brigade, helped by 109th Battery RFA, inflicted sharp losses on the massed ranks of the advancing enemy infantry. The latter took shelter from the rapid fire of the Lincolns behind corn stooks in the fields, which they rapidly discovered offered no protection at all. Having inflicted heavy casualties the British battalion retired through Frameries, where further sharp encounters were dealt with and the retirement to Sars-la-Bruyère continued.[6] The 7th Brigade, beginning their retirement from Ciply, also retired in good order towards Genly. But 2nd South Lancashire Regt suffered serious losses when they were enfiladed by enemy machine guns firing from Frameries.[7]

The really heavy fighting of the day took place to the west of Frameries where it involved Fifth Division and, to a lesser but still significant extent, the Cavalry. It had been well past daybreak before the last of the Division's units which had been defending the canal the previous day reached their Second Line positions. The Division were therefore well behind the rest of the BEF in organising for their part in the planned retirement. Their situation was further complicated by the retirement, beginning at 09h00, of the battalions of 5th Brigade which Haig had loaned the previous day to cover the gap between 3rd and 5th Divisions. The resulting vulnerability of the Division's right flank was compounded by the fact that 19th Brigade, the French 84th Territorial Division and the Cavalry, which had been covering the Division's left flank, had also retired leaving this flank in the air. The Divisional Commander, Major General Sir Charles Fergusson, asked the Cavalry Commander, General Allenby, to stop his Division's retirement to provide some left flank cover. Allenby readily agreed. Fergusson gave instructions for his infantry brigades to retire as soon as they could disengage, the 14th first, followed by the 13th and finally the 15th. These retirements were to have been completed by the early afternoon.

The 13th Brigade were the first to find themselves engaged in heavy fighting. Reinforced by the 1st Dorsets on detachment from 15th Brigade, they were in position round and in the village of Wasmes. The enemy began their assault with a heavy bombardment and then tried to get their infantry out of the village of Hornu and into Wasmes. As usual they were forced to pay a heavy price at the hands of the British musketry and field artillery. But the fighting was intense, sometimes hand-to-hand, and British casualties were not insignificant, especially those of 2nd Duke of Wellington's Regt which amounted to nearly 400. The Dukes had nevertheless succeeded in stopping 6 German battalions in their tracks and were thus able to retire along with the rest of 13th Brigade. They were preceded by 14th Brigade who had only been lightly engaged and who in their turn covered the retirement of the 13th. The two uncommitted battalions of 15th Brigade (in addition to 1st Dorsets, 1st Bedfordshire Regt had also been detached, in their case to 14th Brigade) had already been sent to the village of Dour to form the divisional reserve.[8]

The role of these two battalions, the 1st Norfolks and the 1st Cheshires, was quickly to be changed to one of flank guard as it became apparent that a major German threat was developing against the left flank of the retiring 5th Division. The Germans were advancing in considerable strength from the direction of Quiévrain, Baisieux and Thulin largely unhindered because of the ill-timed retirements of the Cavalry Division and 19th Independent Infantry Brigade. Their aim was to attack between the villages of Elouges and Audregnies. If they could not conclude matters there and then with the annihilation of 5th Division they aimed to force them back into Maubeuge.

Under the overall command of Lt Colonel C. Ballard of the Norfolks the two British battalions were deploying as rapidly as possible between Audregnies and Elouges across the line of advance of the Germans, the Cheshires on the left and the Norfolks on the right. They were supported by 119 Battery of XXVII Brigade, RFA. The 2nd Cavalry Brigade, consisting of 4th Royal Irish Dragoon Guards, 9th Lancers, 18th Hussars and L Battery RHA, which General Allenby had turned around and sent back to the area at General Fergusson's urgent request, had positioned themselves in a hollow behind Audregnies on the left flank of the Cheshires.

At around 12h30 German artillery and small arms fire indicated that the German attack was getting underway. With the British infantry still not fully deployed the 9th Lancers and two troops of 4th Dragoon Guards were ordered to charge north from Audregnies, on either side of the Roman road, to take the German infantry in flank as they advanced in a broadly south easterly direction. The charge was to be a costly failure. After disposing of a few German advance

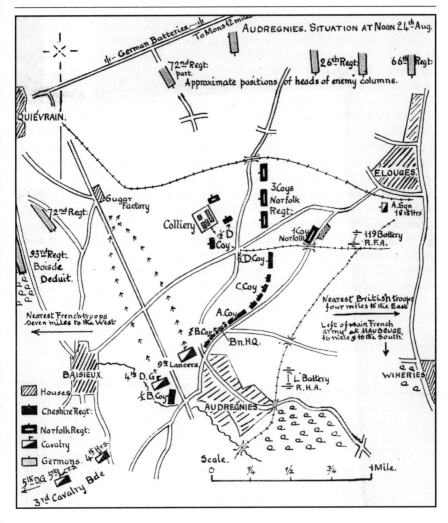

Sketch 8: The Action at Elouges / Audregnies, 24 August 1914

troops the troopers came up against barbed wire fences near a sugar factory which brought them to a halt and then forced them to make a wide sweep in full view of German batteries and machine guns which took a heavy toll. Some survived by taking shelter dismounted in the factory buildings. Others got back to Audregnies or made it to Elouges. The total losses were more than 200.

The charge may however have given the infantry time to complete their deployments. They almost immediately came under heavy pressure from the solid mass of German infantry advancing towards them. Once again the enemy presented perfect targets for the British artillery batteries and the musketry and machine guns of the infantry. But with the bulk of II Corps having put a safe distance between them and the enemy and the growing threat to the flank guard of being enveloped, Colonel Ballard ordered a retirement at around 14h30 and sent messages accordingly to the Cheshires. None of these was received with the result that only the Norfolks successfully extricated themselves. Even they had to leave over 100 seriously wounded behind and abandon the men in an advanced outpost to their fate. The Cheshires fought on despite their mounting casualties. Even when surrounded they continued to fight, only surrendering at around 19h00 when they had exhausted their ammunition. Only 202 officers and men out of a total of 1,000 answered their names at roll call following the battle. The Norfolks' losses were over 250.

The 119th Battery also lost 30 officers and men. But they did succeed in saving their guns despite being under fire from three German batteries. In doing so they earned two Victoria Crosses and two DCMs.[9]

With the ending of the Cheshires' and Norfolks' ordeal the Battle of Mons had fully evolved into the Retreat from Mons as both I and II Corps of the BEF escaped the threat of encirclement and made their ways south. British losses on 23 August had amounted to 1,642 killed, wounded and missing (some of whom would rejoin their units over the ensuing days). The count for the 24th was even higher at 2,590. Only 140 of these were I Corps losses, an imbalance between the two Corps to which the Retreat would add further.[10]

Chapter VI

The Retreat: GHQ and I Corps

he routes and the fortunes of the two British corps were to differ markedly over the two weeks of the Retreat from Mons. The accidents of geography and the fact that II Corps were on the western side of the BEF meant that Sir Horace Smith-Dorrien's troops would once more bear the brunt of the fighting during the retirement. While I Corps had to cope with a number of small scale actions, II Corps had to fight the major defensive Battle of Le Cateau.

The need for the Retreat itself had been brought about not by any doubt in the mindset of the BEF about their ability to withstand the frontal attacks of von Kluck's First Army, but by the growing evidence that the Germans were attempting to get round the BEF's left flank where the only obstacles to their progress between the area of the recent fighting and the Channel were two weak French divisions. Coupled with the retirement of the French Fifth Army which, if not conformed to by the BEF, would expose the latter's right flank, it left GHQ with no option but to retreat. The question was what the Retreat would seek to achieve in addition to extricating the BEF from the threat of encirclement. It was here that the poisonous personal relationship between Field Marshal Sir John French and General Lanrezac was to have significant effects on the military decisions of the former.[1]

Sir John's concern for the welfare of his troops was well-known. Early on in the Retreat he decided it was of paramount importance that his army should be given the opportunity to rest and re-equip by, in effect, withdrawing them from contact with the enemy to an area west of Paris, south of the River Seine. Only after their recuperation would he consider committing his troops to supporting a French counteroffensive. Not surprisingly this came as very bad news indeed to the French C-in-C, General Joffre. He was in the early stages of formulating a plan for the creation of a new French Sixth Army, to be positioned to the west of the BEF. When it was in place and the opportunity offered this new army would spearhead the counterattack. The disappearance of the BEF from the front line at such a crucial time would severely damage the counterattack's prospects of success. Sir John's distrust of Lanrezac had by now extended to a general distrust of the French High Command, including even General Joffre who, up to this point, could with reason be perceived to have presided over nothing but a series of disasters. As a result, when General Joffre outlined his plans to him, Sir John declined to change his intentions for the BEF beyond agreeing that it would not cut across the new French Sixth Army's lines of communication by falling back west of Paris. The BEF would instead fall back east of the capital.[2]

In a further demonstration of his resentment of his treatment by Lanrezac Sir John refused to offer any help to the Frenchman when he turned his army round and fought the Germans to a temporary standstill at the Battle of Guise. As a result of air reconnaissance General Haig had seen an opportunity to strike at the German flank in support of General Lanrezac, but he was forbidden by

Map 3: BEF Retirement from Mons

GHQ to intervene and was even accused of initiating operations with the French. In response to Lanrezac's request for help all Haig could do, in the face of such hostility from GHQ, was offer to cover the French army's flank.[3]

Sir John's attitude took little or no account of the fact that France was fighting a desperate and apparently losing battle for its survival against the German onslaught. Had it been allowed to prevail it could have meant the BEF standing idly by while the French army went down to defeat. This was not only militarily but also politically unacceptable and the Secretary of State for War, Lord Kitchener, intervened. After some face-to-face meetings, which did nothing to improve their personal relationship, Sir John was in effect instructed to conform with the French army's movements and drop all ideas of a unilateral strategy.[4]

The main geographic constraint affecting the cohesion of the BEF during the Retreat was the Forêt de Mormal. This block of woodland was about nine miles long from north to south and three to four miles wide. It was situated between Bavay (or Bavai) to the north and Landrecies to the south. Because it contained no north-south roads or usable tracks it was in effect a no-go area for the retreating BEF which would have to bypass it on 25 August either to the west or to the east or on both sides. For sound practical reasons the decision was taken that II Corps should pass down the western side on its way to overnight positions around the town of Le Cateau and I Corps should march round the eastern and southern edges to link up with II Corps near the French town. The advantages of this decision were that the danger of a flank march by the whole BEF across the enemy front, inherent in going for the western route, was avoided. If the eastern route only had been chosen, the BEF would have become engaged in fierce competition with the French army for the use of the few available roads. The main disadvantage was that, however possible it seemed in theory that the two corps would end up cheek by jowl on the night of 25th/26th, they would in practice be too far apart to be able to offer each other support. GHQ's orders had envisaged making the Bavay-Montay Roman road just northwest of Le Cateau the corps boundary which would have necessitated I Corps, having passed round the south of the Forêt de Mormal, effecting a junction with II Corps west of Le Cateau. But I Corps never got further west than Landrecies by the night in question, as General Haig had warned GHQ would be the case.[5] In effect I Corps were to remain on the eastern side of the River Oise all the way down to La Fère.

Both Corps had begun their retreats on 25 August from the area of Bavay. I Corps were hardly troubled by the enemy during the course of the day apart from the occasional German patrol. The main problem was in trying to sort out priorities with the 3 French divisions in the area also trying to move south, or west. But the bulk of the Corps' two divisions and the 5th Cavalry Brigade had reached positions stretching from Dompierre to Landrecies by early evening. The 5th Brigade, which had been left behind to guard some bridges over the Sambre River until relieved by French units, reached their overnight destination, Noyelles, at about midnight.[6]

It was at Landrecies, during the late evening and early morning of the night of night of 25/26 August, that a sharp action was fought, which is perhaps better remembered for the alleged effect it had on the usually imperturbable Douglas Haig than for the action itself. As the British were settling down for the night in Landrecies, largely under the impression that there was no immediate enemy threat, rumours began to circulate among the local population that the Germans were approaching the town and the neighbouring town of Maroilles. It was about 17h30. Two companies of 3rd Coldstream Guards, of the 4th Guards Brigade, 2nd Division, took up positions where the railway line crossed the road leading into Landrecies from the northwest about half a mile from the town itself. The mounted patrols which were sent out found no sign of the enemy.

No 3 Coy of the Coldstreams were on picquet duty on the road with a machine gun on either flank when at 19h30 they were approached by a body of troops who, when challenged, responded in French. The Coldstream picquet commander went forward to question them. In the course of the exchanges, always in French, the strangers edged forward and suddenly charged with fixed bayonets. The British officer was knocked to the ground and one of the machine guns seized before a volley of fire from the picquet drove the Germans back and enabled the machine gun to be recovered. The picquet was immediately reinforced and the whole of 4th Guards Brigade turned out with 2nd Grenadier Guards moving up in close support of the Coldstreams.

The Germans made repeated charges, all of which were thrown back. At 20h30 the town and the picquet came under artillery fire. The fire ignited some haystacks near the fighting. By the light of the flames the Germans realised that there was only a single thin line barring their way. They managed to bring enfilade fire to bear on this, but still without result. The fighting continued past midnight when the Germans were finally persuaded to withdraw by a howitzer of 60th Battery which was manhandled forward and succeeded in silencing the German guns with its third shot.

The loss of 120 Coldstreams and a similar number of Germans during the action is a good measure of its relative insignificance in the overall scheme of things.[7] But on a dark night it was not easy for Haig and his staff to get a true picture of what was going on. This was reflected in their overreaction. GHQ received a telephone call from Haig's headquarters at 22h00 describing the German attack as heavy from the northwest and asking for help to be sent. GHQ directed Sir Horace Smith-Dorrien to respond by at least sending 19th Brigade to I Corps' aid. Understandably, given his own Corps' situation at this critical time, Smith-Dorrien responded with regrets that he could not help. When he learned of this, Haig ordered the whole town to be organised for defence. Secret papers were to be destroyed. He proclaimed that they would sell their lives dearly. A further message was sent to GHQ at 01h35 describing the situation as 'very critical'.

Haig's uncharacteristically melodramatic behaviour at this time has been put down to the effects of a gastric infection he had picked up a couple of days earlier and had refused to have treated. He was subsequently persuaded to have treatment which consisted of a dose of something which, according to his Intelligence Officer Brigadier General Charteris, must have been designed for elephants. Its effect was immediate and volcanic! But it was also effective although Haig was still suffering the after effects when he arrived at Landrecies. [8]

There was to be a significant military consequence arising from the alarmist reports received at GHQ of the Coldstreams' action. On the assumption that it represented the beginning of strong enemy pressure on I Corps from the northwest, Haig was ordered to continue his retreat in a southern rather than a southwestern direction, thus ensuring the continued separation of the BEF's two corps.[9]

There was one other small-scale clash of arms with the enemy on the night of 25/26 August involving I Corps, this one involving units of 6th Brigade of

2nd Division. A troop of the 15th Hussars had been given the task of guarding a road bridge over the River Sambre on the Maroilles-Locquignol road, about one and a half miles northwest of Maroilles, until they could be relieved by infantry. A second troop were guarding a lock bridge two miles away from the road bridge and a similar distance west of Maroilles. There was no disposition on the part of the local population to believe that there were any Germans in the area, to such an extent that the Hussars were refused permission to destroy some wooden buildings near the road bridge which were obstructing their view. The complacency of the locals was rudely shattered when at around 18h00 the advanced guard of the German 5th Division engaged the Hussars at both bridges. They were easily held at bay for about an hour until they brought up a field gun at the road bridge and, using the very buildings that the Hussars had wished to destroy, got close enough under their cover to compel the Hussars to retire leaving the bridge in German hands.

The 1st Royal Berkshire Regt had only just arrived in Maroilles after a long day's march from Bavay when B Coy were ordered back in the direction they had come to relieve the Hussars at the Sambre road bridge. The advancing B Coy bumped into the retiring Hussars and learned from them that the bridge was now held by the enemy. The Berkshires took up positions on the Rue des Juifs about a mile southeast of the bridge. The Germans were close by and, with a piece of subterfuge, took B Coy's commander prisoner. Perhaps sensing that they were overexposed and vulnerable the Germans then retired back to the bridge. The approach to it for the Royal Berks, intent on retaking it from the enemy, was along a causeway flanked by swampy water meadows which prevented any deployment on either side. By now the whole Battalion had moved up to join B Coy. There are differing accounts of how successful the Battalion's attempts to wrest back the bridge were. The War Diary states without detail that the bridge was retaken by B, D and C Companies after a night attack. The recently published Battalion History endorses this claim although it makes no claim for the bridge as a whole, just the southern end. The Official History states that 'the enemy having barricaded the bridge and put his field gun into position, the Royal Berkshire failed to drive him from it. After a total loss of over sixty men, it was decided to make no further attempt to recapture the bridge until daylight, and to be content with forbidding advance along the causeway.' After the war Field Marshal Haig recalled the incident in a letter as follows:

> A company of the Berkshire Regiment, followed later by the rest of the battalion, was dispatched at once to retake the bridge at all costs. The approaches from the south side led across a narrow causeway. This was found to be commanded by a field gun, and being flanked by bad ditches and marshland it was impossible to deploy. Two attempts to retake the bridge were repulsed. About midnight the 1st KRRC were ordered forward to resume the attack. As nothing more could be done in the darkness the Berks were withdrawn and the 1st KRRC prepared to carry the bridge at dawn. Before the plan could be carried out orders were received for the general retirement to be continued at daybreak.

The weight of evidence therefore points to the probability that the bridge was not entirely, and perhaps not even partially, retaken by the British. But there is no question that the presence of the 1st Royal Berks close to, if not on, the southern end of the bridge precluded its use by the enemy throughout the night. The decision to continue the general retirement at daybreak on the 26th made its possession or non-possession an irrelevance.[10]

GHQ's order to Haig that he should continue his Corps' retreat southwards rather than to the southwest as previously envisaged was modified to give him the option of a more southwesterly route, which would lessen the gap between the two Corps, or a southeasterly route, which would bring his Corps closer to the retreating French. Haig chose to stick with the southern option. His main concern was the perceived threat from the northwest which, if it materialised and was successful, would lead to a breakthrough between the two British corps.[11] Elaborate rearguard and flankguard arrangements were put in place to protect the Corps' retirement on Etreux on the 26th but no serious threat materialised. The same could not be said for II Corps which was this day fighting the Battle of Le Cateau. Any possibility of I Corps coming to the aid of its embattled comrades was precluded by GHQ's failure to keep the two Corps informed of the situation of the other (the two Corps had no means of direct intercommunication).

The 27th was to be a more fraught day for Haig's Corps, especially for the 2nd Royal Munster Fusiliers. The retreat was to continue due south along the Landrecies-Guise road which the French had agreed to leave free for the British. Once more, rear and flank guards were put in place. The rearguard for the whole Corps was entrusted to 1st Guards Brigade. The 1st Coldstream Guards were in position just northwest of a bridge crossing the canal north of Oisy. The 1st Scots Guards and 1st Black Watch were deployed between the Coldstreams and the village of Wassigny where the western flankguard took over. The Munsters were further north than the rest of the Guards Brigade, facing northeast between Chapeau Rouge and Bergues and northwest at Chapeau Rouge itself. Attached to them were two troops of the 15th Hussars and a section of 118th Battery RFA. The Munsters' CO, Major P. Charrier was directed to hold on in their positions until ordered or forced to retire.

After some preliminary early skirmishing the Germans launched unsupported infantry attacks at 10h30 at Bergues and Chapeau Rouge which were dealt with without much difficulty by the well-entrenched Munsters and the RFA guns. At 12h30 the enemy attacks were renewed in greater strength but still unsupported by artillery. This time the pressure was sufficient for Major Charrier to order a gradual retirement from Chapeau Rouge to Fesmy, which was successfully accomplished. Although the Irish musketry effectively deterred close follow up, it was not long before the Germans delivered a strong artillery supported attack of the Munsters' new positions. In the face of the Irish machine guns they drove cattle before them, an ineffective screen as it turned out. In the meantime the troops at Bergues were forced out of their positions but retired in good order towards Oisy.

At 13h00, with the main bodies of the Corps successfully on their way southwards and the Guise road more or less clear of traffic, the Brigade Commander ordered all units of the rearguard to retire at once. Although dispatched by two separate routes the order never reached the Munsters. Nevertheless, with the German attacks growing in intensity it was evident to Major Carrier that the time had arrived for a fighting withdrawal towards Oisy. This began at 14h30. Thirty minutes later, 1st Coldstreams north of Oisy received the Brigade Commander's order to retire and did so, along with 1st Scots Guards and 1st Black Watch, leaving the guarding of the bridge over the canal at Oisy to the detachment of Munsters and Hussars which had arrived in the village from Bergues. Despite being attacked by a cavalry division on their march south the 3 battalions reached Guise virtually unscathed.

The 2nd Munsters, retreating from Fesmy, had almost reached Etreux in the early evening. As they approached the village they came under rifle and artillery

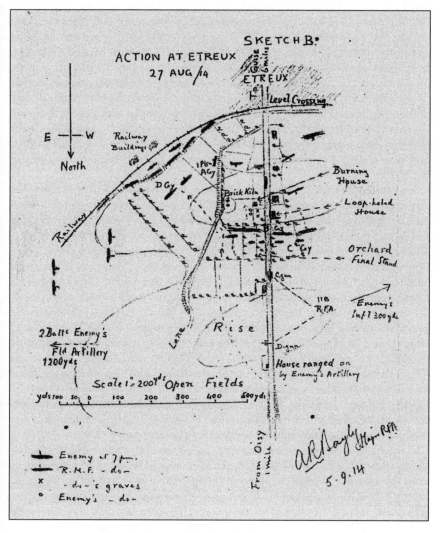

Sketch 9: The 2nd Royal Munster Fusiliers at Etreux, 27 August 1914

fire from German troops who had got behind them and had occupied houses on the northern outskirts. With great courage the Munsters threw themselves into a series of assaults on the German positions in desperate attempts to break through and continue their march south. But by 19h00 these efforts had failed and the Munsters were forced onto the defensive by the growing number of enemy. Major Charrier was killed and a final attempt to break out failed. With German troops pressing in on them from 3 sides and ammunition exhausted the main group of around 250 survivors was finally overwhelmed and forced to surrender at about 21h15. The Munsters' stubborn rearguard action against overwhelming odds, sometimes amounting to 9 enemy battalions, had dealt yet another severe blow to the German timetable as well as giving breathing space to the retreating I Corps which, by the end of 27 August, were over 12 miles ahead of their pursuers.[12]

The bulk of I Corps spent the night of 27/28 August south or west of Guise. During the course of the following day they continued their retreat along the axis of the main road heading southwest from Guise through Mont d'Origny to La Fère. Despite this change of direction there still remained a gap of 15 miles between I and II Corps which it was feared the German cavalry would seek to exploit. The main body of I Corps was relatively untroubled by the enemy all day; the sharpest engagement of the day involved 5th Cavalry Brigade of Brigadier General Henry Horne's flankguard. The Brigade was sent to the west of the River Oise by Horne, and its Commander, Brigadier General Sir Philip Chetwode, held it in readiness in and between the villages of Moy and Cérizy southeast of St Quentin.

As feared, the German cavalry advanced in two columns as if probing the gap between the two corps. The western column was effectively deterred from pressing too hard by Brigadier General Hubert Gough's 3rd Cavalry Brigade which had been sent eastward from II Corps to try to link up with I Corps. The eastern column was successfully ambushed and then routed by 5th Cavalry Brigade which probably inflicted 300 casualties on the Germans, ten times the number of British casualties. Although only a minor action it was to have a significant dampening effect on the offensive ardour of the German cavalry.[13]

Late on the night of the 28th GHQ ordered that the following day should be one of rest for the BEF provided that all units were south of a line from Nesle to Ham prolonged eastwards. It was on the same night that Haig was peremptorily refused permission to co-operate with General Lanrezac in his planned attack at Guise. In the light of the apparent inability of Lanrezac to make progress against the Germans Sir John French ordered a further retirement of the BEF to behind the River Aisne. With the BEF occupying the area between the French Fifth and the newly created Sixth Armies, General Joffre was obliged to abandon any thought of standing and fighting on the Reims-Amiens line.[14]

The I Corps enjoyed an undisturbed day on the 29th and renewed its march southwards at 03h00 on the 30th. Again there was to be very little interference from the enemy; the main problems for Haig's troops were the suffocating heat, the dust and roads choked with refugees. These forced a curtailment of the planned distance to be covered during the day. The same circumstances prevailed the following day. I Corps crossed the Aisne through and to the west of Soissons and halted for the night on the northern instead of the planned western side of the Forest of Villers-Cotterêts. It was during this day that aerial reconnaissance indicated that the German First Army was now moving south instead of southwest and might even be showing the first signs of a move onto a southeasterly course. Von Kluck was apparently discounting any threat to a potentially exposed right flank from the newly created French Sixth Army and the BEF. For Joffre the German move represented the makings of an opportunity. For Sir John French it seemed as if once again the BEF were in the direct line of march of the First German Army. His orders were therefore for the retreat to continue the following day, this despite the pressure he was coming under from Kitchener and the Government at home to conform with General Joffre's plans.[15]

At 04h00 on 1 September I Corps resumed its march south, 1st Division skirting Villers Cotterêts to the east and 2nd Division to the west. By late evening, after yet another day of intense heat, and having marched around 16 miles, 1st Division reached its planned stopping places around La Ferté Milon. The 2nd Division and 3rd and 5th Cavalry Brigades arrived at Betz and the villages between it and La Ferté, about 8 miles to the east. The infantry had scarcely been bothered by the enemy during the day, but the 3rd Cavalry Brigade, which had screened the left rear of the retiring Corps, had been attacked at Taillefontaine and had suffered casualties in sharp fighting which lasted until midday. But the brunt of the day's fighting fell on 2nd Division's rearguard, the 4th Guards Brigade. At the start of the day they occupied two lines north of Villers Cotterêts. The northernmost, between Vivières and Puiseux-en Retz, was held by the Irish Guards and 2nd Coldstreams, and the line further south, at Rond de la Reine, by 2nd Grenadier Guards and 3rd Coldstreams. In support were 9th Battery of XLI Brigade, RFA.

At 10h00 the northern battalions came under attack from a German force of all arms trying to advance in a southeasterly direction. The British response, especially that of 9th Battery, was so effective that the enemy fire died away, It was deemed safe for 2nd Coldstreams to retire to the northern edge of Villers Cotterêts and they did so. But as the Irish Guards were about to follow suit the Brigade Commander warned their CO not to fall back too quickly as it was intended to give the main body of I Corps a long rest during the heat of the middle of the day. It was too late to recall the Coldstreams and at 10h45 the enemy resumed their attack with greater vigour than before. A company of Grenadiers from the second line were sent up to reinforce the Irish. The Germans now mounted a flank attack on the Brigade's second line and were able to penetrate through the wide gaps between the positions of the 2nd Grenadiers' and 3rd Coldstreams' companies. Both battalions, fighting now in isolated groups, fell back very slowly and were eventually joined by the retreating Irish Guards. The slow retirement towards Villers-Cotterêts continued until they linked up with the 2nd Coldstreams in position on the railway line just north of the town. The 17th Battery RFA would have been able to offer supporting fire to the Guardsmen had it been necessary. But the Germans had, at least temporarily, been successfully seen off.

The 2nd Division's 5th and 6th Brigades, which were by now southwest of Villers-Cotterêts, halted to cover the retreat of the Guards Brigade whose rearguard battalion, 2nd Coldstreams, passed through 5th Brigade in mid-afternoon. Towards 16h00 the Germans, advancing southwest from Villers-Cotterêts, engaged in a sharp artillery and infantry duel with the British field artillery, 6th Brigade's 1st King's (Liverpool) Regt and the ubiquitous 2nd Coldstreams. The fighting ended for the day at around 18h00 when 1st King's successfully broke off the action after the artillery's retirement had been assured.

The day's fighting had resulted in the loss of over 300 officers and men of the Guards Brigade (including two isolated platoons of Grenadier Guards which had fought to the last man) and 160 officers and men of 6th Brigade. But significantly higher casualties had been inflicted on the enemy.[16]

It was on 1 September that I and II Corps finally re-established direct close contact. They were to remain in tandem for the remaining few days of the Retreat. Sir John French's force had meanwhile been enlarged by the arrival of 4th Division from England. With the 19th Independent Infantry Brigade they were formed into III Corps which, under the command of Lieutenant General William Pulteney, came into being on 30 August and took up positions to the left of II Corps.[17]

From 2 September onwards contact with the enemy was almost entirely confined to brushes between cavalry units of either side. The general Retreat continued, initially southwestward but then southeast to keep away from the perimeter of the entrenched camp of Paris and to narrow the gap which had widened between I Corps and the French Fifth Army. The change of direction had the risk of offering the Germans the opportunity of taking the BEF in flank but it was becoming clear that the German Corps opposite the BEF had also turned south east and were therefore marching more or less parallel to the BEF. The cavalry were given the task, successfully fulfilled, of ensuring that the Germans did not get near enough to realise the opportunity on offer. With the threat from the enemy seemingly contained the main problem for the British was the continuing extreme heat and growing exhaustion of officers and men. The daily distances covered diminished appreciably as longer rests became necessary to prevent heat-stroke and excessive numbers falling out. Haig decided to send back by rail half of his Corps' ammunition thus freeing up 50 wagons which were used to carry kit and some of his exhausted soldiers.[18]

On 3 September the BEF crossed the River Marne, blowing the bridges behind them. The following day they crossed the Grand Morin river. On 5 September, the last day of the Retreat, the British reached their halting places south-southeast of Paris. I Corps were in and around the town of Rozay. During these early days of September it had become apparent to the Allied Commanders that von Kluck's First Army was becoming more committed to its easterly course. The German General was apparently ignoring the danger this would open him up to from the garrison of the fortress of Paris, the French Sixth Army and the BEF, all of which were poised on his right flank and rear. General Joffre made the fateful decision; the French Sixth Army would attack on 5 September with the French Fifth and Ninth Armies and the BEF joining in on the 6th.[19]

Chapter VII

The Retreat: GHQ, II Corps and Le Cateau

The action at Elouges and Audregnies had successfully parried the German attempt to envelop II Corps and temporarily alleviated the enemy pressure. During the course of 24 August the troops' main enemies were exhaustion and lack of sleep as they trudged to their overnight halt line extending westwards from Bavay to St Waast and thence southwestwards to Amfroipret. The day's march had deliberately entailed the two divisions of the Corps exchanging positions so that 5th Division would now be on the right and 3rd on the left. It was part of a strategy to ensure that the Corps stayed well clear of Maubeuge and to ease the length of the day's march for 5th Division. The 19th Brigade and the Cavalry Division were positioned between St Waast and Saultain, well to the west.[1]

Late on the 24th Sir Horace Smith-Dorrien received orders to continue to retreat southwestwards the following day to a line between the town of Le Cateau and the village of Haucourt, a march of 15 miles and, in some instances, more for his troops. The route to be followed would skirt the western edge of the Forêt de Mormal, the obstacle to the cohesiveness of the BEF. There was some welcome news for Sir Horace; he learned that the newly arrived 4th Division had arrived in the Le Cateau area and would move north to Solesmes to assist in II Corps' retirement.[2]

Despite the arduousness of the previous day for many of the troops, it was planned that the first troops to move off on the 25th should do so at midnight. But there was an unavoidable delay as the French cavalry of General Sordet moved across the planned path of the Corps on their way west. It was not until 03h00 that the main body of 5th Division moved off with 3rd Division following suit at 05h00. The day was to prove largely uneventful for the bulk of the Corps. But the 7th Brigade, which was providing the rearguard for 3rd Division, the 19th Brigade and the 4 cavalry brigades, all of which were deployed on the western flank of the Corps, were to spend the day in running fights with bodies of German troops apparently determined to put the retreating British under pressure without exposing themselves unduly to their foes' by now much respected musketry. A particular flashpoint was the town of Solesmes and the area immediately round it. Several important highways converged there and the British military traffic found itself competing for road space with the large numbers of refugees and their wheeled vehicles, to the serious detriment of the progress of both. The 4th Division had taken up positions just south of the town and were ordered by GHQ to cover the retirement of 3rd Division, 19th Brigade and the Cavalry Division. They were still there as darkness fell and were not able to begin their move southwest to their overnight positions, on a line from Fontaine-au-Pire to Wambaix, to the left of II Corps' planned positions, until 21h00.[3]

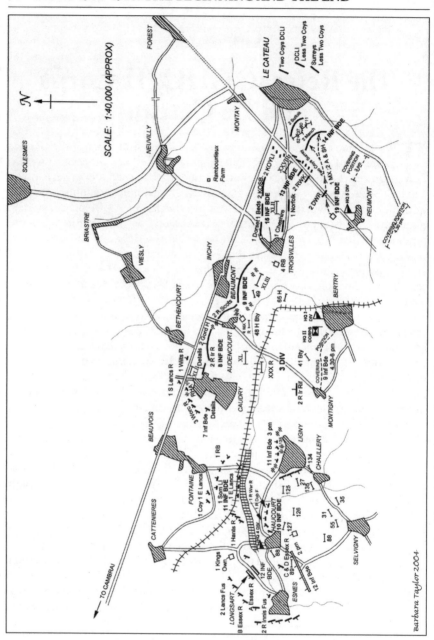

Map 4: Battle of Le Cateau
(Map courtesy of Barbara Taylor)

The main consequence of the enemy's more aggressive posture and the traffic hold-ups, not only at Solesmes but also at Le Cateau, was to make it another very long day for the troops directly involved and to lead to the widespread scattering of the cavalry putting it well beyond the capacity of its commander, General Allenby, to exercise any serious control over its movements. Some units did not make it to their planned overnight halting points until very late at night, if at all. But many did, including the bulk of the 3rd and 5th Divisions.

During the night of the 25th/26th Sir Horace Smith-Dorrien was confronted with the need to make some vital decisions. His orders from GHQ, received at about 21h00, were unequivocal. On the next day he was to continue his march to the southwest to a line between Beaurevoir and La Sablière, a distance for his troops of between 10 and 15 miles.[4] The catalyst for his decision to stand and fight instead was probably the report he received from General Allenby in person soon after midnight on the 26th. Allenby told him that in order for the cavalry to cover the initial stages of the planned retreat they would have to retake some high ground south of and overlooking Solesmes, something which was beyond their strength to achieve. In these circumstances, and with the Germans so close, the day's retreat of II Corps and 4th Division would have to begin under the cloak of darkness to enable them to get away before the enemy attacked. Allenby warned Smith-Dorrien that his division was so scattered and exhausted that it would not in any case be able to provide effective cover for the retreat if it was to be resumed that day.

At around 02h00 Smith-Dorrien asked General Hamilton, the GOC of 3rd Division, whether his troops could be got on the move before daylight. Hamilton told him that some of his units were only just coming in and there could be no question of the Division being formed up and ready to depart before 09h00. After a full discussion with both Allenby and Hamilton, Smith-Dorrien came to the reluctant conclusion that he had no alternative but to stand and fight. He hoped thereby to administer a sharp check on his pursuers which would give his Corps the breathing space to resume their retreat relatively unhindered. Allenby and the GOC 4th Division were asked to place their commands under his orders. Both readily agreed.[5]

Smith-Dorrien immediately sent a lengthy message to GHQ at St Quentin informing Sir John French of his decision and the reasons for it. The fastest means available for its despatch was staff car which took until 05h00 to reach its destination. Aroused from sleep a probably befuddled Sir John composed a reply. It was not in the event sent until 11h05 as it had been discovered that the two headquarters could telephone each other using the railway telephone linking their nearest stations. Henry Wilson thereby conveyed the gist of Sir John's reply to Sir Horace shortly after 06h00. Wilson placed more emphasis on the need to break off the action as soon as possible, reflecting Sir John French's belated concern that the written message had given Smith-Dorrien too much latitude. The message had read in part:

If you can hold your ground the situation seems likely to improve. 4th Division must cooperate. French troops are taking offensive on right of I Corps. Although you are given a free hand as to method this telegram is not intended to convey the impression that I am not as anxious for you to carry out the retirement and you must make every endeavour to do so.

Sir Horace took this, when he eventually saw it, and his conversation with Henry Wilson as endorsement of his decision to stand and fight. Had it been otherwise it would in any case have been too late to revert to an immediate continuation of the retreat.[6] Sir Horace's decision and Sir John's final assessment of it were sadly to lead to a further downward spiral in their already poisonous relationship. But that was for later. On 26 August there was a battle to be fought.

The battlefield stretched from just south of Le Cateau, on the right, in a just north of west direction through the villages of Troisvilles, Audencourt and Caudry, and thence southwest to Haucourt. The main part of the British line therefore ran just south of the dead straight Cambrai-Le Cateau road. In normal circumstances the topography would have greatly favoured defence. But the British expectation had been that the Le Cateau position was to be merely an overnight stop on their retreat. By the time it became apparent, either from the belated receipt of orders countermanding those ordering the retreat, or from the opening of the enemy attack, that they were going to stand and fight that day, there was little time available to dig in and prepare sound defensive positions.

With the caveat that the previous day's rearguards were in some cases only just arriving in the pre-dawn period, the bulk of the troops under Smith-Dorrien's command were in or close to their allotted overnight positions as the day's fighting started. The 5th Division were on the Corps right. The 1st DCLI and 2 coys of 1st East Surreys, of 14th Brigade, had been sent the previous night to positions out on a limb east of Le Cateau near the village of Bazuel. They were there in the hope of making contact with I Corps.[7] Unbeknownst to them this was no longer a possibility as the changed route being taken by Haig's troops was widening the gap between the two corps.

One of the remaining battalions of 14th Brigade, 2nd Suffolks, were placed immediately to the west of Le Cateau across a spur of higher ground. Just to their southwest were 2nd Manchesters and the other 2 coys of 1st East Surreys. Next in line, moving to the west, were two battalions of 13th Brigade, 2nd KOYLI and 2nd KOSB. In close support of the Yorkshiremen were XV and XXVIII Brigades RFA and 37th Howitzer Battery. Behind the two forward battalions, in echelon, were 1st Royal West Kents and 2nd Duke of Wellingtons.

Next came 15th Brigade occupying the line from the left of 2nd KOSB's positions to just north of the village of Troisvilles. On the Brigade's right were 1st Bedfords, with 1st Norfolks behind them, and on the left 1st Dorsets, with the remnants of 1st Cheshires in echelon. The XXVII Brigade RFA were in support east and southeast of Troisvilles.

The British position continued to the west and was occupied by the brigades of 3rd Division. The 9th Brigade were on the right of the Division between Troisvilles and Audencourt. The 1st Northumberland Fusiliers were on the right, 1st Lincolnshires on the left. Immediately behind were 1st Royal Scots Fusiliers with 4th Royal Fusiliers further back in reserve. Close artillery support was provided by XXIII Brigade RFA. Further south were 65th Howitzer Battery and 48th Heavy Battery.

The 8th Brigade were located in Audencourt and between that village and Caudry. The 2nd Royal Scots were in Audencourt, with 4th Middlesex behind them. In the middle of the brigade line were 1st Gordon Highlanders with 2nd Royal Irish Regt on their left closest to Caudry. With the exception of 2nd Royal Irish Rifles, still well to the southeast at Maurois, the 7th Brigade were fully deployed around Caudry. Northeast of the town were 1st Wiltshires and to the north 2nd South Lancashire Regt and 56th Field Coy RE. On the northwestern outskirts were 3rd Worcesters.

The rest of the artillery available to the Division was largely concentrated around Caudry. The exception was XL Brigade which was in position south west of Audencourt.

Temporarily operating as part of Smith-Dorrien's command, the 4th Division were on the left of the British line occupying the stretch between Caudry and the villages of Haucourt and Esnes. Closest to Caudry and south of Fontaine-au-Pire were 11th Brigade. The three forward battalions were 1st Rifle Brigade, 1st Somerset Light Infantry and 1st Hampshires, with 1st East Lancashire Regt close behind. At Haucourt in reserve were 10th Brigade with the Royal Dublin Fusiliers and the Royal Warwicks east of the village and 2nd Seaforth Highlanders and 1st Irish Fusiliers behind it.

The extreme left of the British positions was occupied by 12th Brigade. The battalions were spread out from north of Haucourt to northwest of Esnes. The 1st King's Own (Royal Lancaster Regt) were on the eastern flank with 2nd Lancashire Fusiliers on their left facing northwest. On their left covering the north and west of Esnes, were two companies of 2nd Royal Inniskilling Fusiliers. The other two Inniskilling companies and the four companies of 2nd Essex Regt were distributed in the hamlet of Longsart and between the left flank of 2nd Lancashire Fusiliers and the Inniskillings at Esnes.

The reserves theoretically available to General Smith-Dorrien consisted of the Cavalry Division and 19th Infantry Brigade. One of the main reasons for his decision to stand and fight had been the difficulty the cavalry would have had in screening a continued retreat because of its scattered state. Nevertheless orders had been issued for the 4 brigades under his command to take up useful positions. Two of them, the 2nd and 3rd, were ordered respectively to Bazuel and Mazinghien, to help guard the Corps' right flank. The 1st Brigade were placed about four miles southwest of Le Cateau near the village of Escaufourt. The 4th Brigade were ordered back from their advanced position at Inchy to Ligny, southwest of Caudry, which they reached at dawn. These orders give the impression that the Cavalry brigades were intact and cohesive, but this was only the case with the 3rd and 4th at either end of the British deployment. Parts of 1st and 2nd Brigade were detached from their main bodies, in the vicinity of Le Cateau. It was hoped that they might nonetheless be of help in covering the gap between I and II Corps.

The 19th Infantry Brigade had found themselves caught up overnight in the traffic chaos in Le Cateau. Not having received any countermanding orders they were still intent on continuing the retreat. They were two hours behind schedule, and only just ahead of the Germans, when they finally got clear of Le Cateau and made their way southwest towards Reumont village. It was here that they were intercepted by a messenger with orders for them to stand fast there as part of Corps reserve.

The units of 5th Division only received their orders countermanding the retreat at around 06h00 if they received them at all. The DCLI and East Surreys, who had been sent east of Le Cateau in the hope of linking up with I Corps and were among the non-recipients, began their withdrawal by way of the southeast corner of the town. There, at 06h30, they came under fire from Germans who had somehow got into the area unobserved. With all thoughts of withdrawal abandoned by the British troops they manned a defensive line on the high ground southeast of the town. But the threat of a German breakthrough between the two British corps, with the DCLI and East Surreys separated from the rest of their Corps, was very real. Under cover of a counterattack by the East Surreys which forced the Germans back, they moved eastwards towards Bazuel. When they were strengthened by units of the 1st and 3rd Cavalry Brigades they felt able to resume their attempt to rejoin their Brigade. They began their move westward at around 08h30 and made slow but steady progress against stiff opposition. Two companies of the DCLI lost touch with the main body and made for St Benin to the southwest. The remaining half of the DCLI, with the help of a battery of artillery managed to take the Germans in enfilade forcing them to withdraw to the east. The main body then split up with the DCLI making for Escaufourt which they reached before midday. The East Surreys made for Maurois and the cavalry units went due south to St Souplet. The first, rather half-hearted, German attempt to get round the British right flank had failed.

The 2nd Suffolks were particularly disadvantaged by the late receipt of the order to stand and fight. They were in an exposed position, had neither the time nor the equipment to dig in properly and were to prove overoptimistic in their assumption that the ground to their right would be occupied by the arrival of I Corps. Almost immediately they came under heavy artillery fire which pinned them down. Their position worsened when fresh German guns, firing from just over two miles to the northwest, took them in enfilade. The British artillery did their best to respond but had only muzzle flashes to aim at. It was not until some German skirmishers showed themselves on high ground as they attempted to silence the British gunners that some of the Suffolks had the chance to use their weapons. If they had any effect it was hardly noticeable as the Germans placed more artillery on the high ground east of Le Cateau (which the Suffolks had expected to be occupied by I Corps) thus enabling them to enfilade the British right wing from both flanks. Greatly outgunned the exposed British artillery fought on as, one by one, their guns were silenced and their crews killed or wounded. The Suffolks, and 2nd KOYLI on their left, were also deluged by shrapnel. The 19th Brigade's 2nd Argyll and Sutherland Highlanders came up from Reumont to take up position on the right of the Suffolks just in time to help in dealing with the entry of the German infantry into the battle. As had become familiar to their opponents this took the initial form of massed formations apparently aiming to overwhelm the defenders by sheer weight of numbers. Their advance began at 10h00 on a two mile front stretching from due east of the British right wing round to the north, opposite 13th Brigade's frontage. It was met by concentrated machine gun and rifle fire as well as that of the surviving field artillery and the heavy howitzers further back. The attacking infantry suffered heavily but replaced the fallen and continued their advance with scarcely a pause.

The Suffolks were successfully resisting everything that was being thrown at them but were taking serious casualties. They were reinforced by the Argylls taking over some of their trenches. The 2nd Manchesters had also been sent forward from Brigade reserve to provide reinforcement which enabled the British line to be extended southward. But all 3 battalions were in a serious plight not helped by ammunition shortages and the final elimination of their last remaining close support field gun by German heavy artillery fire. With the Germans growing in strength and pressing harder all the time there appeared to be only one possible outcome as midday came and went. But this was not even considered as the British battalions determined to cling on in the increasingly remote hope of rescue by I Corps. In contrast to what was happening on their right the remaining battalions of 5th Division passed a relatively quiet morning enabling them to dig in more thoroughly than the Suffolks and KOYLI had been able to.

Generally speaking, the 3rd Division had more notice than the other two divisions that 26 August was going to be a day of battle rather than retreat. This was because its headquarters were close to Smith-Dorrien's and its GOC, General Hamilton had been part of the consultation process which had determined Sir Horace's course of action. Although there remained the difficulty of getting orders to widely dispersed brigades and battalions, the Division as a whole were aware by 04h00 of what was to be required of them. The Germans had clearly recognised that there was very little prospect of success for a massed infantry assault on the positions occupied by the 8th and 9th Brigades, which enjoyed good fields of fire. They therefore confined themselves to minor attempts at infiltration which were quickly discouraged and not pressed. Their focus on this part of the battlefield would be on Caudry which formed a tempting salient in the British defences.

The village was defended by 7th Brigade and any notions they might have had that they would soon resume the retreat were quickly dispelled when the Germans, from an early hour, subjected the town to heavy artillery and small arms fire. At 07h00 a vigorous infantry assault began on both flanks of the village, but especially on the Worcesters on the left. So forceful was the German assault for a time that reinforcements were called up from 8th Brigade. These consisted of two depleted companies of 2nd Royal Irish Regt, who moved up at about 08h30 to positions east of the village.

By 09h00 2nd Royal Irish Rifles had finally rejoined the rest of the Brigade when they reached the hamlet of Le Tronquoy, about 1,000 yards south of Caudry. There they entrenched, with 41st Battery RFA unlimbered to their right rear. Thus reinforced, 7th Brigade were able to cope with the German assault, which had in any case diminished in intensity, without giving ground.

Unlike the other two divisions under Smith-Dorrien's command, the 4th Division had only received orders to continue the retreat on the 26th at around midnight, too late for them to be got to subordinate formations before they were countermanded and their earlier orders of the previous evening, to occupy positions round Haucourt, reinstated. In implementing these the Division were to labour under severe disadvantage as they faced the prospect of maintaining the integrity of Smith-Dorrien's left flank. Only in infantry and field artillery was their order of battle complete. They were still without their cavalry component, their cyclists, their engineers, most of their signallers, their train, their ammunition column and field ambulances. The deficiencies were serious, leaving the Division effectively blind, unable to construct proper defences, largely unable to convey orders except by runner or mounted officer, and with limited means to care for wounded. But even more potentially disastrous was the lack of their 60 pounder heavy artillery, which could be so effective in disrupting enemy troop deployments. The Division had also had a rather tough time since it had detrained at Le Cateau station and other stations thereabouts on 24 August. As has already been noted they had been immediately ordered forward to positions just south of Solesmes to assist in the retirement of II Corps. Their march northward began at 01h00 on the 25th and took them 4 hours. The day passed relatively quietly with only light exchanges with the enemy. But it was not until 21h00 that 12th Brigade were able to begin the Division's flank march southwest to their planned overnight positions. The 11th Brigade followed suit an hour later and the 10th at about midnight. The heavy rain which had set in and a pitch black night did nothing to help the brigades find their ways and there were some wrong turnings taken. It was not until 05h00 that it could be safely said that the Division's infantry were all in the positions assigned to them, most of them bedraggled and many hungry.

There was one positive feature from which 4th Division could draw some comfort as they contemplated their immediate future, the presence of General Sordet's French Cavalry Corps on their western flank. Their movement the previous day from east to west across the path of II Corps had been a major contributor to the delays and traffic chaos suffered by the British, especially at Le Cateau itself. But even though as exhausted and bedraggled as many of the British units, the threat that their presence offered was to sow seeds of doubt and uncertainty in German minds as they sought to deal with II Corps.

The 4th Division very quickly felt the effects of their lack of cyclists or cavalry when the enemy launched an attack in strength whose build-up had been undetected. Soon after 06h00 heavy machine gun fire targeted the totally unprepared 1st King's Own who suffered heavy casualties before they were able to respond and contain the German fire. But the Germans were able to bring artillery to bear which caused further casualties among the Lancastrians. Two companies of 1st Royal Warwicks, sent forward from reserve to assist them, also suffered heavily. The Germans then turned their attention to 2nd Lancashire Fusiliers, adding cavalry and infantry in turn to the machine gun fire, in which they enjoyed a great preponderance. When the British Battalion's single effective machine gun proved too hot for them, the Germans moved to positions where they could enfilade the Fusiliers, causing heavy casualties. Two companies of 2nd Royal Inniskilling Fusiliers moved up to reinforce both flanks of the Lancashire Fusiliers, while the rest of the Battalion successfully contained an infantry attack aimed at Esnes.

Even though 4th Division's 12th Brigade had successfully withstood for 90 minutes or more the German surprise attack employing a cavalry division and two infantry battalions, backed by heavy machine gun and artillery fire, the time had come for a retirement to nullify German attempts to get round the advanced British left flank from the direction of Wambaix. The extrication of the battalions concerned was not to prove an easy task. The Royal Warwicks again suffered badly in protecting the withdrawal of the remnants of the King's Own. The 1st Hampshires (11th Brigade), sent up to help the Royal Warwicks, forced a German artillery battery to retire hurriedly by the strength and accuracy of their musketry at long range. The retirement of 12th Brigade to the line Ligny-Esnes was successfully achieved by about 10h00 except for one platoon of the Inniskillings who, all wounded, remained where they were and continued to inflict heavy casualties on the enemy. In order to strengthen II Corps' left flank 1st Irish Fusiliers of 10th Brigade were ordered to occupy a ridge southeast of Esnes. The 2nd Seaforth Highlanders were placed in echelon.

Except for XXXVII Howitzer Brigade, which did not come into action, 4th Division's available artillery support consisted only of field artillery. This provided steady support to the infantry during the course of the morning. But the enemy's huge preponderance in artillery was used to advantage in reducing the exposure of their infantry.

The enemy's artillery strength was, as midday passed, still making matters very difficult for II Corps' right wing. The 2nd Suffolks, the 2nd Manchesters and the parts of the Argylls holding the line here could look for very little hope of reinforcement. Two battalions of the reserve 19th Brigade had been sent west to Montigny to be available should an enemy threat to Ligny develop. This left only the remainder of the 2nd Argylls and all of 1st Middlesex available. They were quickly moved up on the right flank in support. Fortunately however the German infantry showed little disposition to press on with trying to outflank the British defences. Nevertheless the position remained precarious. There being little likelihood of reinforcement or a miraculous intervention from I Corps, the GOC of 5th Division suggested to Corps HQ at 13h20 that he had better begin retiring. In anticipation of such a move the artillery teams were sent forward to recover the guns. Even though these were close to the firing line and under heavy bombardment a number of them were limbered up and made good their escape. But others had to be disabled and abandoned as men and horses were cut down by enemy fire.

Corps HQ's response to General Fergusson's suggestion was to order the two battalions of 19th Brigade recently sent to Montigny back east to Bertry where they were placed at the disposal of 5th Division. At the same time General Smith-Dorrien asked General Fergusson to hang on a little longer, but gave him permission to withdraw as he should think fit. The plan was for 5th Division's and 19th Brigade's retirement to be followed by 3rd and 4th's in that order. The routes and roads to be followed to the southwest were spelled out in the orders prepared by Corps HQ.

The German infantry had by now overcome their reluctance to press the British right wing hard and were gradually gaining ground until only two or three hundred yards separated attackers and defenders. Despite this, 37th Battery of VIII (Howitzer) Brigade managed to get one of their two guns away from under the noses of the enemy. This was to be the last British success on this part of the battlefield. In overwhelming strength the German gradually surrounded the

Suffolks, Manchesters and Argylls. All attempts to make them surrender failed and they fought on until overrun by a rush of enemy from their rear. The end came at around 14h45.

General Fergusson's order to his units to retire was issued at 14h00 but, generally speaking, did not reach battalions until an hour or so later, if then. The message had to be carried by hand across terrain swept by enemy artillery and machine gun fire and it was perhaps remarkable that it reached as many units as it did. One unit which did not receive it was 2nd KOYLI. As a result of the overrunning of the Suffolks on their right they found themselves under strong pressure from the Germans from that direction as well as from the continuing pressure they were under from their front. They were able to inflict great execution on the massed ranks of German infantry which tried to overrun them from the right. But the retirement of other battalions, in conformity with the orders they had not received, left 2nd KOYLI with no cover to their rear or left. This enabled the Germans to outflank the Yorkshiremen. Even though they still presented tempting targets which were taken full advantage of, the Germans were able finally to overrun the survivors of the Yorkshire battalion at about 16h30 by dint of maintaining their pressure from the right rear, resuming their attacks from the front, and opening a new line of attack from the left, which had been left exposed by the departure of 2nd KOSB. The Yorkshire Battalion's losses were very heavy but they had, perhaps unwittingly, held up the Germans to an extent which enabled other units of 5th Division to make a good start to their retirement.

German plans for a wider sweeping movement from east of Le Cateau which, if successful, might have taken retiring 5th Division units in rear, were successfully nullified by a judicious use of the remaining troops available to block the enemy's path. A line running from Reumont to Escaufort through Maurois and Honnechy was put together to back up 3 platoons of the Argylls, 59th Field Coy RE, half of 1st Middlesex and two companies of 1st Scots Fusiliers, who were further forward on the western slope of the valley of the River Selle. It was this grouping that initially stopped the Germans with their long range rifle fire and the assistance of E and L Batteries RHA. The enemy resumed their attack at around 15h30, but again were temporarily brought to a halt, mainly by the RHA guns. Nevertheless the time had come for the forward group to pull back, which they did to positions southeast of Reumont. In the meantime attempts by the enemy artillery to eliminate their British opposite numbers had had very little effect.

By now the delays inflicted on the advancing Germans, which were added to by the accurate fire of 61st Howitzer Battery and 108th Heavy Battery, gave hope that darkness would soon cloak the retirement of the 5th Division's infantry. This was soon underway and proceeded with very little interference from the enemy. The main problem was that units had become thoroughly mixed up. But the first priority was to get clear of the battlefield; sorting out could be left to later.

In contrast to the heavy fighting experienced by much of 5th Division, 9th Brigade of 3rd Division immediately to their left had quickly brought the enemy's attempts to advance beyond Inchy to a complete halt, largely through the dominance of XXIII Brigade RFA. The Brigade received the order to retire at about 15h30, none too soon as the battalion to their right had already begun to withdraw and they needed to conform. The withdrawal of the infantry battalions proceeded smoothly with two of XXIII Brigade's batteries successfully discouraging any German attempts to interfere. Once the infantry had passed them the guns were disabled and abandoned.

To the west of 9th Brigade's positions around and east of Caudry, the enemy showed much greater determination. Their efforts against 2nd Royal Scots and 1st Gordons of 8th Brigade east of the village nevertheless wilted in the face of the British rifle fire. The village itself was subjected to concentrated and heavy artillery fire from about 14h00 which led to a temporary British retirement and its occupation by the Germans. A counterattack by 3rd Worcesters of 7th Brigade, mounted between 14h30 and 15h00, succeeded in reoccupying the southern half of the village but failed to clear the enemy out of the village entirely. It was in any case time to withdraw and arrangements were made for this to be begun using 2nd Royal Irish Rifles and two field batteries as cover. By 16h30 the withdrawal was virtually complete, which was just as well as the parts of 8th Brigade, which had received the order to retire, were doing so, leaving Audencourt village empty. But not all of 8th Brigade had received the retirement order. Nearly all of 1st Gordon, half of 2nd Royal Irish Regt and a handful of 2nd Royal Scots were non-recipients and continued to fight where they stood. Although Audencourt had been under heavy bombardment since early afternoon there was no infantry assault on the village until 17h00. Then, perhaps assuming that there were few, if any, British remaining in the vicinity, the German advance was made in such a way as to expose themselves to the rifle fire of the Gordons and Royal Irish. They were shot down and the advance halted. At about the same time the rest of 8th Brigade, together with 7th Brigade, were on their way to Montigny on the first stage of their withdrawal from the battlefield.

The failure of 3rd Worcester's counterattack to reoccupy the whole of Caudry had meant that the Germans were able to enfilade 4th Division's 11th Brigade's positions between Caudry and Esnes. It was decided therefore to pull them back to positions in front of Ligny. The retiring troops sustained heavy losses as they were obliged to cross open ground on their way back. The enemy infantry were however overeager in their efforts to follow up this success and suffered at the hands of the British artillery. They rallied and resumed their advance. They suffered even more heavily and this time abandoned their attempts to dislodge 11th Brigade from Ligny.

Further south the German attempt to break through with a strong attack towards Esnes had been thwarted by the rifle and machine gun fire of 2nd Royal Inniskilling Fusiliers and their supporting artillery. But there was a clear danger that the rapid build up of German strength in this area would soon open up the danger of the British positions being outflanked and turned to the west. This threat added urgency to 4th Division's need to begin its retirement as soon as II Corps had largely disengaged and begun its retreat. This was the case by about 17h00. With the threat to their left flank growing by the moment the time could have hardly been more opportune for General Sordet's French cavalry corps to appear to the left and rear of 4th Division. Sordet had been ordered by General Joffre not just to cover the British left flank but to intervene in the battle with all the force at his disposal. His response was full hearted. His artillery and cyclists took the Germans in flank as they sought to close with the British. The British left flank seemed secure.

The main activity from 17h00 onwards involved the disengagement and retirement of all the British infantry and artillery units fortunate enough to have received the orders to do so. There was to be surprisingly little attempt on the part of the enemy to disrupt the operation. The drizzling rain that had begun to fall was to bring on an early onset of darkness which seemed to indicate to many German units that it was time to call it a day. Even on the British right flank, where the Germans had scored their most striking success, 1st Norfolks, who were operating as rearguard for the collection of units making up the right wing of the Corps, were surprised to see the Germans stop about 3 miles southwest of Le Cateau on the road linking the town with Busigny. Infantry seemed to have given way to small parties of cavalry seeking, without much success, to harass the British. Even the German artillery's activity was only intermittent. The British right wing's main problem was the congestion on the main artery of their retirement, the Roman road heading southwest from Le Cateau. It was shared by 5th Division and 19th Brigade, but with no German pursuit worthy of the name the congestion sorted itself out and the troops marched steadily towards relative safety.

The retirement of the bulk of the 3rd Division was achieved with even less interference from the enemy than had 5th Division's. To a not inconsiderable extent they owed this to the fixation of the Germans with the British units which, not having received the order to retire, were still occupying their positions in front of Audencourt and between that village and Caudry. For about two hours from around 17h00 the Germans made strenuous and unsuccessful frontal and outflanking efforts to overrun the Gordons, the Royal Scots and the Royal Irish Regt before handing the problem over to their artillery. This achieved nothing as the latter focused their efforts on Audencourt, long since evacuated by the British. Meanwhile the rest of the Division made its unhindered way by way of Montigny and Clary to the area of Beaurevoir, 13 miles southwest of Le Cateau.

The retirement of 4th Division was an altogether livelier affair than that of the other two divisions. It also received a great deal of attention from the German artillery. Fortunately for the Division they did not have to worry greatly about their left flank being turned as it was being very effectively protected by General Sordet's Cavalry Corps. Nor was the German artillery as great a threat as it might have been thanks to a very carefully worked out plan of retirement for the British guns which ensured that some of them were always in position to give covering fire to the others and to the infantry. Thus were many of the guns saved. Although there were a lot of small units of infantry which had become detached from their main bodies there was nevertheless a sufficiency of large bodies to offer cover as they passed through each other on their way out of the forward area. The retirement began at about 17h00. Two hours or so later the last Battalion, 1st Hampshires, were on their way. Once again the Germans did little to pursue or impede the departing British except for some occasional shellfire.

The units which had not received orders to retire were to feature significantly in the lists of British casualties for the day. Having successfully withstood everything that the Germans had thrown at them during the early evening, and their efforts to obtain orders from Brigade or Divisional HQ having come to nought, the CO of 1st Gordons (who, as senior officer present had also assumed command of the Royal Scots and Royal Irish Regt detachments) decided at around midnight to pull out his troops from their assembly point near Caudry. By now the route they wished to take had been infiltrated by the enemy and after a couple of inconclusive brushes with them the British column found itself up against hopeless odds. After a further hour of fighting they were overpowered and the survivors made prisoner.

In the 4th Division area a number of units had found themselves cut off and in danger of being surrounded around Haucourt. Two companies of the King's Own and about half of 1st Royal Warwicks managed late at night to get back on track to rejoin the Division. But some Royal Dublin Fusiliers with stragglers from nearly every British battalion in II Corps, totalling about 200 men, became separated and fought a series of fire-fights as they struggled to rejoin the main body of the BEF. Eventually 78 officers and men succeeded in reaching Boulogne. The rest had become casualties.

Of the roughly 2,000 officers and men who had not retired from the battlefield, generally because they had received no orders to do so, about half became casualties. Their sacrifice had not however been in vain. Their continuing presence on the battlefield until late into the night had distracted and confused the enemy, thereby playing a major part in discouraging pursuit and harassment of the main bodies of General Smith-Dorrien's men as they retired.[8]

In order to derive full advantage from the check they had inflicted on the enemy at Le Cateau, Smith-Dorrien's men needed to put as much distance as possible between themselves and the enemy. The night of 26/27 August would not offer much opportunity for rest or sleep. After marching for distances of around 10 miles, which for many of them took them up to midnight and in some cases beyond, they then had to endure being sorted back into their parent units in darkness, an operation which took up to two more hours. They then had to resume the retreat southwards at 04h00. Leaving aside stragglers, who would be rejoining their units over the coming days, they were leaving behind a total of 7,812 men (and 38 guns) who had become casualties. Heavy though these losses were, they were unquestionably more than matched by the losses inflicted on the enemy. More to the point were the consequences which flowed from the battle for the ability of the BEF to continue the Retreat relatively unthreatened and for the Germans to implement in full the strictures of the Schlieffen Plan.[9]

Chapter VIII

The Retreat: II Corps: the Aftermath of Le Cateau

The combination of circumstances which led General Sir Horace Smith-Dorrien to conclude that he had no alternative but to turn on his pursuers and fight the Battle of Le Cateau has already been described. Sir Horace was fully aware that in so doing he was contravening GHQ's orders that the Retreat should be continued on 26 August. Although by the time he received it the die was cast, he interpreted Sir John French's reply to his message announcing his intentions as an endorsement of them.

> This reply cheered me up, for it showed that the Chief did not altogether disapprove of the decision I had taken, but on the contrary considered it might improve the situation.[1]

Sir John's reply, with its emphasis on the need to resume the Retreat at the earliest possible moment, had been reinforced before it had even been seen by Sir Horace by the telephone call he received from Henry Wilson as the first shots of the battle were being exchanged. Wilson had been instructed by Sir John, already fearful that his written reply had offered Sir Horace too much latitude, to urge retreat rather than battle. Wilson was however quickly won over by Sir Horace's optimistic assessment of the likely outcome of the day and rang off with the words, 'Good luck to you; yours is the first cheerful voice I have heard for three days'.[2]

There is now general agreement among Great War military historians that Sir Horace's decision to turn and fight was not only right but also the only practical option open to him in the circumstances. The distinguished military historian, the late John Terraine, went so far as to describe the Battle of Le Cateau as, '...in truth, not only the most brilliant exploit of the B.E.F. during the Retreat, but one of the most splendid feats of the British Army during the whole of the War'[3]. The Official History's verdict on the Battle was almost as wholehearted in its praise.

> In fact, Smith-Dorrien's troops had done what G.H.Q. feared was impossible. With both flanks more or less in the air, they had turned upon an enemy of at least twice their strength; had struck him hard, and had withdrawn, except on the right flank of 5th Division, practically without interference, with neither flank enveloped, having suffered losses certainly severe, but considering the circumstances, by no means extravagant. The men after their magnificent rifle-shooting looked upon themselves as victors; some indeed doubted whether they had been in a serious action. Yet they had inflicted upon the enemy casualties never revealed, which are believed to

have been out of all proportion to their own; and they had completely foiled the plan of the German commander and of OHL.[4]

Sir John French and the GHQ staff spent 26 August gloomily convinced that Smith-Dorrien's failure to continue the Retreat as ordered could only result in the destruction of II Corps. It was not until the arrival of Sir Horace at GHQ (which, unknown to him, had moved that day from St Quentin to Noyon) in the early hours of the 27th that the gloom was partially lifted with his confirmation that the action had been successfully broken off and the Retreat was once again under way. The meeting between Sir John and Sir Horace was less than harmonious or a meeting of minds. Sir John, who had spent the day convincing himself that Sir Horace's disobedience of orders had been unforgivable, accused him of undue optimism in his assessment of the results of the battle. Sir Horace, whose well-known hot temper had not been improved by the difficulty he had had in locating GHQ in the middle of the night, responded robustly. The two men parted with their mutual antipathy enhanced.[5]

When his official dispatch appeared on 7 September however it looked as if, after further reflection, Sir John had come to accept that Sir Horace had pulled off something remarkable on 26 August. Although it reminded its readers that Sir Horace had been ordered to retire at the earliest possible moment, it concluded by paying him a most handsome tribute.

> I cannot close without putting on record my deep appreciation of the valuable services rendered by General Sir Horace Smith-Dorrien. I say without hesitation that the saving of the left wing of the army under my command on the morning of the 26th August could never have been accomplished unless a commander of rare and unusual coolness, intrepidity, and determination had been present to personally conduct the operation.[6]

If matters had been left there that would have been an end to it. But Smith-Dorrien's conduct continued to rankle with the Commander-in-Chief and by late April of the following year he was telling General Haig that he should have court martialed Smith-Dorrien for his disobedience of orders.[7] Sir John did his best to disown the praise he had heaped on his subordinate, claiming, in his self-exculpatory book *1914*, that the dispatch had been completed hurriedly before there had been time to study all the relevant reports. The book also more or less doubled II Corps' actual losses in men and guns during the battle. It also failed to admit the existence of the message he had sent to Smith-Dorrien on the morning of the 26th.[8]

In fairness to the Field Marshal however it must be said that there were other senior military figures who believed that Smith-Dorrien had been mistaken in taking the action he did. None of these was a senior officer of the 3rd, 4th, 5th or Cavalry Divisions, all of whom had been either privy to the decision or fully supportive of it. But they did include French's Chief of Staff, Sir Archibald Murray, Vice Chief Henry Wilson, and Sir Douglas Haig.[9] In the last case it may be questioned how far his views were based on purely military considerations and how far on a degree of guilt that his overreaction to the events at Landrecies had been at least partially responsible for the unbridgeable distance between I and II Corps on 26 August and the consequent inability of the former to come to the aid of the latter. There may also have been a touch of jealousy at work. Haig's conviction that Sir John French was unsuitable for the command of the BEF has already been noted. It was coupled with Haig's belief that he should be the occupant of that position. One of his two main rivals had already been eliminated through the tragically premature death of Lt General James Grierson. The second was Sir Horace Smith-Dorrien. It would do no harm to Haig's prospects if doubt were cast on the former's judgment and competence.

Haig was not to know that his rival would fall victim to his rancorous relationship with French well before the question of the removal and replacement of the Commander-in-Chief reached its climax following the Battle of Loos, fought in September-October 1915. During the Second Battle of Ypres in April-May of that year, Smith-Dorrien sought permission to shorten his lines by making a minor withdrawal. Sir John seized the excuse and opportunity to dismiss him (and then promptly accepted his successor's recommendation that Sir Horace's proposed withdrawal should be implemented).[10] The loss of this highly competent infantry general can not have served the future fortunes of the BEF well. The malign vindictiveness of Sir John's action, which was widely perceived as being just that, reinforced the growing doubts in the minds of many over his suitability for the position he held. The Battle of Le Cateau, although but one of the *causes célèbres* in the breakdown of the relationship between the two men, was to cast a long shadow in the futures of both and the consequent fortunes of the BEF.

For the moment however personal differences took second place to the need to complete the Retreat successfully and reunite I and II Corps. The skilful disengagement of the bulk of II Corps from the Le Cateau battlefield and the distances covered southwestward by the exhausted troops during the early hours of 27 August had improved the prospects of achieving the former. But there could be no let up if full advantage were to be taken of the check inflicted on the enemy's forward momentum by the events of the 26th. During their acrimonious meeting in the early hours of 27 August, Sir John French had told Sir Horace Smith-Dorrien that the orders issued on the afternoon of the 26th for the continuation of the retirement to the St Quentin (Crozat)-Somme line still held good. This involved minor modifications of the routes being taken by 5th Division and 19th Brigade which Smith-Dorrien put in place on his return from the meeting to his own Headquarters.[11]

Throughout the 27th and the night of the 27th/28th the southerly march of II Corps continued with only spasmodic enemy interference. The morale of the troops was boosted by the availability of food and water, the opportunity for brief rests and the use of road wagons and the railway, where available, to carry the men too exhausted to march further. By dawn on the 28th the bulk of II Corps were south of the River Somme, about 35 miles from the Le Cateau battlefield.[12]

On 28 August the retirement of II Corps continued. This was to prove to be the last day on which distance covered was to be the yardstick of success or failure of a day's operations. Smith-Dorrien's men had in effect shaken off their pursuers. Other considerations were coming to the fore in allied thinking. The French Fifth Army were about to take to the offence at Guise and it was important for the BEF not to retreat so far south as to expose the French Army's left flank. In addition, Joffre's plans for the creation of a new Sixth Army which would spearhead his counteroffensive, subsequently to be known as the First Battle of the Marne, were being implemented. It was vital that he should be able to count on BEF participation and that all notions that the British should fall back, perhaps even as far as Le Havre, to rest and re-equip, should be abandoned. But even Joffre was at this stage content to see a continuation of the BEF's retreat provided that it did not expose his Fifth Army unduly and was continued at a deliberate pace until it reached the area from which they would turn and assume the offensive. Joffre acknowledged that this area was further south than he had originally wished, but the change should enable his plans to be properly implemented. The area he now suggested was on a line between the towns of Noyon and Roye.[13]

Late on 28 August, with air reconnaissance having shown little sign of close German pursuit, Sir John French ordered the BEF to rest on the 29th. The II Corps were by then north and east of Noyon. There was still a gap of about 11 miles between the two corps which was being covered by the cavalry. Mainly in order to narrow this gap II Corps crossed to the south side of the River Oise late on the 29th, blowing the bridges behind them. The river had already been crossed further east by I Corps and the gap was thus reduced to 7 miles.[14]

Any thoughts that Sir John French may have entertained to conform with General Joffre's wishes to end the BEF's retreat on the Noyon-Roye line were put to one side when news filtered through that the French Fifth Army's surprise attack at Guise had not resulted in a German defeat. Even though Lanrezac had inflicted a sharp check on the Germans, which might have become a defeat had there been active assistance from the BEF, the vulnerability of his Army, with its flanks open, had led Joffre to order its retirement, which belatedly began on 30 August. Regardless of Sir John's reaction. this spelt the end of Joffre's plans to hold the German on the Reims-Amiens line. The French Commander-in-Chief could still harbour concerns about the extent of Sir John's commitment to his overall strategy but could only acquiesce as Sir John ordered the resumption of the BEF's retreat on 30 August. The British C-in-C did however agree to slow its pace so as to fill the gap between the French Fifth and Sixth Armies, a commitment which he later regretted and retracted. It was at this point that Joffre invoked the help of his government which resulted in the intervention, already described, of Lord Kitchener with Sir John French.

The BEF's Retreat continued on 30 and 31 August with little interference from the enemy. The BEF were in fact opposite a gap between the German First and Second Armies. The former were pursuing a course well to the west where a number of sharp engagements were fought with the French Sixth Army as that new formation retired. The latter German formation were still trying to regain their balance and come to grips with the French Fifth Army following the shock Lanrezac's troops had given them at Guise. On 30 August the BEF's III Corps, consisting of 4th Division and 19th Infantry Brigade had come into existence. A gap of 5 miles already existed between the new Corps and II Corps which, on 31 August, was partially covered by 1st Cavalry Brigade and L Battery RHA both of which reached the village of Néry as darkness fell.

During the night of 31 August/1 September the German 4th Cavalry Division had crossed through the British lines undetected and bivouacked just to the east of Néry, at Le Plessis-Châtelain. Although tired, depleted in numbers and out of touch with the rest of German IV Corps, they became aware of the British presence in the village and decided to mount a surprise attack in the early morning. Perhaps assuming that surprise and their preponderance of numbers in men and guns would suffice, the Germans were remarkably careless in organising their dispositions. The heavy early morning mist, which was to hamper the German ability to direct their fire accurately, may also have led to them placing some of their artillery on a ridge close to the eastern side of Néry where it was vulnerable to counterbattery and machine gun fire.

The German plan was simply to overwhelm the British with shellfire supported by flanking cavalry attacks. It seemed to lack coordination from the start with machine guns opening up, achieving almost complete surprise but alerting the British before the artillery could join in. A dawn patrol of 11th Hussars had in fact skirmished with Uhlans and galloped back to Néry to report. But they only arrived immediately before the Germans opened up with their machine guns. Nevertheless, the main body of 11th Hussars, who were occupying sturdy stone farm buildings on the eastern side of the village, did have a brief time to man their defences in anticipation of a German assault and were soon returning the German fire coming at them from the ridge to their front.

L Battery RHA did not receive any warning in their exposed positions in a field south of the village. The effects of the German shrapnel and high explosive gunfire from positions about half a mile away south of L Battery's positions were

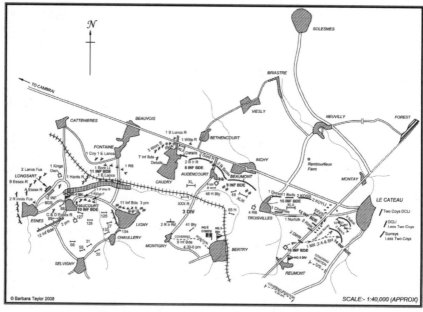

Sketch 10: The Action at Néry, 1 September 1914
(Sketch courtesy of Barbara Taylor)

devastating to men, horses and guns. Within a very short time L Battery's field was a shambles. Despite the shock and the damage however the survivors of the initial onslaught managed gradually to get 4 guns up and ready for action. Three of these were quickly put out of action by the enemy shellfire but not before they had inflicted some damage of their own including the breaking up of a squadron of cavalry which was about to charge. Soon only F Gun was left in operation. Despite many of the crew and their replacements being killed or seriously wounded the gun continued to fire and probably accounted for three of the enemy guns. One of those mortally wounded at this time was the Battery's Second in Command, Captain Edward Bradbury, who had initially rallied the Battery when it first came under fire, and had then helped keep F Gun in action.

Just as F Gun ran out of ammunition I Battery RHA arrived in the village and completed the silencing of the German guns. As the British had no high explosive shells it was difficult to inflict anything more than superficial damage on the enemy guns. They were silenced by the shrapnel fire of the RHA, coupled with the machine gun and rifle fire of the dismounted units of 1 Cavalry Brigade, which made it impossible for the German gun crews to stay with their guns.

L Battery played a key part in frustrating the German 4th Cavalry Division's plans on 1 September. Another key part was played by 5th Dragoon Guards who completely disrupted an attempt by the enemy's 3rd Cavalry Brigade to get round the northern flank of the British defences, by taking them in flank as they made their preparations. The 2nd Dragoon Guards (Queen's Bays) played a similar part on the southern flank of the British defences. They were caught by the initial German artillery onslaught in the same way as L Battery, losing many horses and men. But they recovered quickly and, having ascertained where the bulk of the enemy fire was coming from, brought their machine guns into action, one of their machine gunners, Lance Corporal Frederick Webb, even using his own knees as an improvised tripod to save time. So effective was the machine gun fire that it materially helped L Battery sort out their chaotic situation and ruled out any question of the German cavalry operating from horseback to mount a flank attack from the south east.

But a last attempt was made by two regiments of Hussars of 18 (Hussar) Brigade. Insofar as they had any clear idea of their objective it seemed to be to hit the British defences roughly at the junction of the 11th Hussars and the Queen's Bays The ground over which they charged had not been reconnoitred and it was topography rather than the British reaction that forced them southwards where they only narrowly averted attacking one of their own dismounted regiments of Dragoons in mistake for the British. Although it achieved nothing, the additional presence of the Hussars added to the German build-up south of Néry and caused the 1st Cavalry Brigade commander to look to reinforcing the British presence in the area. He was particularly concerned to dispute possession of a sugar factory about three quarters of a mile due south of the village, from where the Germans would have been able to enfilade L Battery and the Queen's Bays and give fire support to an assault on the British positions. Two small cavalry charges in succession were mounted against the growing German presence in the complex of buildings which made up the sugar factory, the first by a squadron of Household Cavalry of 4th Cavalry Brigade, which had come up to support 1st Cavalry

Brigade, and the second by the Queen's Bays. Although neither was successful in driving the Germans out of the factory, they did prevent any significant advantage being taken of its possession. Two machine guns which the enemy were trying to manoeuvre into the factory were eliminated by I Battery.

In trying to counter the British cavalry and move forward it is alleged that the Germans employed a human screen of Belgian civilians rounded up in the factory buildings. The stratagem failed although inevitably there were some Belgian casualties. The arrival of further British reinforcements in the shape of a company of 1st Middlesex of 19th Brigade finally enabled the British to clear the sugar factory of Germans.

Requests for reinforcements had been sent by dispatch riders as soon as the Germans had begun their attack. Both General Allenby at St Vast and General Snow, the GOC of 4th Division, at Verberie responded with alacrity; the former sent units not only to Néry itself but also well to the south of the village to get round the German flank and cut off their retreat. The latter alerted units to cut off any enemy attempt to retreat northwards. With I Battery RHA completely dominating the German guns, forcing them to abandon 8 of the 12 on the battlefield, the enemy were forced to abandon the field and retreat southwards to avoid being overrun or captured. Not all succeeded in getting away. A charge by 11th Hussars, ably supported by troops of 1st Middlesex, not only secured the German guns but also took some of the gun crews prisoners as well as divisional HQ staff when the German headquarters at Le Plessis-Châtelain was overrun.

Even though they had been a sitting target and had been taken by surprise by a much larger force, the 1st Cavalry Brigade with L and I Batteries, RHA, had pulled off a remarkable victory on 1 September. The enemy 4th Cavalry Division had been drastically reduced in size and effectiveness, having taken heavy casualties and lost most of their guns. The British had also suffered heavily, especially L Battery and the Queen's Bays, but the Brigade remained a fully effective fighting force for the trials which the immediate future would bring. L Battery's casualties in killed and wounded amounted to 55, more than a quarter of their establishment. They also lost 160 of their 220 horses, an early pointer to how appallingly horses were to suffer in the war. But the immense courage the Battery had shown in dealing with the carnage inflicted on them and keeping one gun operative until it ran out of ammunition was recognised by the award of no fewer than 3 Victoria Crosses of which one, to Captain Edward Bradbury, was posthumous.[15]

The action at Néry saw the only severe fighting on 1 September involving units of II and III Corps. The main bodies continued their trudge southwards in intense heat almost completely undisturbed by enemy action.[16] The rearguards of 5th Division and 4th Division did however have to deter enemy attempts to close with the retreating troops. The 5th Division had delayed their departure southwards in the light of the fighting at Néry. Their outposts north of Crépy-en-Valois, southeast of Néry, came under cavalry and light infantry attack at 06h00. This was followed up by an infantry attack from due north just as the Division's retirement was getting under way. The concentrated artillery fire of 119th Battery RFA and the rifle fire of 1st Royal West Kents, 13th Brigade, quickly brought the German attack to a standstill after which the Brigade was able to withdraw without difficulty. At the extreme west of the British line the Germans also attacked the two battalions covering the retirement of the 4th Division's 11th Brigade. They were beaten off after suffering heavy casualties.[17]

It was on 1 September that it was finally made clear to Sir John French by Lord Kitchener, acting with the full authority of the British government, that he must do his utmost to conform with the plans of General Joffre and not continue to pursue his apparent aim of withdrawing the BEF from the campaign for rest and recuperation. From now on the BEF's retreat would be a measured operation which would keep it occupying the area between the French Fifth and Sixth Armies and leave it in a position to take the offensive once General Joffre so ordered.[18]

For the next four days the Retreat would continue virtually unhindered by the enemy. By nightfall on 5 September the BEF were southeast of Paris. The II Corps were in positions in and east of the town of Tournan-en-Brie and III Corps on their left between Ozoir-la-Ferrière and Brie-Comte-Robert. The long Retreat from Mons was over. It had lasted 13 days and had covered 136 miles as the crow flies, but more like 200 on the routes actually followed. The name Mons would disappear from the thinking and ambitions of the BEF for four long year. But the first hesitant steps on the way back would be taken on 6 September 1914, as the Allied offensive known as the First Battle of the Marne got under way.[19]

Chapter IX

'The Angel of Mons'

An enduring feature of the BEF's participation in the Battle of Mons and the subsequent Retreat is the claim, or series of claims, that the British were materially helped at times of crisis in the fighting by supernatural or divine intervention. These manifestations have been usually referred to under the catchall title of 'The Angel of Mons', even though not all of them claimed to feature the presence of angels.

Stories of divine intervention on battlefields have a history as long as battles themselves. The Bible records many instances of the Lord coming to the aid of the Israelites, a familiar one being His help to Joshua in bringing down the walls of Jericho. It would have been a surprise if the mediaeval Crusades had not, by their very nature, offered up many instances of divine intervention which ensured Christian success on the battlefields of the Holy Land. A warrior Saint much invoked in aid by the Crusaders was St George, who made such an impression on the English contingents that they continued to invoke him when they returned from the near east and immersed themselves in wars closer to home. St George soon came to be regarded as England's patron saint. His name was memorably used as a rallying cry by King Henry V outside the walls of Harfleur in 1415[1]. It can come as no surprise therefore that the Saint was often to be a feature of the divine interventions said to have taken place in and near Mons in 1914.

It is perhaps surprising that, in early twentieth century Britain, there were still a very large number of people ready and willing to believe that the stories of supernatural events that were beginning to circulate in the early months of the war described actual happenings. Leaving aside those whose strong religious convictions, or belief in the occult, would always overcome any natural scepticism, there were many others caught up in the unprecedented circumstances of the time who were looking for explanations and reassurance which were not always forthcoming from governmental, military or press sources. This was particularly the case in the early months of the war when, with one notable exception, the public were starved of virtually any indication of what was happening to the BEF in France and Flanders and, for that matter, to the Navy. The one exception was when on 30 August *The Times* was allowed to publish a sensational and exaggerated report describing in highly coloured language an exhausted and shattered BEF in full retreat from Mons.[2] The thinking behind the Military Censor's action in passing and indeed embellishing the report appears to have been that the stimulation it would give to recruitment would more than outweigh the effects of the shock and alarm it would cause. It certainly did give an immediate boost to the numbers volunteering but it also added to a general public unease and anxiety about how the war was going, especially as the Military Censor immediately reverted to the policy of starving the press, and by extension the public, of information, a policy which was to continue until well after the Western Front had settled down into stalemate. It was small wonder in these circumstances that rumour and gossip moved in to fill the void. Rumours and stories of supernatural interventions on the battlefield were seized on as offering assurance that God was on the Allied side and that ultimate victory must therefore be certain.

Considering that the earliest supernatural intervention story concerned the successful withdrawal of 8th Brigade from their salient northeast of Mons on the late evening of 23 August 1914 it is curious that there was no reference to the event or anything similar in the British press until much later. What appears to have prompted a search for such stories was an article which appeared in the London *Evening News* on 29 September 1914 written by one Arthur Machen, a novelist and journalist with a predilection for the supernatural and the occult. The article was a story of pure fiction which was however clearly based on the events in the salient northeast of Mons on 23 August. It described how the British troops had been saved by the appearance of bowmen of the Agincourt period who had inflicted huge casualties on the Germans and dissipated their assault. Its appearance in a newspaper with no specific disclaimer that it was a work of fiction led to the story's widespread acceptance as factual.[3] Machen's persistent subsequent efforts to put the record straight were largely discounted.

Although many were to dispute that the whole Angel of Mons legend derived from Arthur Machen's story, there is no authenticated proof of claims that visions were observed over the battlefields of Mons and the Retreat prior to the publication of the *Evening News* article. General Haig's Director of Intelligence, Brigadier General John Charteris, claimed to have referred to rumours of the Angel of Mons in a letter home dated 5 September but there are question marks about whether this letter was actually written and, if it was, whether its date is correct.[4]

The legend was taken up by a fellow author and journalist of Machen's, Harold Begbie. Although he accepted Machen's insistence that his *Evening News* story had been fiction he disputed his belief that it had begun the whole Angel of Mons legend. Begbie's book *On the Side of the Angels – the Story of the Angel of Mons – an Answer to 'The Bowmen'* appeared in 1915. Begbie's book sought to authenticate the legend largely because it would inspire the war effort and offer comfort to the bereaved. But his selection of supernatural or divine instances lacked forensic rigour.[5] In particular he drew on hearsay evidence and the evidence of a British nurse, Phyllis Campbell. The youthful Nurse Campbell had been largely educated in France and, at the outbreak of war, joined a French nursing unit. She claimed that she had been told, by both British and French soldiers whom she nursed, of supernatural interventions on the battlefields, particularly around Vitry-le-François, during the Battle of the Marne.[6] In addition to the publicity her stories received through Harold Begbie and the *Occult Review* magazine she recorded them in a booklet entitled *Back of the Front* published in late 1915. The high regard in which she was held as a youthful and heroic nurse at the Front helped boost the public acceptance which her stories found. That she was never able to produce first hand corroboration of them was largely overlooked at the time even though Arthur Machen, for one, pointed it out. Further positive publicity for the Angel of Mons was also frequently to be heard from British church pulpits.

The reported sightings which can be grouped together under the general heading of 'The Angel of Mons' took many forms. Arthur Machen's story featured

Agincourt-era bowmen. Other claimed sightings featured angels, angels with bows, the warrior Saints George and Michael and the soon-to-be canonised Joan of Arc.[7] Under the heading 'The Legend of the Angels' the Mons Tourist Office's current *Battlefield Guide* describes the appearance of angels in the form of archers towards midnight on 23 August 1914. They came out of the sky and stopped the Germans thus enabling the beleaguered battalions of 8th Infantry Brigade, which were in danger of being surrounded and cut off, to retreat safely in the darkness. This version seems to derive largely in time and place from Arthur Machen's story although his bowmen have been elevated to angel archers. There is no mention either of the enormous casualties said to have been inflicted on the Germans by their celestial foes in Machen's story.[8]

The only other serious claim of divine intervention during the Battle of Mons itself involves the appearance of a line of angels between 1st Lincolns and the Germans as the former were acting as rearguard for the retiring Third Division. But that was not to be the end of it. More and more claims of divine intervention at Mons and subsequently were to be made as soldiers spoke to each other, to nurses and wrote home usually recounting what they had been told by other soldiers. These claims frequently featured St George clad all in white on a white horse with a flaming sword. His, and angelic appearances generally, seemed to be at times when British units were about to be overwhelmed; they invariably resulted in the confused retreat of the enemy. When German soldiers involved in these events were subsequently captured it was claimed that they frequently said they had observed large masses of British reinforcements approaching the action which had caused them to break it off and retire. According to the claims, these reinforcements were figments of their imagination or were phantom units conjured up by divine intervention.

In the case of French claims of supernatural events, for example those recounted by French soldiers to Nurse Phyllis Campbell, St George is usually replaced by St Michael or Joan of Arc. But for the British the white clad warrior was St George. Coincidentally, the English patron saint plays a large part in the history and contemporary life of the town of Mons. In a ceremony called *Le Lumeçon*, which is held every Trinity Sunday, the slaying of the dragon by St George is re-enacted in the centre of the town. This tradition dates back to the 14th century and probably indicates that the legends of St George brought back from the Crusades by the English also percolated to this part of Belgium.[9]

Despite the passage of over 90 years the legend of the Angel of Mons still exerts a powerful hold on the imaginations of many. The question of whether there is any truth behind it or not will probably never be resolved to the satisfaction of everyone. But for the average objective and dispassionate 21st century observer the circumstances surrounding the claimed supernatural visitations would probably call into question their authenticity. Considering the impact they are supposed to have had it is odd that they are not referred to in the War Diaries of the units concerned. Nor are they ever mentioned, except perhaps as a passing curiosity, in German accounts of the period. Given that on a significant number of occasions the visitations are supposed to have disrupted German attacks and sometimes forced hasty retreats, this is surprising. They are almost always claimed to have happened when British units were on the point of being overwhelmed by superior

German forces. As has been noted, these occasions were not that frequent in the period of the Battle of Mons and the Retreat. Even though the British were usually outnumbered their musketry had quickly taught the Germans, especially their cavalry, to be wary. Many of the British troops were puzzled that they were being ordered to retreat when they were coping more than adequately with the enemy threat. Nevertheless the continued skirmishing and endless marching in extreme heat, coupled with sleep deprivation and inadequate food supplies were to leave many of them exhausted and overwrought and ideal candidates for wild imaginings and hallucinations.

Sceptics from Arthur Machen onwards have made much of the fact that the accounts of visitations which were published or circulated by word of mouth or in letters were virtually never first hand experiences. Generally speaking they reported the experiences as having happened to others and were often at third or fourth hand. Human nature being what it is, the stories fed on themselves and were embellished at every retelling. The flood of publicity which the visitations received in 1915 is indicative of the momentum the legend was building up. There were no published accounts contemporaneous to the events they describe and even this short passage of time would have distorted recollections.

It is curious that the visitations all took place in the early days of the war. If they were an indication of divine support for the Allied cause it must be wondered why the interventions did not continue throughout the war. It goes without saying that there would have been many occasions on which they would have been most welcome. As for the visions themselves at least some of them seem to have been based on an imaginative interpretation of unusual cloud formations and light conditions.

Whatever view is held of the authenticity of the manifestations there can be little doubt that they were widely believed to have been genuine at the time. This belief did no harm and probably gave some consolation to the many bereaved. It also helped sustain national morale, through very dark periods in Allied fortunes, with the certainty it seemed to offer that the Allies would ultimately emerge victorious.

Chapter X

The Western Front 1914-16

On 6 September 1914 the strategy devised by General Joffre, in the wake of the disaster of the French Plan XVII[1] and the relative success of the German Schlieffen Plan[2], became fully operational. The newly created French Sixth Army continued with the attack they had begun the previous day. On their right the BEF and the French Fifth and Ninth Armies[3] went over to the offensive.

Although the growing German threat to Paris would have required a robust French reaction whatever the circumstances, the favourable conditions in which in fact it was made had been largely created by the German First Army Commander von Kluck's decision to abandon the wide sweep round the west of Paris, called for by the Schlieffen Plan, in favour of a turn to the southeast from positions northeast of the capital. His intention was to close the gap which had opened up between the German First and Second Armies. But his army's change of direction had the effect of presenting their rear and right flank to the allied armies which he had mistakenly discounted as no longer presenting a serious threat. The French Sixth Army's attack on 5 September forced him to turn part of his army to counter it and for a time it looked as if the French would suffer a serious setback. But the titanic efforts which the Military Governor of Paris, General Joseph Galliéni, made to strengthen the Sixth Army, including the moving of over 6,000 men to the front by Parisian taxis, retrieved the situation and became the stuff of legend.

The result of the allied offensive, known as the First Battle of the Marne, was that the Germans were forced into hasty retreat as they sought to prevent the Allies thrusting through the gap between their two armies. The retreat was only saved from turning into a rout by the caution of the allied pursuit, notably that of the BEF. Nevertheless, in this final abandonment of the Schlieffen Plan the Germans had lost their best chance of winning the war.

The pursuit took the Allies back over the Rivers Marne and Aisne, the latter of which was crossed on 12 September. It soon after became apparent that the Germans were now well dug in in pre-prepared defensive positions along the natural defensive barrier of the Chemin des Dames Ridge just north of the Aisne, and intended to retreat no further. At the same time the dangerous gap between the two German armies was closed by the arrival of the Seventh Army, newly created largely from units which had become available following the fall of Maubeuge on 7 September. The First Battle of the Aisne, which began on 13 September, consisted of a series of allied attacks on the German positions which achieved very little. German counterattacks also made little progress as the contest declined into trench warfare. Both sides thereupon began to seek to outflank the enemy by a series of western side-steps which were to become known as the 'Race to the Sea'. When this was reached, with neither side having succeeded in outflanking the other, the opposing trenches stretched in an unbroken line from the Channel to the Swiss border. The pattern for the next three and a half years of Western Front warfare had been established.

As soon as it became clear that the fighting on the Aisne had reached stalemate Field Marshal French sought Joffre's agreement to the BEF relocating at the western end of the Anglo-French line where pre-war planning had always been envisaged it should be. The creation of the French Sixth Army west of the BEF had upset this arrangement. It clearly made sense for the BEF to occupy an area where it could protect its own lines of communication back to the Channel ports through which it was supplied from Britain. In making the move the BEF would be better placed to assist in plans for the defence of Antwerp and to attack in an area where it was believed the Germans were absent or numerically weak. Joffre consented and the transfer of the BEF began on 1 October, initially to the area between Béthune and Hazebrouck. By the time the transfer was complete it was clear that Antwerp could not be held, which freed the 7th Infantry and 3rd Cavalry Divisions to join the BEF as IV Corps. This additional Corps enabled the British line to be extended northwards to Ypres where it linked up with the Belgians. There were also French divisions in the area.

Sir John French and the French Commander of Army Group North, General Foch, agreed plans on 10 October to advance against the enemy in the confident expectation that weak points would be found for exploitation. On the same day Antwerp fell. The Germans also occupied the city of Lille on 10/11 October which forced the BEF advance, which began on the 10th, to take a more northerly route than planned. For 10 days the BEF made steady but unspectacular progress, although it was becoming increasingly apparent that the German presence in front of them was a great deal stronger than had been anticipated. On 20 October the Germans turned the tables and attacked with five and a half corps backed with heavy artillery, greatly outnumbering the Allies. Their plan was to capture Ypres on their way to breaking through to the Channel. For the Allies the battle became one of stubborn defence along the whole of a line stretching from Bixschoote, five miles north of Ypres, to Givenchy and La Bassée, about 30 miles south. Despite occasional brilliant counterattacks, notably 2nd Worcesters at Gheluvelt and 2nd Oxford & Bucks Light Infantry at Nonneboschen, the Allied lines were pushed back. In the south the village of Wytschaete and the Messines Ridge fell. But the Germans failed to take Ypres despite enormous and costly effort. When the battle ended on 22 November the Ypres Salient had been formed with the Germans in possession of the high ground on three sides of the town. But by now for political and emotional reasons the sensible course of giving it up and creating a more defensible line further back could not be contemplated. The Salient was to prove a huge drain on the BEF's resources, both human and material, for the rest of the war.

The First Battle of Ypres, as the fighting from 10 October to 22 November became called, resulted in at least 135,000 German casualties, far outnumbering those of the BEF at 58,155. But the latter figure was out of a strength of a little over 90,000. In effect the BEF, as originally constituted and which had first taken the field at Mons, had been destroyed. But despite the heavy casualties of the first few months of the war the BEF's losses were numerically light compared to those of the French and Germans. Nevertheless, unlike those two countries, there

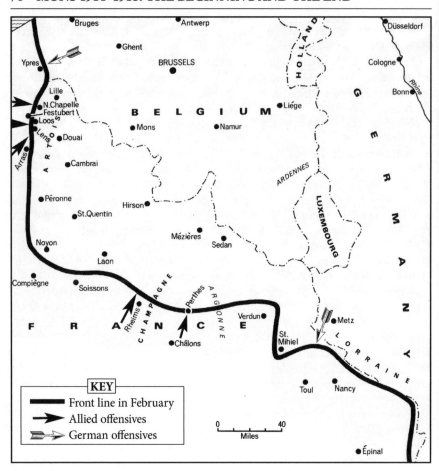

Map 5: Western Front 1915

was virtually no pool of trained manpower, especially at the junior officer/NCO level, from which to draw replacements. Lord Kitchener's decision to channel the respondents to his national call for volunteers into divisions of a New Army, meant that it would be some time before any reinforcement could be looked for from that source. In the meantime all that was available were a few divisions made up of regular battalions hastily being returned from garrison duties in the colonies, the Territorial Army, the Indian Army and one Canadian division. All of these were to find themselves on the Western Front in 1915. A further major problem which was to bedevil the BEF was the shortage of suitable artillery for static warfare, notably heavy guns and howitzers, and the shells required for them. Not only were the shells available largely shrapnel when high explosive was the main requirement, but they were being produced in pitifully inadequate quantities. It is estimated that in 1915 Britain was producing 22,000 shells per day compared with French production of 100,000 and German of 160,000. And to compound the problem the British shells were proving unreliable with a high proportion of 'duds'.[4]

After the blood letting of the first few months of the War the end of 1914 found both sides coming to terms with the new concept of trench warfare and giving urgent thought to how to break the apparent stalemate. On the German side the decision was taken to adopt a largely defensive posture in the west and focus on defeating the Russians in the east. By contrast defence was never conceived of as an option by the Allies; for General Joffre, it was merely a question of when and where he should mount his offensives with, if at all possible, increasing participation from the BEF which had been reconstituted as a two-Army force at the end of 1914 with I and 11 Corps being upgraded to First and Second Armies, each of three corps.[5]

The year 1915 was to prove the last full year in which the French were incontrovertibly the senior partner and this fact, to a large extent, was to determine where and when the BEF would attack during the year. Even in the one case when the British attacked in isolation, at Neuve Chapelle, a major stimulus to the decision to do so was a perceived need to demonstrate to the French that the BEF was attack-minded and keen to play its full part.

By the beginning of February Joffre had settled on his grand design for 1915. He planned 3 large offensives which involved his armies advancing northward from their positions between Verdun and Nancy in Lorraine; northward from around Reims in Champagne; and eastward from north of Arras in Artois towards Vimy Ridge. The Champagne and Artois attacks would, if successful, eliminate the German Noyon Salient. It was the Artois strand of his strategy which would concern and involve the BEF.[6]

Joffre had begun his attempts to eliminate the Noyon Salient in December 1914. Separate attacks were launched at both ends of the Salient as well as directly against Noyon. But progress was minimal and casualties heavy. When the attacks were suspended on 17 March 1915, the French had suffered nearly 90,000 casualties.

As the fighting was subsiding in Champagne the BEF had on 10 March launched the first set piece battle of the war in which they took the offensive. The Battle of Neuve Chapelle was originally conceived as a joint Anglo-French attack but Joffre cancelled French participation when the BEF declined to take over a length of French-held line north of Ypres.[7] Sir John French nevertheless decided to go ahead with the British part of the attack. He wished to show the sceptical French that the BEF were keen to play their full part and could be a potent attacking force as well as an effective defensive one. A successful attack would also convince a sceptical Field Marshal Kitchener that the German lines could be breached.

Neuve Chapelle is a small farming village, about 14 kilometres southwest of Armentières. It was a tempting target for the British. The German line at this point formed a salient about two kms to the west of the low but strategically important Aubers Ridge. This 10 kms long feature gave the Germans an overall view of the British lines and kept them relatively drier. But their strategy of seeking a decision on the Eastern Front in 1915 had led them to reduce their front line strength in France, especially opposite the BEF; they shared the French scepticism about the offensive ardour of the British. The BEF would thus achieve a significant numerical superiority at the start of the battle. Only one and a half German battalions faced the 15 assaulting battalions.

The offensive was entrusted to Haig's First Army. His plan called for the Indian Corps and IV British Corps to pinch off the German salient, capture Neuve Chapelle and seize Aubers Ridge. Following a short, but violent, artillery bombardment lasting 35 minutes the infantry would assault, relying on speed and surprise. The assaulting battalions were thoroughly trained in their tasks.

The three-day long battle proved to be a major disappointment. It began promisingly enough with a generally effective short bombardment which achieved the hoped-for surprise. But the infantry assault did not go entirely to plan. In line with the doctrine of a broad front approach one brigade was refused permission to forge ahead when a genuine opportunity offered, . The Germans took advantage of the lessening of pressure and the onset of night to reinforce their defences and were thus able to repulse very easily the British attacks on the second day. The third day was dominated by German counterattacks which achieved little at great loss. But they did dislocate British plans for further attacks which, when they took place, were also largely ineffective. The battle was called off late that night. British casualties were nearly 13,000 of whom almost 4,000 were dead. German losses were probably rather greater.

On 22 April the main fighting shifted north when the Germans launched the Second Battle of Ypres, which was to be one of their rare major attacks on the Western Front during the years 1915-1917. The German assault was primarily aimed at reducing the size of the Ypres Salient and at disrupting suspected Allied plans to launch their own offensive. It also offered the opportunity to introduce a new feature into modern war – the use of 'asphyxiating', or poison, gas.

Both the French and British contrived to discount ample warnings that the Germans were planning to use gas against the Salient. The Germans had not yet perfected the means of delivering the gas by artillery shell. It had instead to be released from cylinders placed in the front line when the wind was favourable. Zero Hour had constantly to be postponed because of the lack of this requirement.

On 22 April the northern bulge of the Salient from the Ypres-Diksmuide Canal, round the north of Langemarck to the Poelcapelle-St Julien road was manned by two French divisions of poor quality, the 87th Territorial and the 45th Algerian. To their right was the recently arrived Canadian Division, part of IV Corps of the BEF Second Army.

Around the middle of the day the wind suddenly shifted to the right quarter and at 17h00 the German bombardment began and the gas was released. Gas clouds formed on either side of Langemarck, then joined up and rolled inexorably towards the French lines. The effect on the French troops was cataclysmic and soon those not overcome where they stood were flooding back towards Ypres, joined by many civilians. The Canadians could see and smell the gas but were largely unaffected by it. They could do little to prevent the subsequent advance of the German infantry which moved forward about 4 kms and dug in. At this stage the Germans could have done very much as they pleased.

The subsequent days of the battle were to highlight the very worst aspects of senior allied generalship. The allied commanders, General Foch and Field

Marshal French, were completely in the dark about the situation on the ground and spent the next few days ordering unrealistic counterattacks which either never took place or did so with inadequate preparation, no artillery support and exhausted troops, with predictable results. The BEF command structure virtually disintegrated and the battle largely consisted of confused hand-to-hand fighting by units of battalion strength or less.

The remainder of the battle consisted of a series of gradual, clumsy, forced and costly withdrawals of the line around Ypres until 25 May when the battle ended with the Salient reduced to about one third of its original size. The Allies sustained 70,000 casualties, the vast majority of whom were BEF. The Germans lost around 35,000.

Fortunately for the Allies the Germans had not been able to exploit the unanticipated success of their new weapon in tearing open such a wide gap in the allied lines. If they had taken full advantage of the surprise the use of poison gas had afforded them they could have inflicted a severe defeat on their enemies and possibly deprived the BEF of the use of their Channel ports. But their own underestimation of the new weapon's shock effect and the strategic decision to concentrate all available reserves on the Eastern Front at this time deprived them of the means to exploit their initial success to the full.

An unfortunate consequence of the battle for the future of the BEF was that the Second Army Commander, General Sir Horace Smith-Dorrien, was relieved and sent home because of alleged shortcomings in his conduct of the battle which owed little to the facts and a great deal more to Sir John French's poisonous antipathy towards him.[8]

Even as the fighting around the Ypres Salient dragged on, General Joffre launched the First Battle of Artois on 9 May. His plan called for a major assault by the French Tenth Army on Vimy Ridge. Following a five day bombardment by 1,200 guns, the French infantry went over the top. Despite heavy losses XXXIII Corps, commanded by General Philippe Pétain, captured Carency, Neuville St Vaast, La Targette and the Bois de la Folie. The Moroccan Division broke through the German line and took Vimy Ridge, having advanced four kms in just a few hours. They were exhausted and desperately in need of reinforcement but the reserves were too far back to arrive before the following day. Their problems were compounded when they came under heavy fire from their own artillery, and a German counterattack retook the ridge in the evening. In the following days the Germans also retook the villages of Carency and Neuville after bitter house-to-house fighting. Despite these setbacks the offensive continued, with the French seeking to capture Notre Dame de Lorette, Ablain-St Nazaire and Souchez. All three were eventually taken, Souchez not until June. General Ferdinand Foch, the Army Group Commander, ordered the offensive ended by mid-June, by which time the battle had cost the French 102,533 casualties of whom 42,108 were dead.[9]

The British supporting role in the First Battle of Artois was fought in two segments, the Battle of Aubers Ridge, which began simultaneously with the French offensive and lasted just the one day, and the Battle of Festubert, which was fought from 15-27 May. The main purpose was to tie down German troops and prevent the movement of their reserves southwards to confront the French.

The Battle of Aubers Ridge was fought over the same ground as Neuve Chapelle by the same army, Haig's First. The planning attempted to draw on the lessons of the earlier engagement, but the Germans had done likewise. The short, surprise bombardment which preceded the infantry assault proved ineffective this time against the greatly strengthened enemy defences. The infantry paid the price and only a few isolated units managed to infiltrate the German forward defences. Attempts to repeat unsuccessful assaults were perforce abandoned or proved abortive in the shambles to which the British forward trenches had been reduced by casualties trying to get back and reinforcements trying to get forward. Apart from the fighting necessary to extricate troops in lodgements in the German lines, the fighting was over by the end of 9 May. The most worrying aspect of this disastrous day, which had cost the British 11,619 casualties against only 1,550 German, was the growing evidence of a major shell shortage coupled with defective ammunition and worn out guns.[10]

There could be no question of leaving British participation in the First Battle of Artois at that. The French offensive was still continuing and British support was still needed. The main changes in the British approach for the Battle of Festubert were, first, that the short surprise bombardment was abandoned in favour of one sustained over two days. (Given the worn state of the insufficient number of British guns and the inadequate and defective supply of shells the effect seemed unlikely to be greatly beneficial, as proved to be the case.) Secondly, strictly limited objectives were set by General Haig, advances of 1,000 yards in two separate attacks.

The artillery bombardment began on 13 May and the infantry assault two days later. The attack by 2nd Division and an Indian Brigade broke new ground by being made at night. It was only partially successful however and resulted in serious losses on the left of the assault. The attack by 7th Division went in at dawn the following morning but was halted by strong German defences. Haig sought to reinforce the limited success of 2nd Division in follow-up assaults but the battle declined into an attritional struggle which left the British, after the 12 days the battle lasted, content to consolidate the small, and tactically valueless, areas of ground gained. Once again the losses strongly favoured the defence. British casualties were 16,648 and German about 5,000.[11]

The Second Battle of Artois was fought largely over the same ground as the First. Joffre planned it as support for a major French offensive in Champagne. The main French thrust was again towards Vimy Ridge. The battle began on 25 September and by 29 September a division of the Tenth Army had managed to reach the plain leading up to the ridge despite heavy losses sustained at the hands of a formidable German defence, which prevented any lasting gains elsewhere. Notre Dame de Lorette was fully secured and fighting raged once again over Souchez before the ruins of the village were secure in French hands. The offensive concluded in early November. French casualties amounted to 48,000.

General Joffre had once again sought the support of his British allies for his Artois offensive, requesting them to mount a simultaneous attack in an area just north of the German-occupied mining town of Lens. Both Sir John French and Sir Douglas Haig considered the proposed battlefield entirely unsuitable for offensive operations and said so forcefully. But they were overruled by Lord

Kitchener, who allowed himself to be persuaded by Joffre, that not only was the ground suitable, but a British attack there was essential if the French offensive were to succeed. Whatever Joffre's views on the suitability of the terrain, the facts were that it was almost devoid of cover and dead flat with such high ground as there was firmly in German hands. In addition the Germans possessed most of the ideal observation points provided by the slag heaps and winding gear towers of the many coal mines in the area.[12]

Joffre's overall plan had called for a 96 hour bombardment prior to all the assaults going in. While the French enjoyed a sufficient density of guns to have allowed a reasonable hope that the bombardments on their front would achieve their objectives of cutting the German wire, damaging their defences and destroying their morale, there was little hope that the British, with only half the gun density and a chronic shell shortage, would achieve any of these aims. Unsurprisingly Haig and one of his Corps Commanders, Lt General Sir Henry Rawlinson, were gloomy at their prospects of success.

Haig decided to attack on a six-divisional front between the La Bassée Canal in the north down to the town of Grenay in the south. In addition, two feint attacks would be made north of the La Bassée Canal by the Indian Corps. In order to compensate for his shortage of artillery Haig decided to use 'asphyxiating' gas during the initial assault, in what would be its first use by the British.

The Battle of Loos began when the gas was released at 05h50 on 25 September and the infantry began their assault 40 minutes later. The success achieved seemed to be in direct proportion to the effectiveness of the gas. On a day when the wind conditions were essentially not suitable for its use it proved most effective at the southern end of the British assault, where the wind was least unhelpful, and decreasingly so the further north it was employed. In several place it harmed the attackers by blowing back into their trenches, and caused no problem to the defence. The southernmost Division achieved all its objectives and the one next to it, charged with capturing the vital Hill 70, would have done so had inexperience and the loss of most of its officers not led to disorientation and confusion. Little success was recorded further north. But essentially the success or failure of the attack had hinged on the capture and retention of Hill 70, which was not to be achieved.[13]

To the generals the results of the first day seemed gratifyingly positive. Severe inroads had been made into the German defences which seemed ripe for exploitation by the original attacking divisions and the reserves. This assessment however took little account of the exhaustion and decimation of the troops involved on the first day. One sixth of the attacking force had become casualties. The assessment also took no account of the fact that overnight the Germans had managed to rush up nearly seven divisions to reinforce their shaky defences.

Haig claimed that the first day had seen possibilities for exploitation by the reserves, reserves which had been held too far back to intervene in the battle. Their handling would spark great controversy. For reasons which are not entirely clear Sir John French decided to keep them under his control and not place them under Haig. He then left them well behind the battlefield so that when they were called forward they had huge distances to march over unfamiliar country, arriving at their jumping off points tired, hungry and thirsty, and 24 hours too late to exploit any opportunities that had arisen on the first day of the battle. When they were thrown into the battle on the second day without adequate maps or artillery support they were scythed down in great numbers to no effect at all.[14]

Even though the battle was to continue until 14 October with small scale losses and gains being recorded, any serious hope of success had been confined to the first two days. When the battle concluded British casualties amounted to around 60,000 for a maximum penetration of the German front of one and a half miles on an 8,000 yard length of front. German casualties were about half those of the British.[15]

Almost predictably the French Champagne offensive, in support of which the Second Battle of Artois, including the Battle of Loos, was fought, was a costly failure. Little ground was gained at a cost of 138,000 French dead in a month.

The main fallout of Loos was that his conduct of it wore thin the remaining patience with French's tenure as Commander-in-Chief of the BEF. He did himself no good by producing a mendacious dispatch on the battle, which, when added to the embarrassment he had caused the Government by his hostile leaking to the Press over the shell shortage (which was by now the 'Shell Scandal'), and his unfair dismissal of General Sir Horace Smith-Dorrien from the command of Second Army, led to his own dismissal in December 1915. His successor was Haig, who had done much to undermine French with his criticisms in private correspondence with, among others, the King. Nevertheless French's dismissal was justified as he had convincingly demonstrated that he was not up to the job.

With the conclusion of the fighting in Champagne and Artois in October, the 1915 campaigning season drew to a close. Attention focused on 1916 at an inter-Allied Conference convened at Chantilly on 6 December. It was agreed that the main allied effort on the Western Front in the summer of the coming year should be a joint Anglo-French offensive to be launched in the Somme Département where by then the junction between the two nations' forces would be situated. The offensive would be predominantly French but with a large British input consisting mainly of Kitchener New Army divisions which by then should be adequately trained and prepared for their role.[16]

But the Germans threw the allied plans into disarray when they launched an offensive against the fortress city of Verdun on 21 February 1916. This was the brainchild of the German Chief of Staff von Falkenhayn who, in a memorandum submitted to the Kaiser in December 1915, identified Britain as Germany's main enemy and advocated a two-pronged strategy to weaken Britain's appetite for the struggle. One prong was unrestricted submarine warfare; the other, the knocking of France out of the war by attacking her at a place she would feel obliged to defend to the last man. That place was Verdun. The purpose of the offensive would not be so much to capture Verdun as to draw the French army into a cauldron where it could be 'bled white' in the Verdun 'mincing machine'.[17]

The ring of fortresses surrounding Verdun had led the French to discount the possibility of a German offensive there, to the extent that their garrisons had been reduced to small numbers of indifferent quality troops. Worse, much of their ordnance had been stripped out for use elsewhere on the front. German security prior to the offensive being launched was so effective that had it not been for a week's delay in the German timetable caused by heavy snow and mist, the surprise would have been total. As it was, the French picked up signs of German intentions in the last few days. These were fed back to GQG, which made desperate attempts to shore up defences and draft more troops to the area, but too late to prevent initial disaster. Following an intense bombardment by the greatest concentration of artillery seen to that date, the Germans assaulted with nine divisions of the German Crown Prince's Fifth Army. Although stunned and greatly outnumbered, the French put up a heroic defence which slowed up the Germans and inflicted heavy casualties. But the German advance was inexorable, its highlight being the capture of the supposedly impregnable Fort Douaumont, the principal fort of the Verdun system, on 25 February. The capture was achieved by a mere handful of German soldiers thanks to an almost incredible series of blunders by French commanders. (Its retaking on 24 October would cost thousands of French lives.)[18]

The French called on General Philippe Pétain to assume command of the defence of Verdun. He instituted measures that made matters more bearable for the French troops and progress for the Germans more difficult to achieve. He set up a reliable supply system based on the road between Bar-le-Duc and Verdun which ensured that fresh troops, their food and equipment and ammunition would reach the front and tired troops and the wounded could be brought away. The road became known as *La Voie Sacrée* (the Sacred Way). Pétain also introduced a system of *roulement* (rotation) which ensured that the front line troops were relieved on a regular basis after only short periods of front line squalor and horror. This system meant that almost every unit of the French army did a tour of duty at Verdun, many more than one. Pétain inspired his troops with an Order of the Day which contained the memorable *'Courage ... On les aura'* (Have courage ....we'll get them). Although frequently mistakenly attributed to Pétain the even more memorable *'Ils ne passeront pas'* (They shall not pass) was coined by his successor in command at Verdun, General Robert Nivelle.[19]

The Germans widened their assault front and continued to attack against ever more stubborn resistance. Following the failure of an attack on 11 July they decided to go over to the defensive leaving them about five kilometres from Verdun itself. This was not however to be the end of the fighting as the French were intent on recovering the ground and forts they had lost. Under the new commander Nivelle, assaults were launched which recovered most of the ground and the Forts Douaumont, Vaux and Thiaumont. The fighting ended on 18 December making it the longest and arguably 'worst' battle in history. The French had suffered nearly 400,000 casualties of whom 162,308 were killed. German losses were nearly 340,000 of whom over 100,000 were killed or missing, The German plan to bleed the French army white had come massively unstuck as they allowed themselves to be drawn into a battle of attack and counterattack.[20]

The intensity of the fighting at Verdun clearly called into question the ability of the French army to lead the planned Somme offensive. At the same time the need to relieve the pressure on the French at Verdun made it essential that it should be launched at the earliest possible moment. Haig and Joffre agreed that the offensive should now become a British one with French support. 15 BEF and five French divisions would form the first wave of the attack. Because of Verdun the planned start date was brought forward to late June.[21]

The Fourth Army was created in March 1916 to take over the Somme sector from the French and carry out the Somme offensive. Its command was entrusted to General Sir Henry Rawlinson, an infantryman.[22] It would be supported by a diversionary attack towards Gommecourt in the north by two divisions of the Third Army (which had been created on 1 July 1915), and, in the south, by the French. A Reserve Army of 3 British cavalry divisions commanded by Lt General Sir Hubert Gough was set up to exploit any breakthrough.[23]

Cavalryman Haig believed that a real breakthrough was possible, and looked to the capture of Bapaume and a subsequent northward wheel of Fourth and Reserve Armies to roll up the German defences. Infantryman Rawlinson, however, had no real belief in a breakthrough, or the cavalry's ability to exploit one should it occur, and only looked to the capture of Pozières Ridge, the highest ground on the battlefield. Rawlinson's objective was, very belatedly and at enormous human cost, to be achieved; Haig's never was.[24]

General Rawlinson planned a five day bombardment to cut the German wire, destroy their artillery and defences and extinguish all life therein. It began on 24 June and was subsequently extended to seven days. Mines laid under enemy strong points were detonated at Z minus 2 minutes. The infantry were to walk in extended line to occupy the German trenches, nine fortified villages and 11 redoubts on an 18 mile front. The French were to advance on the right flank on an eight mile front.[25]

The result was an almost unbroken disaster. Montauban on the right was taken quickly and relatively easily. Mametz was also captured on the first day. The Germans had to evacuate Fricourt on the first night because the salient had become untenable. The only other success was the 36th (Ulster) Division getting into the Schwaben Redoubt. But they had to evacuate it that night.

Of the 66,000 troops in the first wave, 30,000 became casualties in the first hour. There were 57,470 casualties on the first day of whom 19,240 were killed or died of wounds. The 2,152 listed as missing may additionally be largely presumed dead. The casualties were the equivalent of six full divisions. By contrast German losses for the day were 8,000, of whom fewer than 6,000 were killed or wounded.

The reasons for the tragedy of 1 July 1916 were not hard to find. The inexperienced British were up against seasoned German veterans familiar with the area and well dug in. The length of the British bombardment sacrificed any hope of surprise. But most importantly the bombardment failed to achieve its aims of destroying the German wire and dugouts. The battle was essentially a race between the two sides to occupy the German front line trenches, a race the British did not even realise they were in. With the Germans manning their front line machine guns as soon as the barrage lifted and the heavily laden British infantry walking slowly towards them making no attempt to use any cover available, the slaughter was inevitable.[26]

Following the disaster of the first day the two Fourth Army corps north of the Albert-Bapaume road were transferred to the Reserve (later Fifth) Army, which assumed a largely defensive posture for the next three weeks. The remaining three corps of Fourth Army meanwhile sought to exploit their relative success of the first day with follow-up attacks. Despite the initial brilliant success of a night attack

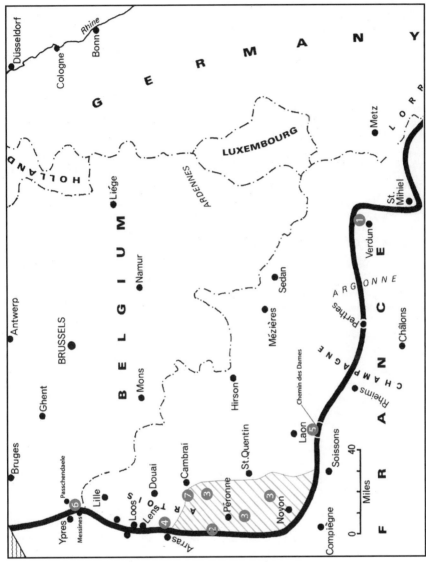

Map 6: Western Front 1916–1917

Legend

1. Verdun: German offensive and French counter-offensive February–December 1916
2. The Somme: Anglo-French offensive July–November 1916
3. Voluntary German withdrawal February–April 1917
4. Arras: British offensive April–May 1917
5. Chemin des Dames: French offensive April–May 1917
6. Third Ypres (Passchendaele) British offensive July–November 1917
7. Cambrai: British offensive and German counter-offensive November–December 1917

on the German Second Line at Bazentin Ridge and the introduction of tanks to the battlefield at the Battle of Flers-Courcelette, the attacks of both Fourth and Reserve Armies declined into a series of attritional slogs in deteriorating weather. When the appalling weather and total exhaustion brought the Somme campaign to an end on 18 November after over 20 weeks the maximum advance the Allies had recorded was 12 kilometres. British casualties totalled between 400,000 and 420,000 of whom 127,751 were killed. French casualties were between 190,000 and 203,000 and German between 437,000 and 680,000. By the end of the battle Germans had been killed in about equal numbers to the Allies, almost certainly reflecting their decision to counterattack whenever the British and French captured ground.[27] Ironically, early the next year the Germans were to withdraw voluntarily to well to the east of the Somme battlefield.

As GQC and GHQ began considering their options for 1917 two events intervened which would have important consequences for the Western Front. The first was the replacement of Joffre as French Commander-in-Chief by General Robert Nivelle, the hero of Verdun. The second was the replacement of Herbert Asquith as British Prime Minister by David Lloyd George. Joffre's fall was caused by the series of disastrous campaigns he had presided over since the outbreak of war alleviated only by the 'Miracle of the Marne'. The last straw was his failure to anticipate the German attack at Verdun despite the warnings he had received. In contrast to his predecessor, Lloyd George gave every promise of being an interventionist Prime Minister in the running of the war. He was already deeply sceptical of the pre-eminence of the Western Front in military thinking and determined to avert further bloodlettings like the Somme. In very short order his interventions would lead to a sharp downturn in the relationship between the Government and the military.

Chapter XI

Mons Occupied: Part I

In common with the majority of Belgians, the realisation that the Germans had invaded their country came as a terrible shock to the citizens of Mons. They had convinced themselves that in the event of war the belligerents would respect Belgian neutrality. Even if they did not, the fortifications of Liège and Namur would keep at least the Germans at bay.

Once it became clear that Belgium was at war with Germany the press and church vied with each other to convey reassuring messages which filled the void left by the absence of any hard news. As far as Mons was concerned it was only the arrival of the British army in their midst and rumours of Uhlans nearby that gave the man in the street a first indication that the war might be getting closer. The Mons *Garde Civique*, a citizen paramilitary organisation, had been activated when the town's Belgian army garrison had been mobilised and left for the front in the first days of the war. They had been actively employed since then guarding the property of German nationals, railway lines and other potential targets for sabotage. Perhaps better informed than most on what the immediate future might hold, the Mons authorities had instructed the *Garde Civique* to deposit their arms and ammunition in two separate goods wagons at the railway station on the morning of 21 August. They were also ordered to hand in their uniforms and equipment at their town headquarters. The *Garde* personnel very reluctantly complied. The stationmaster saw to it that the two wagon of arms and ammunition were dispatched to Antwerp, out of reach of the Germans. The Mons authorities also instructed private citizens to hand over all firearms and ammunition in their possession at the *Conservatoire de Musique*.[1] In taking these two steps the Mons administration were demonstrating a realistic recognition, or premonition, of the German taste for reprisals against the civil population, should they be given the slightest pretext.

Once the *Montois*[2] had got over treating the newly arrived British as a spectacle, they set to with a will to help them build up the defences of the area by digging trenches, felling trees and erecting barricades. That these measures and the British presence would be insufficient to save Mons from German occupation became apparent as Sunday 23 August wore on. The village of Nimy was the first place in the Mons area to experience at first hand the brutality of the invader. Being situated just south of the canal crossings, which had only been wrested from the British at very high cost, it suffered the full fury of the frustration and anger felt by the Germans. Claiming that they had been fired on by villagers, the Germans shot at least 13 of them out of hand and torched 30 houses or more.[3] The Germans also took around 500 hostages, including women and children, to use as a human shield in their advance towards Mons. When they reached the *Grand-Place* in the centre of the town they were met by a delegation of local notables led by Mayor Jean Lescarts, who declared Mons an open town. For his pains he and the other notables were incorporated into the human shield, from which the Germans at this stage released the women and children; it was then driven southwards down the *rue de la Chaussée* and *la Grand-Rue*. At the bottom of the latter street was a road block manned by 1st Lincolns who opened fire, taking care as far as possible to avoid hitting any civilians. In the ensuing panic 13 of the hostages were shot, allegedly by their guards as they tried to escape. Five died, the rest were wounded. Mayor Lescarts made good his escape, only lightly wounded.[4]

An indication of the impact the fighting had had on the local population can be gleaned from the diaries of the *Congrégation des Filles du Sacré Coeur de Jésus* whose convent was situated just off the direct route from Nimy to Mons, the route which the Germans followed after their successful crossing of the Nimy road bridge. The unnamed nun who kept the diary demonstrates on every page the intensity of her devotion to her vocation and an almost equally intense detestation of the Germans. What follows is a free translation of part of her diary entry for 23 August.

At Nimy, we have learned since, civilians had fired on the enemy; horrible reprisals followed. A number of inhabitants were shot and killed or so badly wounded that they died shortly afterwards. Several houses were torched but the flames stopped before reaching our Maison du Sacré-Coeur. We poor Sisters fled and took refuge in the cellar of a neighbouring house.

Towards 4am some louder explosions than the earlier ones were heard close to us, The shells found in the square attested to the fact that even if we might have escaped death, the solid walls of our dear House would not have been able to resist a similar broadside. Bullets had penetrated by the windows; several had pierced bed-frames and lodged in the bedding. The Jesuit Rector, who at the request of Reverend Mother, had come to offer us reassurances, was as disquieted as were we. He advised us to spend the night in the basement or at the very least on the ground floor. We brought down mattresses and blankets and improvised dormitories in the corridors furthest from the direction of the firing.

While we were having supper the bell rang. It was two Sisters du Bon Pasteur who implored us to offer asylum to 18 Sisters and 60 orphans from their Convent, which was under threat from the spreading of fires from neighbouring houses and from British and Prussian shells. Our big hearted Mother could not refuse to help those less fortunate than ourselves. A third corridor was converted into a dormitory for the orphans and cooking pots of potato soup prepared.[5]

With the last vestige of a British presence in Mons having disappeared with the withdrawal of 1st Lincolns the *Montois* sought to adjust themselves to German occupation. To the great annoyance of the Germans they initially and fearfully stayed indoors leaving the streets deserted. They were ordered to resume their normal activities immediately. To ensure that there was no active resistance to the occupation the Germans took local notables hostage, four at a time, for periods of three to four days each, until 30 October when the measure was suspended.[6]

The *Sacré-Coeur* Convent had been converted into a temporary hospital and was sent around 20 wounded soldiers to look after of whom five were British. The latter had to be treated as prisoners but, as they were kept separate from the Germans, the Sisters were able to slip them a few treats.[7]

Only three days after the Germans took over the city the inhabitants were ordered to hand over all arms still in their possession after the town authorities' attempt to anticipate this requirement. This was part of an understandable effort by the occupiers to ensure that any capacity for resistance or trouble making was nipped in the bud. As the war went on the Germans were to become more and more obsessed by fears of espionage. Decrees and orders would be handed down confiscating private telephones, cameras and typewriters, all perceived as of possible use to saboteurs or spies. In addition kite flying would be banned as would the laying out of laundry to dry on open grassy areas. A total night-time blackout was eventually instituted.

Another casualty of the preoccupation with sabotage and espionage were homing pigeons. Pigeon racing had been a popular sport in Belgium prior to the war. In the first days of the occupation the residents of Mons were ordered to kill their pigeons and take their remains to the Town Hall (where they were to be collected and used for food for the wounded troops). Not everyone responded to this order and it was subsequently repeated. But eventually the Mons authorities were able to negotiate an arrangement whereby all the remaining pigeons were kept alive and housed in the Mons cavalry school. This fell through when there was insufficient food for them and the owners were allowed to take them away and keep them in their pigeon lofts under strict control. But overall the homing pigeon population fell by 40%.[8]

On 13 September the *Sacré-Coeur* diarist recorded her feelings on the first three weeks of German occupation.

> They are the masters and make us feel it at every opportunity: nothing can be done in town without their permission; each day posters are put up on the walls: it is the Mayor, by order of the German commander, who enjoins the citizens to keep a visible light on the outside of their dwellings at night; to place a full bucket of water outside in the evening; to take to the Town Hall all their pigeons for use to feed the army (a measure which almost provoked a riot amongst a people excessively attached to homing pigeons). From 8pm it is strictly forbidden to *Montois* to move around the town. All vehicles, above all luxury vehicles, are to go to the masters, just like our railways and our telegraph and telephone lines. Finally, their lives are guaranteed by 4 hostages under strict guard at the Town Hall. Units of 10 to 15,000 Prussians are all the time passing through the town on their way to France. Usually they pass the night here and it is no longer unusual to receive visits prior to midnight of groups of Prussians looking for accommodation; one cannot even think of rejecting them. Thanks be to Providence, the *Sacré-Coeur* has not up to today had to endure the chore of putting up or feeding the enemy. God preserve us to the end![9]

Perhaps even more starved of hard news than they had been prior to the arrival of the Germans, the *Montois* at first clung on to the hope that an allied victory would ensure that their misfortune would be short lived. But their hopes faded when, on 11 September, the Germans marched about 24,000 French prisoners through the streets of Mons. They were the garrison at Maubeuge which had surrendered four days previously and, as such, were mainly territorials aged 35 or more. The Germans ordered the Montois to stay indoors in order to avoid the danger of demonstrations of sympathy with the French troops. Nevertheless the locals did contrive to pass bread, fruit and chocolate to them.[10]

Inevitably, with little prospect of a transformation in their fortunes, the people of Mons resigned themselves to getting back to as near normality as circumstances permitted. They could at least count themselves fortunate that none of the worst examples of German atrocities of the first few weeks of the war had been visited upon them. The German approach to the territories they occupied had none of the winning of hearts and minds about it. Their approach was perhaps best encapsulated in the ancient Roman precept *oderint dum metuant* (let them hate as long as they fear). They were determined to suppress any latent popular opposition to their occupation and took the draconian measures of executing civilians out of hand and burning down houses believed to have sheltered those firing on them. To a large extent these measures were a gross overreaction. There must have been occasional cases of Belgian (and French) civilians firing on the invader, but subsequent investigation has shown that such firing usually came from uniformed allied troops. A case in point was the town of Tamines where on 22 August 383 civilians, including many women and children, were murdered and 240 houses burned down after German troops came under fire from French units occupying the heights to the south of the town. An even worse instance was at Dinant a day later where 674 civilians were massacred and 1,100 houses destroyed. There was no apparent cause for this outrage on a picturesque and innocent town of about 8,000 inhabitants. It seems to have fallen victim to a combination of indiscipline and intoxication in the German troops who occupied the town.

In general however a root cause of the German behaviour was an obsession with *francs-tireurs*. The Germans had suffered at the hands of these irregular guerilla fighters in the later stages of the Franco-Prussian War after they had bested the French regular armies in the field, and were inclined to attribute every incident in the early weeks of the war to their reappearance. They had meted out summary justice to those they had caught in 1870-71 and did so again in 1914. The essential difference was that in 1914 the *francs-tireurs* were a figment of the German imagination, certainly as far as Belgium was concerned. In many cases it has been shown that drunken German soldiers may accidentally have fired on their own side and Belgian civilians were used as a convenient scapegoat.

German atrocities in Belgium in the first few weeks of the war resulted in a total of over 5,500 civilians being killed and in appalling incidents of vandalism, such as the destruction of the Louvain Library, being recorded. The allied propaganda machines had been gifted a catalogue of outrages with which they could blacken the name of Germany around the world. The main problem they had to overcome was one one of incredulity. Many people could simply not believe that the army of a so-called civilised country could unleash such unprovoked atrocities on the civilians of neighbouring countries.

But leaving aside the German use of a human shield on 23 August the town of Mons itself was to escape any visitations of German brutality in the early weeks of occupation. Some neighbouring communities were not quite so fortunate. Mention has already been made of the atrocity at Nimy on 23 August. There were others on the same day at Flénu, Jemappes, Quarégnon and Ville-Pommeroeul. At Flénu, six kilometres southwest of Mons, 12 civilians were murdered and 12 houses burned down; at Jemappes, a similar distance west of Mons, 11 civilians were killed and an unknown number of houses burned down; at Quarégnon, seven kms southwest of Mons, 66 civilians were murdered and 137 houses destroyed; at Ville-Pommeroeul, 15 kms west of Mons, 14 civilians were murdered. In all these places, there had been close engagements with the BEF and it seems likely that the civilians fell victim to the German paranoia about *francs-tireurs*.[11]

Mons' geographical position as one of the closest major towns to the fighting areas, while at the same time being well to the rear of them, meant inevitably that it would become a major centre for sheltering German troops. As a Belgian garrison town it already had some of the facilities that the Germans required but its development into a headquarters centre and military hospital area put considerable pressure on the municipal authorities and individual citizens. Empty buildings were quickly commandeered and barracks, school buildings, hospitals, the *Conservatoire* and other municipal buildings were taken over. Even this wholesale commandeering was insufficient for German requirements as the major headquarters moved in. Citizens were obliged to maintain a bed ready for an unexpected guest and were eventually ordered to keep their ground floors free and move upstairs. To make matters worse they were expected to provide meals for those billeted upon them. Inevitably there were complaints about the conduct of their unwelcome guests and claims for recompense. These were supposed to be adjudicated by the competent authority. But such complaints were discouraged by several plaintiffs being sent to jail or heavily fined for allegedly slandering the German Army.[12]

Once it became clear that the Province of Hainaut would be well to the rear of the battle zones, the Germans organised its governance. The Province was placed under a governor and split into 4 administrative districts. Mons was one of these (the others were Thuin, Tournoi and Charleroi). Each district was commanded by a Chief of the Military District (*Kreischef*). The senior civilian official was the District Imperial Civil Commissioner who was responsible for supervising the Belgian communal governments and bureaucracies in his area. It was only at the level of communal administration that Belgian officials continued to function although even here they were largely operating under the direct supervision of the Military *Kommandantur*, whose staff were, in the case of Mons, working from the Town Hall. All higher levels of administration were subsumed into German structures.[13]

Until 1 January 1917 Mons was in the area of Belgium which was under the overall control of the German Governor-General, who headed a non-military administration. The areas of Belgium near the Front, described as *Zones d'Etape*, came directly under military administration. On 1 January 1917 Mons became a *Zone d'Etape*. This harsher regime meant, for example, that deportees could be sent to military areas rather than only to Germany. The *Sacré-Coeur* diarist had no doubt that it was not good news:

> So there it is: we are separated, not only from the rest of the universe - that was done a long time ago - but from our own compatriots. Since midnight, Mons is separated from the Government General of the illustrious Von Bissing [the Governor-General] and reunited to the region of *Etapes*. What will that mean for us? If it can be judged according to the experience of Tournai and Maubeuge, the misery is only just beginning. May God protect us![14]

Mons was to become of increasing military importance to the Germans. An important rail, road and canal hub, it became a centre through which German army units passed on their way to and from the front. Belgian spies, operating on behalf of allied intelligence were able to pass on valuable information on German troop build-ups, perhaps presaging an offensive, simply by watching the rate of arrival and departure of trains at Mons. The city assumed even more importance when it became the General Headquarters of the German Army as well as the Headquarters of the German Northern Army Group under the command of Crown Prince Rupprecht of Bavaria. In the former role it meant that senior army commanders, from the Kaiser down, were to spend long periods in residence in the town.

The German Army Headquarters were set up in the residence of a Madame Armory in the Place du Parc. It was here on 11 November 1917 that one of the most momentous meetings of the war was to take place. It consisted of a gathering of 49 German generals under the chairmanship of Quartermaster General Erich Ludendorff and gave its approval to the latter's proposed strategy for 1918 which would result in the German spring offensives. and the ultimate exhaustion and defeat of the German Army exactly a year after the meeting. Perhaps the most interesting aspect of this meeting was the light it shed on the German decision-making processes. That it was held in Mons rather than Berlin was surprising. That the Kaiser and Ludendorff's ostensible superior Field Marshal von Hindenburg played no part, equally so. It clearly demonstrated the lack of any political control over the army by this time. The decisions taken ran quite contrary to the growing desire on the part of the politicians for an end to the war through a negotiated peace. Ludendorff was not ready for this and his view prevailed.[15]

For the citizens of Mons the presence of such VIPs in their midst was a dubious honour as it made the town a target for allied air raids. Aerial bombardment took a while to develop and the first air raid on Mons did not take place until 28 July 1916. Thereafter 10 further raids were officially recorded, two of which dropped only leaflets.[16] The *Sacré-Coeur* diarist however paints a picture of almost nightly raids from the beginning of August 1918 onwards. The noise of aircraft engines and anti-aircraft fire would rouse the Sisters and force them to take shelter in a rear kitchen where, for no very good reason, they felt safer. There they would pray loudly until the danger passed. The diarist was under the impression that the allied aircraft were trying to destroy the coal mines west of Mons whose production was sustaining the German war effort. In her view they were doing little material damage. But they were causing civilian fatalities.[17]

One of the earlier raids had other unfortunate repercussions for the *Montois*. On 8 April 1917 Crown Prince Rupprecht's residence was targeted. The information that he was in residence was traced back to a Dutch newspaper whose source could only have been a *Montois*. Even though Rupprecht was unhurt the town was fined 500,000 Marks and put under curfew from 18h00 to 06h00 for 15 days. Only people with a specific pass issued by the German *Kommandantur* were allowed to move about and even the compliant newspapers normally allowed were banned.[18] For his part Rupprecht moved his residence and headquarters, taking up occupation of the *Maison Losseau* in the *rue de Nimy*.[19]

One of the more frustrating aspects of the situation in which the *Montois* now found themselves was the lack of information, or at least reliable information, about what was happening in the war at large. As has been noted they were not well-informed of developments prior to the occupation of their city, but that could be ascribed to fast-moving events and the usual fog of war. Once occupied they had the options of resigning themselves to total ignorance, to accepting uncritically the German version of events or to finding some means of getting the information they craved from allied or impartial sources.

For their part the Germans calculated that their best method of keeping the people of the occupied areas quiescent and resigned to their fate was to convince them that there was no hope whatsoever of their current situation being reversed and that any thoughts of resistance or revenge were therefore pointless. This could best be achieved through a complete monopoly of printed sources of information which would be either German or, if not, would toe the German official line. The latter might be preferable as it could be made to seem more objective than it actually was.

One of the Germans' first acts was to suppress the local free press. This initially forced the *Montois* to read the news posters which the Germans attached to the side of a sentry box in front of the main porch of the Town Hall. All too often these were able to contain facts that were both truthful and unpalatable. But it soon became clear that all news was being given a heavy pro-German gloss often at odds with the odd snippet of factual information that was somehow percolating through to the town along with the products of an inevitably flourishing rumour mill and the contents of the secretly produced and distributed anti-German news sheets *La Flandre Liberale* and *La Libre Belgique*. The Germans soon found that their news posters were being ignored and concluded that they needed to operate through the local press. They would therefore allow it to resume publication provided it toed the German line. They consulted Mayor Lescarts who urged that the local press should be allowed to publish without comment not only German communiqués but also those from Belgian, French and British sources. Unsurprisingly this advice was rejected. The Germans next tried to recruit the proprietor and two senior editors of the *La Province* newspaper, even offering to let them read foreign newspapers but under close German supervision. The offer was declined.

The Germans then called a meeting of all the local editors, journalists and reporters in the hope of persuading them to work together on a joint newspaper.

This appeal also fell on deaf ears. At this stage the Germans gave up on the press professionals and turned their attention to individuals who might be tempted to turn their hand to journalism on the grounds of a perceived duty to keep their fellow citizens informed or simply for financial gain. Anyone who responded positively ran the risk of being branded a collaborator especially as the Germans had every intention of imposing strict censorship on the newspapers' content. In this way the Germans succeeded in getting four newspapers launched. Only one of them, *Les Nouvelles de la Région de Mons*, lasted more than a few weeks.

Probably through the efforts of the nascent Belgian resistance, copies of the London *Times* would sometimes get through to Mons, often several weeks late. These were avidly sought after and were passed surreptitiously from hand to hand. But the Germans became aware of their presence and cracked down hard on anyone caught bringing them in. The supply dried up.

The only non-German foreign newspaper allowed in was a pro-German Dutch publication *Nieuwe Rotterdamsche Courant*. Despite its anti-allied bias its journalism was good and its articles, duly translated from the Dutch in Mons, found a ready readership.

A Monsieur Declerq, the owner of the Café Rubens in Mons got into the habit of scanning the publications permitted by the German censor for any articles favourable to the allied cause. He would translate these, add his own commentary designed to build up the hopes of his fellow citizens and put them on display in his café where they attracted a large and appreciative readership. When the Germans became aware of this he was arrested, heavily fined and jailed for several months. On release he resumed his activities and was again incarcerated.[20]

The economic framework of the Imperial German war strategy had been laid out in the Von Rathenau Plan, named after its author, a German businessman. Essentially it called for the whole German economy to be placed on a war footing and the available resources of the occupied territories to be taken over for the benefit of the Empire. Once Britain had confirmed its belligerency the German government were well aware that a Royal Navy blockade would be put in place, the effects of which they planned to alleviate by drawing on the occupied territories for the necessary means to sustain the vitality of the German economy.

The full implications of this for occupied areas such as Hainaut would take time to be felt. Initially the German occupation authorities were anxious for the normal economic activity of the Province to be resumed. This meant that the early increase in unemployment caused by some enterprises closing at the onset of war was rapidly reversed so that by April 1915 the number of unemployed in Mons was fewer than 1,000. However the figure more than doubled over the next two months. Mons' experience was being reflected nationwide as the German exploitation of Belgium's economic assets began to bite. The Germans sought to put all the blame for the rise in unemployment at the door of the Royal Navy and the 'laziness' of Belgian workers. Although the blockade was depriving some Belgian factories of essential raw materials there was general understanding of the British position. Had raw materials for Belgian factories been excluded from the blockade they would have been very quickly seized by the Germans for their own ends.

The Germans contended that unemployment benefit and charitable handouts encouraged the stay-at-home attitude of some Belgian workers. There were indeed some workers who refused to work but they were largely employees of factories or industries which had come under German control and were taking a stand on the grounds that they had no wish to help the German war effort. In the case of many miners their patriotic grounds for withholding their labour were reinforced by a credulous belief that the Germans would cut the cables of their cages as they descended to the coal faces.

Another case which affected Mons directly was the railway network. The town's railwaymen resolutely refused to work. As an important centre for military rail traffic this represented a considerable inconvenience for the German authorities who brought increasing levels of pressure to bear on the recalcitrant workers. Efforts were made to cut off the funds sustaining the workers. A Monsieur Paquet was sent to jail for six months for organising the distribution of 'secret' funds for the benefit of the workers. The railway offices were repeatedly searched in efforts to locate the cash being used. In August 1916 a large number of workers were arrested in overnight raids and shortly thereafter deported to Germany under the terms of a decree which had been promulgated on 15 August of the previous year. The decree stated that any unemployed person had to accept work related to his skills or face deportation. To some extent the threat that this decree represented had been nullified by the Mons authorities instituting a programme of public works which soaked up a number of those who would otherwise have been vulnerable. The Germans sought to wreck this manoeuvre by enforcing bureaucratic requirements on the local authorities.

To some extent the deportations had the required effect and the numbers of Belgian workers signing up for work at the *Deutsches Industrieburos* increased. The Germans needed more workers for the mines of the Mons area and were able to attract some. But it was not to prove to be the end of the deportations; they were, if anything, to increase.[21]

The German authorities quickly put in place a framework for taking possession of goods and equipment which they decided they required under the von Reichenau blueprint. Insofar as Mons had very few factories the German requisitions of raw materials and machinery did not affect the town directly. But the factories put out of business obviously ceased to call on the banking and commercial services they had sourced from Mons thus reducing employment in those sectors.

As the centre for the *Borinage* coal industry Mons suffered from the German determination to exploit the coal for their own purposes. Although Germany was self-sufficient in the fuel, it needed the Belgian coal for military requirements and, less importantly, to barter with third countries for food and raw materials. Large tonnages, amounting to roughly half of total production, thereby ceased to be available to fulfil domestic Belgian requirements. The problem was exacerbated by a war-long drop in production which was of approximately 22% per annum in the Mons area, not dissimilar to that in other mining districts. The drop was caused by the fall in employment in the industry, by industrial unrest occasioned by wages falling behind inflation, and by shortages of essential equipment and spare parts. This last problem arose despite the fact that the central authority established by the Germans to run the industry (*Kohlencentrale*) was supposed to ensure that the industry was given priority in the allocation of such items as lubricating oils, explosives and oats for the pit ponies. The fall in production led to extreme hardship especially during the very severe winter of 1916-17.[22]

A metal for which the Germans had a pressing need was copper. No fewer than 12 decrees were issued in Mons concerning this vital raw material. Initially all stocks held in the city were seized. It was not long before household goods, such as kitchen equipment containing the metal, also had to be handed over. (The *Montois* were to prove quite adept at concealing items from the searching German *Gendarmerie*. The Sisters of the *Sacré Coeur* were given absolution in advance in case they found it necessary to dissimulate to throw the searchers off the track. The Sister diarist recalled one of the Sisters positively chiming at every move with all the copper bedpans she had about her person. The searchers nevertheless departed empty-handed.)[23]

As a further gesture of vandalism by the occupiers, the town's bronze statues were removed and melted down. After the war it was discovered that many of the machine tools and other industrial equipment which had been seized and carted off to Germany had been stripped of their copper content and then left to rust. It is estimated that the Germans obtained nearly 70 tonnes of copper from Mons from their seizures. The occupiers also grabbed any tin, aluminium and lead, as well as more exotic metals, that they came across.[24]

Paradoxically, given their need for an efficient railway system to sustain their front line war effort, the Germans also carried off locomotives and goods wagons from Mons. Not even the town's schools were safe; many of them lost their laboratory equipment.

In the first month of the occupation a decree was issued ordering the *Montois* to hand over all their bicycles. By 30 September only 200 had been handed over and the Germans made it clear that they wanted 1,500 as well as all motorcycles and cars. They were to be handed over on the *Grand-Place*. Some owners were subsequently able to recover their cars , but the majority of them were cannibalised for their spare parts. The confiscation of bicycles bore down particularly heavily on the city's workers who were often dependent on them to get to and from work.[25]

As regards livestock and agricultural products the Germans were to make similar depredations. Inevitably horses were a prime target. Under a series of progressively more demanding decrees the *Montois* were required to hand them over. Even when an owner was allowed to keep one he was required to hand over the horsehair. As a result of the German confiscations, coupled with poor diet for the remainder caused by the shortage of oats, and the spread of equine disease, the horse population collapsed. The *Montois* were reduced to using bovines to haul their carts and wagons. Not that cattle were exempt from German demands. Their meat and milk were required to feed the German population and army. The Belgian population of cattle fell by more than 40% during the occupation. The pig population fell by 75% in the same period.[26]

Dogs also suffered from German requisitions and disease, especially rabies. On 18 January 1918 all Mons dog owners, not previously deprived of their animals by the occupiers, were required to take them to Binche for an inspection.

The best looking animals were handed over to the German army vets. Those in poor condition were slaughtered by hammer blows in front of their owners unless they could afford a bribe of 10 Marks to save them.[27]

One of the major problems which would be suffered by the inhabitants of Mons, along with the rest of Belgium, was food shortages. The war would disrupt the normal arrangements for food distribution which, when coupled with an overall drop in domestic production and imports, and the seizures by the occupiers, ensured that there were rarely sufficient supplies at manageable prices. Even before the war large numbers of Belgians had tended to live from hand to mouth and were not well placed to cope with the galloping inflation which shortages entailed. This pool of underprivileged Belgians would be enlarged by the large numbers of members of the lower middle class who would see their usual means of earning a living disappear as a result of the commercial disruption caused by the war.

It will come as no surprise that the occupants' requirements in agricultural produce bore down heavily on the unfortunate *Montois* and the country as a whole, becoming progressively more onerous as the war continued. The Germans had very quickly made known that they would be making requisitions from the town of Mons. The citizens were ordered, after only 3 days of occupation, to hand over all oats, yeast (and petrol) in their possession. The town as a whole was called upon to deliver 10 tonnes of flour per day to the army, equivalent to 5,000 two kilo loaves. These goods would all be paid for, but at prices determined by the occupiers. To encourage compliance the German authorities promised not to impose the burden of a war indemnity on the town.

Nationwide worse was to come. The occupiers took possession of the entire 1915 harvests of oats, hay, barley and winter barley leaving the producers with only 2.5 kilos per day for each person and horse belonging to their household. Rigorous measures were put in place to ensure that no production was siphoned off and deadlines were set for compliance. In 1917 Mons was collectively punished for missing a deadline for the handing over of rye. The citizens were no longer permitted to feed the cereal to cattle and millers were forbidden to accept the cereal from the town for milling. Rye, along with wheat, maize, chicory, onions, potatoes, and sugar, had also become subject to seizure and expropriation. So too were stocks of imported products such as tea, coffee and cocoa. As shortages became more severe the Germans extended their requirements to products such as acorns, chestnuts, beechnuts and, for use as animal feed, weeds, leaves, stinging nettles and reeds.

As far as cereals required for bread making were concerned the German authorities claimed that their seizures would be used to meet the requirement of the local population, and were merely intended to stop profiteering and a black market developing. Nevertheless the severe shortages which ensued and the deterioration in quality of the bread that did find its way onto the market indicated that these claims did not tell the whole story.[28]

German interference also led to problems over the supply of another vital commodity, the humble potato. Because it technically contravened their centralised control of the market the German authorities cancelled a contract that the Mons authorities had entered into for the delivery of 1,500 tonnes of the vegetable. This action led to a major shortage in the city lasting several months. German efforts to ensure that Belgian sugar production benefited only the German domestic market and not third countries or, to any great extent, Belgian consumers, led to a tax structure which made the product very expensive. (The proceeds of the tax were used to offset the costs of the occupation administration.)[29]

On 15 August 1917 the occupiers issued a decree calling for all wine stocks to be handed over to the *Kommandantur*. Exempted were communion wine and reasonable stocks held by restaurants, hotels, cafés and pharmacies. Private individuals and invalids were allowed to retain sufficient for personal use. The Germans indicated they would pay a fixed, but very low, amount per bottle regardless of its quality. A good number of Mons businesses and individual citizens had well-stocked wine cellars. Vintners were particularly vulnerable and one lost his entire stock of 450,000 bottles. The *Montois* went to some lengths to keep at least their best bottles out of German hands, some by burying them, others by walling up their cellars. Others did their best to drink their stocks before the deadline for handover, perhaps with the aid of friends and colleagues. This was charitably described as *saôulerie patriotique* (patriotic drunkenness). But essentially the Germans got hold of most of the city's wine stock.[30]

Throughout the occupation the Germans were to make use of communal fines both to raise useful sums of money and to deter hostile acts against them. Mention has already been made of the fine, and other measures, imposed on Mons after Crown Prince Rupprecht's residence was bombed in April 1917. The Mons authorities were obliged to seek loans from citizens to enable the fine to be paid.

In 1915 Mons and the commune of Jemappes were jointly fined 100,000 Marks following an alleged attempt to derail a train near a level crossing. Jemappes would find itself in trouble once again when it was fined 25,000 Marks after some of its citizens gave food to British prisoners of war.

Rather more bizarrely some individual leading citizens of Mons who were governors of the communal college, were fined for refusing to ring the belfry bells following the German victory at Caporetto. Mayor Jean Lescarts was fined only 20 Marks but some of his colleagues received fines of up to 3.000 Marks.[31]

Mention has already been made of the use by the Germans of deportations as a threat to force back to work the unemployed Belgians, whom they deemed to be 'lazy', but were in fact largely withholding their labour in their desire not to help the German war effort. Although this remained one of the ostensible reasons for the mass deportations that got underway in late 1916, the policy was in fact driven by other, more pressing considerations.

By what turned out to be an oversight, civilian deportations had not been banned by the Hague Convention of 1907. Indeed they were not even mentioned as it had not occurred to anyone that such a policy would ever be pursued. When the Germans began to put in place the legal framework under which such deportations would take place, they sought to justify them on the somewhat cynical grounds that they would improve the economic conditions of the occupied country by providing work, food and money to the deportees. In fact the real German aim was to exploit Belgian manpower for the benefit of their own economy and war machine. Such exploitation *was* a direct contravention of the Hague Convention.

On 14 August 1915 the occupying authorities issued a decree stating that all Belgians refusing to do work of 'public interest' for which they were suitable would be jailed for 14 days. The following day appeared the decree aimed at the 'lazy' unemployed, who would be subjected to severe, but not specified, penalties. On 15 May 1916 a further decree stated that anyone refusing to work would be liable to deportation to a place where they would be obliged to work.

As 1916 continued Germany was coming under increasing pressure. The army was heavily engaged at Verdun, on the Somme and on the Eastern Front. The country was therefore placed on a total war footing with large numbers of the civilian workforce being called to the colours. Attempts to replace them with women, the underage and the old did not suffice and the decision was taken that the slack would have to be taken up by importing manpower from the occupied areas to places where they were required for industrial or military tasks.[32]

Given that it had already happened in other communes of the Province of Hainaut, there was widespread realisation in Mons that it would not be long before mass deportations of *Montois* would begin and that the Germans would almost certainly not follow their own rules of targeting the 'lazy' unemployed. This even though the town fathers had received German assurances that the rules would be observed and that, furthermore, no deportee would be forced to do war-related work. The German authorities remained unmoved by protests from the USA, Spain, Holland and the Vatican about their actions in Hainaut, and by a letter addressed to them by the Parliamentary *députés* and senators for the region protesting about the deportations and defending the refusal of mayors to supply them with lists of the unemployed.

The individual *Montois* vulnerable to deportation sought to use the time available to them to build up stocks of food and clothing. Many of those actually unemployed sought to obtain certificates of employment. It was not uncommon to find former employees of the Belgian railways carrying such certificates supplied quite fictitiously by the coal industry. Others bit the bullet and took up jobs with, for example, the German-run railways, preferring this to the greater evil of forced labour.[33]

On 14 November 1916 posters went up in Mons calling on all men of 17 and over to present themselves at Nimy Town Hall at 09h00 on Thursday 16th. Anyone failing to attend would be treated as unemployed. The following day a supplementary poster excluded members of the liberal professions and the sick from the summons. By the appointed hour around 8,000 *Montois*, most accompanied by wives and children and carrying a bag containing food and clothing, had congregated in the square outside Nimy Town Hall. A first sorting freed members of the communal council, employees of the charity caring for Belgian prisoners of war and the elderly. By the early afternoon, following detailed questioning, 659 had been selected for deportation and were taken immediately in groups of 100 to Nimy station for entraining for Germany. The *Montois* themselves were convinced that chance and luck played the major part in whether or not they were selected. But although the Germans appeared to pay little regard to their stated criterion of employed or unemployed, they did consistently apply another, that those selected should be skilled workers. Only 200 of those chosen were unemployed, 58% were under 30 years of age and a further 24% under 40. The age groups favoured not only ensured that the Germans got the fittest men but also removed them as potential recruits for the Belgian army. The Germans paid no regard to marital status. In addition to wives, the deportees left behind them a total of 508 children. Most of these now fatherless families would inevitably become dependent on welfare.[34] The *Sacré-Coeur* diarist immediately made clear her view of this latest development.

> A sad sequel to a glorious day despite everything [15 November was the King's birthday]. The men of Mons must go to a control centre at Nimy to be examined and then sent to Germany or be released, according to the caprice of 'experts'. This is the abominable system that was brought into effect throughout the country a fortnight ago. Under the specious pretexts of ridding Belgium of useless mouths and procuring work for the unemployed in Germany, so that they do not lose their manual aptitudes, they are making each day levies en masse of men of all ages and social classes. They are being sent to Germany to occupy there the places of Teuton workers who can then be put into uniform and armed with a rifle![35]

For the next five months there was no further mass deportation and it was possible for the people of Mons to hope that the Germans had shelved the policy. This appeared to be the case when, in response to a letter dated 14 February 1917 signed by the Catholic Primate of Belgium, Cardinal Mercier, and other Belgian notables protesting against the roundups of human beings for dispatch to Germany, the Kaiser responded favourably on 17 March. But this proved to be a false dawn; German military exigencies intervened.[36]

Thanks to lamentable French security the Germans had become aware that the French were planning their major Chemin des Dames offensive. In partial reaction to this the Germans decided to press ahead as urgently as possible with the completion of the Hindenburg Line, which would form their main bulwark against allied offensives until it was finally breached on 29 September 1918. They needed labour quickly to do the necessary spadework. The nearest available pool was Belgium. In rebuttal of claims that the Kaiser had apparently broken his word it would be cynically pointed out that the All Highest had only promised not to deport Belgians to Germany.

On 15 April 1917 the German *Kommandantur* ordered the Mayors of Mons and the *Borinage* communes to hand over lists of their citizens. These people would be placed at the disposal of the German military. Despite the clear threat of military reprisals if they refused to comply, the Mayors did refuse. The following day a notice was put up ordering all men aged from 17 to 45 to report to the Mons cavalry camp. Exemptions were made for teachers, priests, doctors and employees of the German administration. Members of the liberal professions lost their previous exemption.

On 17 April 1,400 of those who presented themselves were singled out and spent the next four days undergoing further examination. After that 378 were dispatched to Douai; the rest were released.[37]

The last German attempt at a mass deportation of *Montois* began on 14 June 1917. The summons to the cavalry barracks had been made by posters and provoked a rush of *Montois* to obtain certificates of employment. The affected age group was extended to 15 to 60. Veterinarians, uniformed police and French evacuees were added to the list of exemptions. On arrival at the barracks those summoned were grouped by age. Those possessing valid certificates of employment were immediately released. The initial sorting resulted in 1,500 being detained of whom 500 were released later in the day. One of those summoned was Mayor Jean Lescarts. He introduced himself as such to his interrogator. who told him there was no longer a mayor of the town and put him under armed guard.

The Germans were becoming uncomfortably aware that their methods were building up considerable hostility among the people of Mons. A military detachment bringing a group of potential deportees from Jemappes to Mons was confronted by angry *Montois* who were only dispersed by mounted *Gendarmerie* with sabres drawn. Whether because of this or the growing international pressure to stop the deportations, the German authorities suddenly released all those who had been held in custody overnight. This would almost mark the end of their attempts at mass deportations from Mons.[38]

But the Germans had become aware that there was more than one way to skin a cat. The deportations would continue but from the summer of 1917 onwards they would involve only small numbers at a time. This would avert the gathering of large, and potentially angry, crowds and would enable the numbers taken to correspond precisely with requirements at any given time. The effectiveness of the new German approach is shown by the Mons deportation statistics. Mass deportations totalled 1,037; limited deportations 1,414.[39]

One exception to the cessation of mass deportations took place in February 1918. It involved boys aged between 15 and 17. The attempt at a mass deportation in June the previous year had lowered the minimum age of those summoned from 17 to 15 and the one in February 1918 confined itself to this age group. Quite what the German rationale was for targeting young boys is not clear. It could have been as simple as it being the only remaining age group with suitable people available. 265 of the summoned 600 were deported. It raised a predictable storm, which did not prevent the Germans planning further deportations. A last one in the last few days of the war was simply designed to move boys of near military age away from areas where they might be recruited by the advancing allies. After an adventurous few days the end of the war brought their trials to an end.[40]

There were also concerns that the Germans might be casting an eye on mobilising the female population. Rumours started alarm bells ringing, but the Germans were apparently able to recruit sufficient volunteers, as a result of a poster campaign, to obviate any need for compulsion.[41]

A final imposition on the occupied was the creation in February 1918 of groups 60 to 70 strong who would carry out assigned tasks of local value. The communal authorities had to select the personnel for these *Equipes volantes* (mobile teams) from lists given to them by the German authorities. In the case of Mons, these were heavily weighted towards the middle classes as most manual workers had been deported. There were in all 378 members of these mobile teams. They were used to load and unload coal wagons, to package and dispatch goods to front line soldiers, and in the construction of concrete underground shelters for the German army. Unlike the deportees members of the mobile teams could return home when a given task was completed.[42]

The first wave of Mons deportees, who were sent to Germany, were accommodated in labour camps at Meschelde and Frankfurt-am-Main. Most of them refused to work despite the pressures exerted on them. Useless to the German war effort and expensive to maintain, many of them were repatriated where, if they were unlucky, they found themselves caught up in the second wave of deportations. This wave, organised under the German military administration of a *Zone d'Etape* which Mons had become, suffered altogether harsher conditions. Most found themselves in front line areas in France. The food was bad, the work exhausting. The health of many broke down. No statistics for Mons are available but there is no reason to suppose the levels of sickness were out of line with those of deportees from other Belgian towns, which averaged 40%. Although only 33 Mons deportees are recorded as having died, the true number is almost certainly much higher.

Home leave was occasionally granted. But if the deportee failed to return, or if he decided to escape from his work camp, it was his family and his commune which suffered, the latter having to choose a member of the former to replace the fugitive. This measure proved very effective in discouraging desertion.[43]

Chapter XII

Mons Occupied: Part II

The shortage of food was a constant preoccupation of the citizens of Mons throughout the war. The two main vital necessities to sustain a reasonable level of nourishment were bread and potatoes. The Mons authorities quickly introduced a system of bread distribution and rationing which, despite occasional severe shortages, dramatic increases in prices and a deterioration in the quality of the end product, generally speaking served the city well, despite the inevitable grumbling. Twice a week heads of families had to present themselves at a local depot to collect a ration based on the number in their household. The ration would vary according to availability but averaged 300 grammes per head. Supplementary rations were supplied to certain categories such as manual workers, pregnant women, nursing mothers, and the sick. A free distribution was made to the 3,000 indigent families in the town. The price of the bread rose steadily during the course of the war. It went up 58.2% in the first year. But the really severe rises took place in the last few months of the war as distribution systems broke down as the German retreat gathered pace.[1]

The potato market was to prove even more volatile than that for bread. The producers had been obliged to declare all stocks they held above 50 kilos to the new German *Bureau d'Approvisionnement en Pommes de Terre* which had been given responsibility for collection and distribution of the vegetable. In mid 1916 even those Mons producers with less than a hectare of land devoted to planting potatoes were ordered to register with the Bureau.

The first serious disruption in supply came in the last quarter of 1915 when the German authorities decreed a maximum sale price which they pitched very low. They backed this by arresting anyone caught selling at an excessive price. These apparently altruistic measures were in fact designed to tempt producers to keep their potatoes in stock and not market them, thus making them an easy prey for German requisition. By the end of 1915 there was a severe shortage of potatoes which was to last until the 1916 harvest. The Mons administration tried to combat this shortage by declaring war on black marketeers with undeclared stocks. These, when found, were confiscated and released to the market. In addition the administration tried to obtain supplies from Holland and the Ardennes region. When the Dutch supplies arrived the Germans managed to siphon off a large quantity for their own purposes, to the great frustration of the municipal authorities.

With stocks available to the town of Mons already low at the beginning of 1916, the situation was not helped by a very bad harvest in the autumn of that year. By the onset of the worst winter for many years, in which temperatures dropped to minus 20 degrees Celsius, stocks were virtually exhausted. The fate of the attempt by the Mons authorities to overcome the situation by the purchase of 1,500 tonnes of the vegetable has already been noted. In desperate attempts to keep famine at bay the population turned to kohlrabi (turnip cabbage) and swedes as substitutes until the former ran out. With potatoes having virtually disappeared there was no controlling the price. The official price rose from FB 0.08 per kilo in October 1915 to FB 0.30 in December 1917. But more realistically the black market·price rose from FB 0.34 per kilo in February 1916 to FB 2.00 in December 1917.[2]

The plundering of the Belgian livestock herds by the occupiers was a major contributory factor to the severe shortages of butter, milk and meat experienced throughout the war. But it was not the only cause. The disruption of normal commercial interchange cut Mons off from its usual sources of supply in northern France and Holland. But more deleterious and reprehensible was the attitude of local producers who sought to maximise their profit by abandoning normal outlets in favour of the black market. Efforts to regulate the market were largely unsuccessful. Butter virtually disappeared, as did milk, in the latter case with particularly harmful effects to small children.[3]

Meat was a less important feature of the Belgian diet in the early twentieth century than it has subsequently become and efforts to regulate its marketing were rather more successful than those for dairy products. The problem here was largely one of price. Despite attempts to set maximum prices, these rose inexorably. During the course of the war, for example, the cost of a kilo of beef rose from FB 2.50 to FB 32.00.[4]

Eggs also disappeared from the usual outlets. No attempts were made to regulate their marketing and the price of an egg rose from FB 0.05 in August 1914 to FB 1.40 in December 1918.[5]

The result of the shortages in the food supply and the galloping inflation which hit prices was that hunger was ever present in Mons throughout the war. While it is almost certainly true that no-one actually died of starvation, there was a great deal of suffering. Even the most robust were worn down by their dietary deficiencies which left them open to sickness and epidemics and must in many cases have led to premature death. More and more families and individuals became dependent on public welfare as what money and savings they had were swallowed up in paying the inflationary prices demanded by the market. Even those with money could only buy what was available and many products ceased to be available for lengthy periods of time.

Although never able to offset completely the deficiencies in food and other necessities caused by the war, various organisations, international, national, communal and private, were to make significant contributions to alleviating the sufferings of the Belgian people. In anticipation of what was to come a national aid committee, *Le Comité de Secours et d'Alimentation*, had been formed in Belgium itself in the first month of the war.[6] This might have proved a quixotic gesture had it not been well-placed to act as the distribution arm of the Commission for the Relief of Belgium (CRB) which was established in October 1914 under the patronage of the United States, Spain and Holland. Its Executive President was a future President of the United States, Herbert Hoover and its Brussels representatives were the American and Dutch Ministers to Belgium. It was essential that whatever this organisation supplied for the relief of Belgians did not simply enable the Germans to remove equivalent amounts from the local economy; the Commission was sufficiently high-powered to extract German agreement, however reluctantly given, to this. The Commission was to have a significant impact. By July 1915 it had supplied nearly 137,000 tonnes of foodstuffs and significant quantities of clothing and footwear to Belgium and would continue the good work throughout the war. When the United States declared war on Germany in April 1917 the Commission's work was continued by Spain and Holland.[7]

The Belgian national aid committee had access to established internal structures to facilitate the reception and distribution of the aid being provided by the CRB. In the four years of the war it thereby partially provided for the food needs of 10 million individuals as well as providing broader help for the truly destitute. It operated through 10 provincial committees one of which was the *Comité Provincial de Hainaut*, based in Mons, but responsible for all of Hainaut Province. A local subcommittee took care of Mons itself.

The working capital for the national committee was raised by public subscription in Britain and the USA. The distribution of the aid was organised by the national committee which sold the goods to the provincial committees and used the proceeds to finance their aid fund. The provincial committees were supposed to raise the money to make their purchases from the generosity of their well-to-do local citizenry. Those of Hainaut unhappily proved very reluctant to stump up and threats had to be used. These were implemented when those refusing to contribute were publicly named and made to pay three or four times the asking price for their bread.

The local committee operated the outlets which distributed the goods to the public. Their non-seizure by the Germans was assured by the presence of representatives of the CRB. Several outlets were opened in Mons in suitable public premises such as schools and barracks on days notified in advance to the public. These notifications gave details of the products that would be available and the prices. The prices charged to those who could afford to pay were much lower than elsewhere, but a strict rationing system was operated. Unsurprisingly in the circumstances enormous queues usually formed outside the outlets and there were instances when riots were only narrowly avoided.[8]

From the start of its operations until June 1917 the CRB supplied 91,895 tonnes of foodstuffs to Mons. If the figures for the country as a whole are an accurate guide, 60% of this total consisted of wheat, around 6% each of rice and flour. Peas, beans, fat and potatoes also featured but in much smaller quantities. Regrettably the supplies of given products fluctuated, disappeared and reappeared which made controlling the prices that much more difficult. Nevertheless the operation was undoubtedly successful in alleviating, if not eliminating, the threat of starvation.[9]

The local committee also had the responsibility for assisting the most deprived in their communities. The national committee identified a certain number of special cases on which the local committees should focus. Examples were payment of benefit to the unemployed, supplying milk to infants ('*La Goutte de Lait*'), providing aid for the homeless, running soup kitchens and several others. The Mons local committee was established under the name *Les Magasins Communaux de la Région de Mons*. Like the more commercial operation of the local committee, their efforts to aid the most deprived sectors of the population were able to offset partially their sufferings.[10]

Another source of succour for the least well-off was a private initiative called 'Croix Verte'. Its aim was to supply as many people as possible with meals at rock-bottom prices. The first canteen was opened on 21 December 1914 and was followed in the course of 1915 and 1916 by 4 others. They were staffed by well-to-do ladies and girls. The movement's linchpin was a Monsieur Jean Houzeau de la Haye and its President was Madame Lescarts, the wife of the Mayor. In the course of its operations it delivered more than 1,500,000 meals at a cost of FB 2,500,000. Once again it could only contribute to an alleviation of the suffering, not eliminate it altogether.[11]

There were many other instances of private charitable initiatives operating in Mons during the war. There was a strong belief that, in the face of the adversities brought about by the occupation, all differences of social class, religion and political allegiance should be set aside in the cause of L'Union Sacrée. This ideal worked remarkably well in practice although there were inevitable cases where, for example, a pro-Catholic bias might be detected. The private initiatives emanated almost totally from the well-off haute bourgeoisie of Mons, understandably given that they had the money and the leisure time to devote to them. They also traditionally saw good works as a duty imposed upon them by their privileged positions in society. They were not above demonstrating a rather paternalistic attitude to those they were helping, for example in criticising recipients of financial handouts for spending some of the money on cinema tickets instead of food.

The main areas on which the private charities focused were on the welfare of babies and small children and their mothers; on the petit bourgeois who had seen their fixed incomes rapidly depreciate in value as inflation took hold; and on Belgian prisoners of war languishing in German POW camps. The work they did was of immense value and very effective. Despite the general deprivation, for example, the rate of infant mortality in Mons dropped significantly during the war years.[12]

In the midst of all this suffering and deprivation there were some who benefited greatly. They were mainly agricultural producers, the majority of whom turned their backs on the legitimate markets in favour of the high prices to be obtained for their produce on the black market. The withholding of their produce from the proper outlets did much to ensure that price inflation would spiral ever upwards to their even greater benefit.

From a practical point of view taking advantage of the black market raised considerable difficulties for a potential customer. As the farmer or market gardener refused to bring his produce to town, the customer had to go into the countryside to obtain it. The journeys became longer as time went on and the suppliers nearest to the town ran out of product. The customers too had to run the gauntlet of German military police checks intended to stamp out the market. Particular targets were the housewives, farmers and other regular users of the Mons-Casteau road. But despite a regular stepping up of their activities the German military police were never able to put an end to the black market altogether. Considering that everyone in Mons was well aware of the activities of these people through the publicity attaching to the prosecutions of those who were caught, it is of interest that there was very little apparent public disapprobation. This was perhaps a recognition of the inevitability of a black market in the circumstances and the part it played in supplementing the goods received from legitimate sources; in other words it was generally seen as a necessary evil.[13]

Dishonesty was not confined to black marketeers. There were many instances recorded of attempts to defraud the *Comités* by the falsification of ration cards in order to obtain more portions. One well-organised fraud succeeded in buying large quantities of rice in small individual portions and then selling it on to the Germans at considerable profit. The perpetrators were eventually caught and imprisoned.[14]

In the last two years of the war another challenge to the charitable impulses of the *Montois* was to arise when the Germans expelled the citizens of northern areas of France which were getting too close to the fighting for comfort. From March 1917 to January 1918 Mons was forced to play host to around 1,000 citizens of the towns of Douai and Cambrai. They responded with great generosity, initially housing the evacuees in public buildings and later billeting them on individual volunteer families. Food was found for them out of the meagre amounts available for the *Montois*' own needs.

An even worse situation arose in September 1918 when the first of no fewer than 5,600 French evacuees were foisted on the *Montois* at virtually no notice. 1,300 arrived on the 8th and many of the rest the following day. A large number of critically ill arrived by barge. The refugees were generally speaking in a very poor state having walked all the way with their remaining possessions piled into carts and wagons. But once again the *Montois* rose to the challenge despite the fact that the fragile arrangements for the supply of food were coming under increasing pressure in the light of the general German retreat, which was well underway. The Germans tried to foment tensions between the evacuees and their hosts by claiming in a letter to Mayor Lescarts that they had received complaints about the poor reception which the evacuees had experienced. In rebutting this Monsieur Lescarts was able to point to a letter of thanks which he had received from the evacuees' leaders. He suggested that the German information had come from corrupt sources.[15]

As the citizens of Mons tried to come to terms with the fact that the German occupation was going to be a feature of their lives for the foreseeable future they had to determine what attitudes they should adopt towards the occupiers. From the outset the German presence had a deleterious effect. Many *Montois* found that they were out of a job as workshops and businesses closed. It might have been expected that the consequent enforced idleness would have resulted in an increase in criminal behaviour, or at least delinquency. But such statistics as there are and the recollections of some who lived through it are that, if anything, the opposite was the case. Recorded violent crimes such as murder and rape fell, as did robberies. The question must be asked whether the fact that the policing of the town had been taken over by the Germans might have inhibited the citizens from reporting crimes. It is perhaps an indication that crime was not fully reflected in the statistics, that the Town's authorities mobilised citizens to cooperate with the German police in carrying out night patrols to prevent thefts from garden plots. Nevertheless the occupation does seem to have ushered in a period of moral rigour; divorce, for example, practically ceased.[16]

Inevitably, the presence of large numbers of troops brought with it a significant upsurge in prostitution. This became such a threat to physical, as well as moral, health that the German civil administration set up a sort of Vice Squad to try to deal with it. The evidence shows that the problem was virtually entirely one affecting the German garrison; Mons citizens taking advantage of the ladies was almost unheard of. Nevertheless the Mons authorities were made responsible for all the costs involved in hospitalising and treating the prostitutes who succumbed to venereal diseases.[17]

There were broadly three ways in which the people of Mons could deal with the German occupiers. They could collaborate openly, or adopt a middle of the road approach of being neither for nor against the occupation. Or they could resist, either actively of passively. Those who opted for collaboration were few in number. There were occasional cases of citizens being denounced to the Germans authorities by fellow citizens, but these denunciations tended to be in pursuit of a personal agenda rather than because of any ideological sympathy with the occupiers. The same probably applied to the authors of the plentiful denunciatory anonymous letters received by the Germans.

Being neither for nor against the occupiers and doing nothing suited those, such as the black marketeers, who were prospering under the occupation. They took the line of everyone for himself and managed to shut their minds to any harm being done to others. As in the case of open collaborators there were relatively few of these.

To their great credit the majority of *Montois* took the line of resistance, albeit in most cases a passive resistance. Prior to the war, buffeted by national and linguistic politics, the majority of Belgians had become disenchanted with patriotism and indifferent to the trappings of the state and the monarchy. The German invasion however restored national unity and patriotic fervour. The citizens felt a need to safeguard their honour and dignity in the face of the injustice inflicted upon them. '*Patrie et Roi*' once more became watchwords. Their patriotic fervour took the Germans by surprise. They had regarded Belgium as an invention of the Great Powers with no soul or meaning of its own. But they soon saw a need to take measures to prevent public outpourings of patriotic feeling, which would eventually confine these to churches and club premises. For a start, celebration of the King's birthday was forbidden.[18]

The citizens of Mons took an early opportunity to demonstrate to the Germans that they were unhappy with their new lot. On 22 February 1915 they celebrated George Washington's birthday in the *Grand-Place*. This was in gratitude for the American food aid which was already making a difference to their lives. The Germans took umbrage at the display of American flags and even pursued children carrying them.

The Germans also reacted to the way the citizens of Mons observed the first Belgian National Day under occupation on 21 July 1915. The main churches held funeral services for the death of the country's independence. All the schools and shops closed for the day and private houses remained shut up. The rare pedestrians wore their Sunday best and nobody went to work. On the day itself the Germans did nothing.[19] But in anticipation of further protests on the upcoming first anniversary of their invasion of Belgium they put in place measures which raised the ire of the Sister diarist of the *Congrégation des Filles du Sacré-Coeur de Jésus*, on the day itself.

> Did they fear the conquered on this anniversary of their odious triumph? Or did they want to save themselves from the shame which the silent protest of 21 July must have caused them? Yesterday. posters were put up forbidding for today all gatherings, demonstrations, flying of flags or insignia. They enjoined all private individuals to be indoors by 8 pm and public establishments to close by 7 pm. They will be obeyed. Would all these banned manifestations constitute the expression of our pain, our patriotism and the revolt of our souls against abominable oppression? We Belgians know how to suffer in silence as we await patiently the hour of retribution.[20]

A few weeks later, at the beginning of November, the same Sister was complaining that the vexations caused by the German occupation were continuing and its severity was growing. Executions and jail sentences were growing more numerous with less and less justification. It was no longer possible to go out of doors without an identity card. Anyone doing so ran the risk of imprisonment or a fine.[21]

The *Montois* also managed to demonstrate their solidarity with the allied cause by organising a pilgrimage to the main burial place of British soldiers killed in the defence of Mons in August 1914. Its religious overtones may have saved it from being banned.[22] It was during church services that the opportunity was frequently taken to demonstrate the congregation's patriotism. The services often doubled as a manifestation of opposition to Germany. Even non-believing political party adherents would swell congregations to demonstrate national solidarity on appropriate occasions such as the mass said in honour of the men shot at Casteau. The Belgian national anthem might be sung, (and sometimes the *Marseillaise*) and cries of '*Vive le Roi*' might be heard. So annoyed did the Germans become at this provocative behaviour that they banned the singing or whistling of the French national anthem. The only occasion when the Germans interfered in the Church's affairs was when they prevented a pastoral letter by the Cardinal Primate being read in the churches. Cardinal Mercier's letter started innocently enough by recommending that the faithful should abstain from hostile acts against the enemy army which would not be in the general interest. But he continued by affirming that the German administration was not a legitimate authority and was not owed esteem, loyalty or obedience.[23]

Manifestations of resistance such as those described would at worst lead to a few days in prison for the participants. But for those who engaged in active resistance the end result could be death. Significant numbers of Belgians were prepared to take this risk. Unlike the Belgian resistance networks in the Second World War, which drew their recruits from all levels of Belgian society, those of the First World War consisted almost entirely of people from the upper strata of society. There seemed to be an unwillingness on the part of these people to call upon the working classes out of an apparent unease that they could not be trusted. Another contrast with resistance activities in the two wars is that in the Second, everyone knew that resistance was taking place, whereas in the First, this only became generally known after the Germans mounted show trials of some of the resistants they had apprehended.[24]

Active resistance got under way very soon after Belgium was occupied. It took three major forms. The first was the obvious one of providing information to the Allies on movements of German troops and equipment to and from the Front. Those best placed to provide this were people whose homes were close to a railway station, main railway lines, important bridges or canals. If their profession gave them the expertise to evaluate what they were seeing, for example if they were senior railway managers, so much the better. Because of its proximity to the Front, the reports of the Mons resistance were of special value to British and French military intelligence. In addition to information on troop movements the Belgian resistance was to prove invaluable in pinpointing German ammunition and fuel dumps.

It is very probable that the Mons administration dabbled in the Resistance too. The Head of the local water company found that he had been given an assistant accountant for whom there was no real work. He quickly inferred he had been placed there to gather information and thereafter pointed him in the right directions to carry out his spying.

The second main activity of the Belgian resistance was acting as a conduit for banned printed matter such as British and French newspapers and the clandestine Belgian news-sheets *La Libre Belgique* and *La Flandre Liberale*. But perhaps more important was the service it set up in early 1915 under the name *'Mot de Soldat'*. This service enabled families who had soldiers serving with the Belgian army in the southwestern tip of the country to correspond with them. It was organised in great detail. A Mons family would write its message on a thin sheet of paper measuring 11 x 9 centimetres. It would be addressed using the soldier's two letter initials and his service number. It would then be delivered to a secret resistance collecting point (there were 7 in the Mons area, know as *îlots*). From there it would be taken to a central collection point in Brussels where it would be put with others in bundles of 1,000, which weighed precisely one kilo. They were then spirited across the Dutch border and sorted out before being delivered to Belgian army headquarters. The same process also operated in reverse. The operation was fraught with danger especially for those carrying the mail across Belgium or trying to cross the Dutch frontier.

The very efficient German counterespionage service managed to break up the operation on several occasions. The early months of the war during which the Germans had operated against the resistance relatively moderately gave way in the late summer of 1915 to out and out severity. The Germans had not appreciated the misplaced joy with which the Belgians had greeted the perceived victories of the French in Champagne and the delight with which they mistakenly foresaw their imminent liberation.[25]

The third main activity of resistance networks was helping young Belgians who wished to join the Belgian army to escape from occupied Belgium, usually into Holland. The German takeover of much of Belgium at the beginning of the war meant that a great number of Belgians approaching military age found themselves behind the German lines before they quite realised what had happened. Young *Montois* were among those keen to get away. The Germans were equally determined to prevent them from doing so. One way of achieving this was to deport the young men concerned. If they managed to avoid this fate there was still the challenge of getting out of the country. Once Mons became a *Zone d'Etape*, in effect a military district, this became even harder and the first step was to reach a part of Belgium still under the Government-General. The boundary ran through the nearby township of Maisières. Once through there the popular route was via Brussels where the aspirant soldier would be picked up by the resistance. Thereafter he would be passed from hand to hand until he made it into Holland. The last stage, the crossing of the frontier was undoubtedly the most difficult. All along the common frontier the Germans had constructed a triple fence combining barbed and electrified wire. Guard posts were placed at 500 metre intervals. But even this daunting physical obstacle proved insufficient to prevent successful escapes. The Germans resorted to putting pressure on the families of potential escapees. Parents were made responsible for ensuring that their sons did not leave their local area. If they failed to do so they would be imprisoned. But the German records were not always up to the task and many managed to escape without endangering their parents, through various ruses.

The Germans then turned their attention to the networks helping the escapees. Those caught were sentenced to forced labour. But even this did not work. Finally the Germans instituted a system under which each month enemy citizens had to report to an office to verify their continued presence in the area. Failure to turn up entailed severe reprisals on the commune which was made responsible for the people involved. This measure appears to have proved the most effective in discouraging flight.[26]

Even before the war the German secret service had put in place in Belgium agents who would, in the event of an occupation, be able to report signs of disaffection or resistance. In the case of Mons, a Mademoiselle Pippine arrived as a German teacher for the young daughters of top families. Thus handily placed she was able to report throughout the war to the German *Kommandantur*. Even though the families concerned soon realised what she was up to, fear of reprisals prevented them from showing her the door. Several thereby paid the price of their liberty.[27]

On the wider stage, as part of their crackdown, the German counterespionage service decided to bring captured members of the resistance before military tribunals. These courts martial sat in various places in Belgium according to need. They were dominated by Military Prosecutors, one of whom named Stoeber had a particularly malignant reputation. The panel of officers forming the tribunal were completely subordinate to the Prosecutor. Scant regard was paid to impartiality or providing the defence lawyers with the evidence against their clients. The proceeds were conducted in German with no interpretation permitted. In effect they were show trials designed to intimidate the Belgian public.[28]

At least 12 citizens of Mons were to be executed by German firing squads during the war for espionage activities. One of the most notable of these was an architect, Philippe Baucq, who was executed with Nurse Edith Cavell at the Belgian National Rifle Range in Brussels on 12 October 1915. Even though she was British, Nurse Cavell, as a Red Cross nurse, had been allowed by the Germans to continue her pre-war work at the Berkendael Institute in Brussels where she had been Matron since 1907. In September 1914 an engineer from Mons, Herman Capiau, visited the Institute, met Nurse Cavell and told her that following the Battle of Mons and the subsequent Retreat, several allied soldiers had become separated from their units and trapped behind the advancing Germans. He said that the Germans were shooting any allied soldiers they found, together with any locals who had helped them.

Capiau became aware that Nurse Cavell had already sheltered two British soldiers, Lt Colonel Dudley Boger and CSM Frank Meachin of 1st Cheshires, who had escaped from the hospital to which they had been taken after being wounded and captured at Elouges. (Colonel Boger was subsequently recaptured and spent the war in Germany as a POW. CSM Meachin got back to England through Holland.) On his return to Mons, Capiau told the Prince Reginald de Croy and his sister Princess Maria de Croy, whose château near Mons had become a sort of collection point for British soldiers separated from their units, and French and Belgians of military age who wanted to enlist in their respective armies. Philippe Baucq was a member of the network led by the Prince. He organised guides for the fugitives.

Over the course of a year the network organised the escape of around 200 allied soldiers. Most of these passed through Nurse Cavell's hands. But on 31 July 1915 the Germans arrested two members of the network. Nurse Cavell and Baucq were subsequently taken into custody. Nurse Cavell had always recognised that her activities could result in a death penalty if she were detected. But her motives were purely humanitarian; if she had not helped the fugitives evade capture they would have been shot. Baucq resolutely refused to talk but was eventually tricked into admitting his guilt. Both were badly treated in detention and were sentenced to death after travesties of trials. The Germans determined to carry out the sentences without delay. In a final cruel twist Baucq was allowed a final visit from his wife but only on condition that he did not tell her that he was about to be executed. When she said good-bye at the end of the brief visit she did not realise that she would never see her husband again. Baucq was also refused the comfort of a priest prior to his execution. Stoic to the end he refused the traditional bandaging of the eyes. The sentences were carried out in the early hours of 12 October 1915 and both bodies were buried close to where they died.[29]

The leader of the network, Prince Reginald de Croy, had received sufficient warning to make good his escape before he could be arrested. His sister was less fortunate and was eventually sentenced to 10 years hard labour. Herman Capiau had also been swept up and received 15 years hard labour. Both of those imprisoned were released when Germany surrendered.

Three other *Montois* were executed in Brussels on 6 November 1915. One of them was Charles Simonet, a former newsagent. His work for the resistance consisted of collecting together information supplied by agents and transcribing it in invisible ink for onward transmission to British GHQ. He also did some spying of his own, spending long periods at Mons railway station looking for anything which might be of value to the British. When he was arrested on 16 May his guilt was attested to by a letter of congratulations from British GHQ which was found on him. He was taken to Brussels but was to return several times to Mons under escort in the hope that he might reveal the identity of his collaborators by some gesture or reaction. He was even taken back to his family home where again he was not allowed to reveal the certain fate that awaited him. He was executed in the company of his Mons comrades Joseph Delsaut and Jules Legay.[30]

Mons became the scene of a major court martial on 29 February 1916 when 39 alleged resistants were tried in the Mons theatre in the *Grand-Place*. The defendants had been picked up during a widespread German operation aimed at breaking up the resistance network which was spying on German troop movements by railway in various centres and passing on the information to the Allies. The German operation had certainly succeeded as far as the Mons network was concerned.

The main aim of holding this massive show trial in Mons was to cower the local population. But it seemed to demonstrate a greater attachment to justice than was usually the case in such trials. Seven of the defendants were acquitted, and the majority of the rest received prison terms ranging from 4 months to 15 years. Of the 15 death penalties demanded by the prosecution only 7 were handed down. As usual in such cases these were carried out with minimal delay. At dawn on 2 March the condemned men were taken to the communal rifle range at Casteau where, having been given a sight of the coffins and freshly dug graves awaiting them, they were shot. They met their deaths bravely with one of their number, a notary called Léonce Roels shouting, '*Courage mes amis! Nous serons vengés. Vive le Roi!*' The only stain on the Belgian conduct was the betrayal by the head of the railway network, Lampert, of his colleagues in return for his life.[31]

The Sister diarist of the *Sacré-Coeur* recorded the strong emotions roused locally by these executions.

When will the horrors of foreign occupation end? This morning at 6 am at Casteau camp the execution of seven good patriots, guilty of having served their country, took place. May God have pity on their souls... and pardon their iniquitous executioners.[32]

And a week later.

Yesterday, a moving visit to the graves of the executed men. This morning, we took part in a funeral service, celebrated at the request of the Mons Bar, for the victims of 2 November. A noble protest. The defenders of the martyrs and the entire town came together at the Collegial of Saint Waudru to demonstrate their pain, their admiration and their hatred of tyranny.[33]

Despite the dislocation caused to everyday life by the occupation, the citizens of Mons had somehow got to carry on in as normal a way as possible. In one area they received rather more cooperation from the occupiers than they were to come to expect generally. The municipal authorities were keen to get the schools reopened and fully attended at the earliest moment after the German arrival, to ensure that as little of the school year as possible was lost. In addition, neither they nor the Germans could face with equanimity the prospect of idle and bored youth roaming the streets of the town.

During their takeover of the town many school buildings had been commandeered by the Germans for use as barracks. The schools had not as a consequence been able to reopen on schedule after the summer holidays. But the Germans quickly slimmed down their accommodation requirements and were able to agree with the municipal administration that the schools should reopen on 1 October, The pupils of schools whose premises had been retained by the Germans for their own use would have to double up with other schools whose premises the Germans had vacated.

The resumption of public education did not proceed at all smoothly. Many parents decided to keep their children at home until things had fully settled down. Many of those who did send their children back withdrew them hastily when a rumour spread that the Germans were visiting the schools and injecting the pupils with poison! Absenteeism became such a problem that the German administration felt the need to post up a reminder that universal education remained compulsory. The town fathers decided that adult members of families with children between the ages of two and 14, who were not attending classes, would not be considered for jobs within their gift. This threat had to compete with the belief of many parents that in the straitened economic situation it could be more profitable to have their children work rather than attend school.

The problem of absenteeism was not confined to the younger pupils. At senior level, many of the students were not locals but from other parts of Belgium and even from abroad. The difficulties of moving around the occupied country prevented many of these from rejoining their courses. Others had departed for the front.

But the numbers undergoing public education at all level picked up quite quickly following the severe decline recorded in early 1915. The buoyant numbers continued until 1917 when numbers dropped significantly. They would not recover until after the war. There were several reasons for this sharp downturn. The Germans had had to retake possession of some school premises for use as medical facilities for the increasing number of wounded from the fighting around Ypres. Other premises had to be used to house the large number of evacuees arriving from northern France. The mass deportations also involved significant numbers of senior students. In broad terms pupils probably lost on average a year's schooling.

On the other hand adult education courses organised by the town administration proved popular especially with the unemployed who took the opportunity to repair the gaps in their formal education. Of particular use were gardening courses for householders who could set up a kitchen garden, and nursing courses for young ladies.

Although all of the above refers to the public education sector the experience in the private, largely Catholic church, sector was broadly similar. The Jesuits also participated with enthusiasm in the adult education programme.[34]

With large numbers of Mons citizens finding themselves involuntarily with more leisure than they were accustomed to, how it might be filled was a constant preoccupation. As already noted some returned to their studies; others immersed themselves in the work of the charitable organisations. Many were looking for distractions to take their minds off the distressing realities of their situation. There was a general sentiment that simple enjoyment would be wrong when some of their compatriots and allies were fighting and dying not many miles away. The traditional festival days fell victim to this sentiment. The efforts to celebrate publicly George Washington's birthday and the King's birthday, with their obvious patriotic, and anti-German overtones, were rapidly stopped by the occupiers, who did not, however, deny themselves the pleasure of noisy celebrations to mark the Kaiser's and Bismarck's birthdays. German attempts to draw in the Mons public by public open-air performances by military bands enabled the *Montois* to demonstrate their disaffection by ostentatiously staying away from the venue while the concert was in progress and then turning up in large numbers once it was over.

A way to salve the general conscience in respect of not seeming to enjoy themselves when compatriots were fighting and dying, was to ensure that a large percentage of the entrance fees, or all the profits, from events should go to charity. In this framework the administration organised many sporting occasions including cycle races, football matches, cross country races, swimming galas, athletics meetings and pelota tournaments. Theatrical performances were also organised in arenas which had not been requisitioned by the Germans for their own purposes.

But for those who had no money and were dependent on charity, these occasions were closed to them. Even worse they found themselves frowned upon if they spent what little money they did have on a cinema ticket or in a café. Both the town administration and the charitable organisations threatened those who succumbed to such temptations with withdrawal of their benefits. The main free leisure service open to such people was the public library. This saw a huge increase in its clientèle as they took advantage of it.[35]

It would have been surprising if in these stressful times there had not been a resurgence in religious devotion. In the early days of the war attendance at mass rose markedly. But it was not sustained possibly because of the difficulties the faithful were finding in replacing their 'Sunday best' in the light of the growing shortages of clothing and shoes. There may also have been a fear that closely packed congregations were an ideal breeding ground for infections, a concern which probably grew with the arrival of the French evacuees in their midst.[36]

As 1917 gave way to 1918 there was a growing feeling among the people of Mons that the war was heading for its decisive phase. It still remained virtually impossible to get reliable news of what was going on on the battlefields, but the Germans were not slow to trumpet their successes in the spring and early summer of 1918 in the press they controlled. But it slowly became clear that the German successes had not proved decisive. In June the Sister diarist of the *Sacré-Coeur* commented on the state of German morale.

> Uncertainty and ignorance on the subject of external events, except that we have learned that the Germans are marching rapidly towards Paris after a significant advance in France! However there is talk of great demoralisation

among their troops, and we read it on the faces of the troops passing though Mons. Where is the pride and enthusiasm of the first months of the war?[37]

In contrast to what seemed to be happening to the Germans, the British offensive of 8 August which, despite German censorship, soon became known about in Mons, did seem to signify a fundamental change and gave a huge lift to the town's spirits. By early October two German communiqués made it clear to the *Montois* that the Germans were losing the war and that liberation could not be far away. But it would still be more than a month before that great day arrived.[38]

Chapter XIII

The Western Front
January 1917–July 1918

Prior to his dismissal General Joffre had reached broad agreement with General Haig on the allied strategy for 1917; there would be no great changes in their approach or aims from those of 1916. But before detailed plans could be finalised Joffre was replaced as French Commander-in-Chief by General Robert Nivelle. A Gunner, Nivelle had come to prominence during the Battle of Verdun. Almost as soon as General Pétain had restored order out of the chaos of the early days of the defence of the fortress city, Nivelle had replaced him.

In addition to his military skills, Nivelle was a very good communicator who had a natural charm. The French Government, long resigned to the taciturnity of General Joffre, and alarmed at the ever growing casualty lists with little prospect of improvement whilst he remained Commander-in-Chief, warmly embraced Nivelle and his confidence that he could win the war with one massive offensive.

On the other side of the Channel David Lloyd George had replaced Herbert Asquith as British Prime Minister. He had been at the heart of the political conduct of the war from the outset. He had been Minister of Munitions, with responsibility for improving shell production, and prior to becoming Prime Minister, Secretary of State for War in succession to Lord Kitchener, who had been lost at sea on his way to Russia. Unlike Asquith it was certain that Lloyd George would be an interventionist. Appalled by the casualty rates on the Western Front and the apparent lack of anything positive to show for them, the new Prime Minister believed he should conceive and pursue a strategy that would marginalise the Western Front and reduce the scope for Haig and his generals to amass huge casualty lists in further fruitless offensives.

The Prime Minister concluded that Haig's freedom of manoeuvre would be curtailed if the BEF were subordinated to the French. Almost certainly, like the French politicians, his judgment had been impaired by the charm and plausibility of General Nivelle, augmented in his case by the latter's panache and his fluency in English. After a period of intrigue, and at the expense of poisoning military-political relations, Lloyd George partially achieved his aim when Haig was subordinated to Nivelle, but for the duration of Nivelle's planned offensive only. It was also agreed that if the Nivelle offensive were to fail, Haig would then be able to launch his own offensive from north of the River Lys, and would be supported by the French.[1]

At their first meeting on 20 December 1916, Nivelle outlined to Haig his plan for a rapid victory, specifying that if the looked-for breakthrough had not occurred within 48 hours he would call off the battle. Over the next few weeks details of the Nivelle Plan emerged. He planned to repeat, on a much grander scale, the tactics that had proved so successful for him at Verdun and achieve the breakthrough and defeat of the Germans that had eluded the Allies so far. He proposed a massive French offensive, the main thrust of which would start off between Soissons and Reims, sweep over the Chemin des Dames and head north, through St Quentin towards Cambrai and the Belgian border. The main French attack would be supported by a British advance eastwards from Arras and a subsidiary French attack starting off between Roye and Soissons and heading northeast. These supporting thrusts were intended to draw the Germans away from the main French onslaught northwards. Within 48 hours, according to Nivelle, the attacks would link up leaving the Germans in disarray.[2]

The British operation would mainly involve Sir Edmund Allenby's Third Army supported by Sir Henry Horne's First Army on its left flank, and by Sir Hubert Gough's Fifth Army on its right. The thrust of the Third Army attack would be eastwards towards the area of Cambrai where it would link up with the French. The initial assault would be mounted by 10 divisions of Third Army advancing from positions around Arras and supported by First Army's assault on Vimy Ridge. The Fifth Army would attack towards the village of Bullecourt and the Hindenburg Line at a slightly later date. The main British attack would precede that of the French by a week.

Two days after the United States declared war on the Central Powers, the Third and First Armies attacked simultaneously in the predawn hours of a bitterly cold Easter Monday, 9 April. They were initially assisted by a blizzard blowing in the Germans' faces. The Third Army's attack achieved some degree of surprise. Allenby's centre units achieved an advance of three and a half miles, up to that point the BEF's greatest one-day advance on the Western Front. There had been just a slight window of opportunity for the elusive breakthrough but the weather, and the state of the ground churned up by the artillery, effectively prevented the cavalry exploiting the situation.

The Third Army offensive was resumed on the next 2 days but progress became more and more difficult in the face of the artillery's problems in moving up their guns over ground they had all too successfully churned up, and the Germans' hardening defence and counterattacks. In effect, most of what the Third Army were to achieve was accomplished on the first day.[3]

The First Army's assault on Vimy Ridge was a triumphant success. Largely entrusted to the Canadian Corps, whose four divisions went into action simultaneously for the first time, they were in complete possession of the allegedly impregnable Vimy Ridge within three days. Their success had been based on meticulous planning, detailed training, the exploitation of tunnels secretly dug to convey the assaulting troops to their jumping off points, a highly sophisticated artillery programme and surprise. It firmly established the Canadian Corps as the leading shock troops of the BEF and was the first of their many future triumphs which would culminate in the liberation of Mons 19 months later.[4]

The Fifth Army's planning for their share in the battle was greatly complicated by the Germans' highly secret withdrawal to their new defensive system, the Hindenburg Line (*Siegfried Stellung* to the Germans). The operation, codenamed *Alberich*, began on 9 February and was completed by 20 March. Thousands of French civilians, many of whom were to end up in Mons, were uprooted from their homes as the Germans carried out a scorched earth operation. The Fifth

Army realised something was up when their patrols failed to find the enemy where they expected them. Gough ordered his troops forward to close the gap and, he hoped, disrupt construction of any new defence system.

Neither the *Siegfried Stellung* nor the secondary *Wotan Line* (known to the Allies as the Drocourt-Quéant Switch) were likely to be complete before the anticipated Allied offensive was launched. The Germans therefore fortified several key villages in front of the new system to hold up the British advance. Gough decided to gamble that the Germans would not defend the village of Bullecourt in force and planned to pinch it out. In fact Bullecourt was especially sensitive to the Germans, being close to where the Hindenburg Line and the Drocourt-Quéant Switch linked up. They intended to defend it fiercely. The stage was set for some of the most savage fighting of the war. Gough launched his attack on 11 April, 2 days after First and Third Armies. It ended in the bloody repulse of V British Corps and I ANZAC Corps. Three days later a German counterattack at Lagnicourt surprised the Australians. But they rallied sufficiently to drive the Germans back and inflict heavy casualties.[5]

General Nivelle's offensive was launched on 16 April. Not only were the Germans alert to the imminence of a French offensive but, through captured documents, they were fully aware of the details of the French plan of attack. Their new strategy of defence in depth, and the confusion caused by their withdrawal from positions which the French were planning to bombard and assault, meant that they were not badly affected by the preliminary French bombardment. For their part the French infantry were ill-served by an ineffective creeping barrage and unsuitable tanks. The result was disaster.

Despite Nivelle's undertaking to win the battle in 48 hours or give up, it was to drag on into the next month. Although there were some successes the offensive had manifestly failed to live up to the high expectations so rashly fostered by Nivelle. This led to open disaffection in the French ranks, rapidly turning to mutiny. Soon only two divisions could be considered totally reliable. Fortunately the French managed to keep this information from the enemy. Inevitably Haig came under great pressure from the French to continue the Battle of Arras, when there was little military point in doing so, so as to keep the Germans distracted.[6] At a time when he wanted to focus his attention and resources on his proposed offensive north of the Lys, he had instead to continue the battle further south.

The second phase of the Battle of Arras, known as the Second Battle of the Scarpe, was launched on 23 April. Third Army's renewed offensive made little progress at the cost of over 8.000 casualties. Allenby tried again on 28 April but achieved little. All three British armies engaged in the battle attacked again on 3 May. The day proved to be a serious disappointment with little to show for the three armies' efforts except long casualty lists. The Battle of Arras was to continue intermittently and inconclusively until it was brought to an end on 17 May.[7]

On 7 June, implementation of Haig's cherished 1917 strategy began when the Second Army assaulted Messines Ridge. Haig had long seen strategic possibilities for an offensive from the Ypres Salient. He foresaw it capturing the ridges on three sides of Ypres, then advancing northwest to Roulers and Torhout, then north to the Belgian coast. Simultaneously with this last step, British units on the Belgian coast would advance from Nieuwport to overcome the German defences

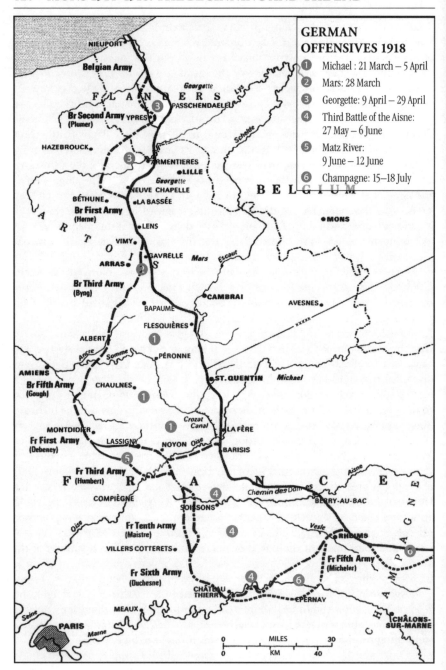

Map 7: German Spring Offensives

at Middelkerke. There would also be an amphibious landing on the Belgian coast behind the German lines. All three operations would converge between Ostend and Zeebrugge, liberating the two ports and driving the Germans northwards. They would thereby be deprived of two submarine bases and suffer a great strategic, and possibly terminal, defeat.

The first stage of this strategy was the seizure of Messines Ridge south of Ypres. Sir Herbert Plumer's Army achieved a stunning success. A huge concentration of guns pounded the German defences for over two weeks prior to Zero Hour at which point 19 mines laid and primed under the German front lines were detonated simultaneously in the largest manmade explosion in history to that date. Confronted by only a few dazed German survivors, the infantry quickly overran and consolidated their objectives. Casualties were sustained over the ensuing days as the attackers sought to advance further, but when the battle ended after a week it had opened the way for the full implementation of Haig's strategy.

But Haig had already planted the seeds of his strategy's failure by his decision, taken over a month earlier, to give the leading role to Sir Hubert Gough and his Fifth Army, rather than Plumer and his Second. Instead of the relatively rapid follow-up which the latter might have been able to achieve there was to be a pause of over six weeks before Gough, distracted by his problems at Bullecourt, was ready.

On 31 July, following a two-week long bombardment, nine divisions of Gough's Fifth Army went over the top on a 14,000 yard front east of Ypres. They were supported by two French divisions to the north and a Second Army diversionary attack to the south. Despite some initial success, the failure of Gough to give sufficient regard to repeated strictures by Haig on the prime importance of securing the Gheluvelt Plateau, led to the offensive becoming bogged down, literally as well as figuratively, as heavy rain turned the battlefield into a quagmire. Even the passing back of responsibility for the offensive to Plumer and the Second Army in mid-September could not stop the battle turning into an attritional slog with its overall strategic objectives well beyond the capacities of the attackers to achieve. By the end of the first week in October the ambition of Haig and his two Army Commanders was confined to the seizure of Passchendaele Ridge as an adequate outcome to the offensive. With the ANZACs having joined the rest of the two armies in exhaustion by mid-October, Haig was forced to call on the Canadians to complete the job. On 4 separate days over the period 26 October to 10 November the Canadians gradually advanced, capturing Passchendaele village on 6 November and, 4 days later, completing occupation of the Ridge.[8]

The Third Battle of Ypres (or Passchendaele) was over. It had achieved none of its strategic objectives and had been prolonged long beyond the point when it had become clear that they were inachievable. It had been fought in appalling conditions of mud and squalor. Even in attritional terms it could hardly be deemed successful. British losses matched those of the Germans and their morale had probably been worse affected.

There would be one further attempt to break through the German defences before the end of 1917. On 20 November Sir Julian Byng's Third Army launched the Battle of Cambrai, the first battle in history in which massed tanks were employed. The objectives were to break through the Hindenburg Line, to capture

Cambrai and Bourlon Wood and to exploit towards Valenciennes. 476 tanks were to take part of which 324 were battle tanks.

So successful was the initial assault that church bells were rung in Britain after the first day to mark a great victory. But the celebrations were premature. Only 92 tanks with exhausted crews were available for the second day of the battle and it quickly reverted to the usual artillery/infantry struggle. The attack came to a halt on 29 November. On the following day Third Army were caught unprepared by a major German counterattack which took as much ground as had been lost in the British advance. The battle ended a week later.[9]

By the time the battle was over it was becoming increasingly apparent that the strategic initiative was passing over to the Germans. The conclusion of hostilities on the Eastern Front would soon enable them to transfer large numbers of relatively fresh but battle-hardened divisions to the Western Front at a time when the Allies were suffering manpower and morale crises. The bloodletting of Passchendaele, roughly equating to the loss of about 12 divisions by the BEF, had persuaded Lloyd George that repetitions could best be avoided by starving Haig and his generals of the human raw material they consumed so prolifically. By the beginning of 1918 the effects of this were becoming so painful that divisions were of necessity reduced in size from 12 to 9 battalions each with all the pain to cohesion and morale that this entailed. Only the Canadian Corps' divisions escaped this surgery.[10]

At the same time the French were only in the early stages of recovery from the nadir of the mutinies and were a long way from resuming their willingness to assume the offensive. In addition, the build-up of the American Expeditionary Force in France was proceeding painfully slowly and it could not be counted on for a significant contribution until the second half of 1918 at the earliest. The realisation was sinking in that the BEF and its Allies would have to look to their defences over the next few months before there could be any question of resuming the offensive other than in strictly limited and local operations. It had been a long time since the BEF had been called upon to fight a major defensive battle but, as 1917 gave way to 1918, this was the prospect that faced the BEF and their French allies.

The Prime Minister's efforts to circumvent what he saw as the dead hand of Haig and his generals on the conduct of the war moved a step forward in early February when he engineered the setting up of an Inter-Allied Supreme War Council at Versailles. This brought about the resignation of General Sir 'Wully' Robertson, the Chief of the Imperial General Staff, and close Haig ally. He was unable to accept the dilution of his role implied by the existence of the Supreme War Council. He was replaced by Sir Henry Wilson despite an unequivocal warning from Haig direct to the Prime Minister and the Secretary of State for War that Wilson was distrusted by the Army, hardly an ideal qualification for its military head.

By 10 March, GHQ Intelligence was anticipating that the main blow of the long anticipated German offensive would fall on Third Army in the Arras-Cambrai sector, with a possible diversionary operation against First Army further north. But by 17 March GHQ Intelligence thought a German attack was no longer imminent.

Only four days afterwards, on the 21st, the Germans opened the *Kaiserschlacht* (Kaiser's Battle) by launching *Operation Michael*. As had been anticipated a major assault was made on Third Army on the Cambrai front. But an even heavier assault fell on the British Fifth Army further south in the Somme area. Sir Hubert Gough's army had only recently taken over much of the sector from the French and were weak in numbers. The Germans, helped by a mist cloaking their movements, a sophisticated artillery programme, overwhelming force and refined infantry tactics, advanced rapidly. There was no diversionary attack on First Army.

Haig's first priority was to reorganise the BEF in the light of developments in the Fifth and Third Army areas, where the immediate crisis was unfolding. A major concern had been the negative response he had received to his request for help from the French C-in-C, General Pétain, who saw his priority as blocking the German route to Paris and not keeping the two allied armies in contact with each other. Haig concluded that it was essential that a Supreme Allied Commander should be appointed to overcome the problem of the pursuit of narrow national self-interest by the Allies. At an inter-allied conference at Doullens on 26 March the momentous decision was taken to appoint General Ferdinand Foch to coordinate the actions of the allied armies on the Western Front. A week later Foch's role was expanded to cover the 'strategic direction of military operations' making him in effect Supreme Allied Commander, or *Generalissimo*.[11]

Two days after the 26 March meeting the German Seventeenth Army launched the two-pronged *Operation Mars*, an attack northwestwards (*Mars North*) and westwards (*Mars South*) on both sides of the River Scarpe towards Arras. Ready to receive the assaults were Third and First Armies. BEF intelligence had predicted accurately both the extent and timing of the German assault. When the German barrage erupted at 03h00 it fell on largely empty trenches. Nevertheless the sheer weight of the German heavy artillery bombardment, which included phosgene gas, put great pressure on the British defences. Despite the great strength in numbers of the German assault in the south, it only succeeded in pushing back the Third Army defenders a short way before the attack petered out with heavy losses. In the north, after stubborn resistance and the infliction of heavy casualties, the British were forced out of the Forward Zone of their defences but stabilised their positions in the forward area of the Battle Zone. Here they successfully repelled all further attempts by the enemy to get forward. Like *Mars South*, *Mars North* had failed.[12]

The main problem for Haig and his army commanders was to determine precisely where the next German blow might fall. As March gave way to April it was felt that the enemy would still try to envelop Arras from the southeast and northeast, but that they might possibly extend their assault northwards to the La Bassée Canal.

A shift north had obvious attractions to the Germans. It would mean them attacking where the British lines were only 50 miles from the Channel, with the area in between chockfull of vital infrastructure and logistics for the BEF. A northward wheel, once the British lines had been breached, would put the Germans in possession of the last remaining French coalfields in Allied hands. The French were understandably nervous about this.

On 5 April the Germans had brought *Operation Michael* to an end in the Somme area. Despite the vast amount of ground that had been captured, unprecedented by Western Front standards, it had proved to be a blind alley for the Germans. Even if they had not been finally held up just to the east of Amiens their offensive was leading nowhere of vital strategic significance. Once they had breached the British defences they should have wheeled north to roll up the British lines and threaten the Channel ports. Instead, prevented from doing so by the stubborn defence of Third Army, they had continued westwards. But their success did lead to the dismissal of the British Fifth Army Commander, Sir Hubert Gough. He had almost certainly merited sacking for his Army's poor performances in the Battles of Arras and Passchendaele. But, despite overwhelming odds, he had conducted his Army's retreat in *Operation Michael* very competently. Nevertheless the Government at home were looking for a scapegoat. If it were not to be Haig, it had to be Gough. So Gough paid the price.

The German offensive in the north against First Army was given the codename *Georgette* in recognition of the fact that it had been scaled down from the originally planned *George*. The scaling down had been necessitated by the unanticipatedly high demands on their resources generated during *Michael*. The German strategy was to break through the British lines and seize the vital railway junction of Hazebrouck. If circumstances were propitious the advance might even be continued to the coast. A second prong would capture the important Flanders heights of Mount Kemmel, Cassel and Mont des Cats and force a British withdrawal from the Ypres Salient.[13]

The German attack was prefaced by a heavy bombardment of the rear areas of the First Army's Portuguese and 55th Divisions which began at 04h15 on 9 April. Singled out for attention were Allied artillery batteries, road junctions and headquarters. It was sufficiently effective to inflict severe disruption on command structures. The bombardment included the intensive gas shelling of Armentières. From 08h00 it concentrated on the Portuguese and British front positions, with trench mortars joining in 10 minutes before the infantry assault began at 08h45.

The assaulting German infantry were helped by a heavy mist which lay over the battlefield. It did not begin to dissipate until the early afternoon. The main thrust of their attack fell squarely on the Portuguese, although both 55th and 40th Divisions on either side, were rapidly and heavily engaged. Many of the Portuguese of the 3 weak brigades manning the front lines had not waited for the infantry assault; they had begun heading for the rear during the German bombardment, some as early as 07h30. By 10h00 the vast majority of the Portuguese had passed through the front line of the Battle Zone (being hastily manned by British reserves) on their way to the rear and out of the battle.

By 11h00 the battlefield was virtually empty of Portuguese troops and guns. The speed and extent of their disintegration had not been anticipated. Nor had their failure to demolish bridges and other vital points in their rapid retreat. The British were consequently left with insufficient time to implement fully their emergency contingency plan which was to try to contain the German advance about 3 miles behind the original front line.[14]

The 55th (West Lancashire) Division were to receive great acclaim for their successful defence of Givenchy and Festubert during this and the ensuing days.

As long as they held their ground, the enemy's scope to exploit their breakthrough of the Portuguese positions to the north would be inhibited. Realising that the Portuguese had collapsed, the division formed a defensive flank facing north. They came under attack from elements of 3 German divisions. But none of the divisional strongpoints was overrun and counterattacks quickly re-established the division's line virtually in its entirety by nightfall.[15]

Held up on their left by 55th Division, and by 40th Division on their right, the German attackers nevertheless made considerable progress through the centre where the 2 tired and depleted British divisions, brought up to plug the gap left by the Portuguese, fell back slowly. But by the end of the day, the German timetable had already fallen behind. Their plan had called for them to be across the River Lys along the whole length of their assault by this time. Instead they had only secured one small bridgehead of the far side of the river. Nevertheless the British position was serious and losses had been heavy. With all available reserves committed, First Army were holding a thin line around the edge of a German crescent-shaped penetration 10 miles wide and 5 and a half miles deep at its furthest extremity.

The 10 April brought no respite for Horne's hard-pressed troops as the enemy's Sixth Army maintained the pressure on First Army's attenuated defences. At the same time, the German Fourth Army launched an assault on General Plumer's Second Army by advancing towards the Messsines-Wytschaete Ridge. For both British armies it was a day of desperate defence. Even though it did not prove possible to stop the enemy from advancing, their progress was much slower than they had planned. They had failed to pierce the British front or drive a wedge between First and Second Armies.

Even though an optimist may have detected signs that the usual norm of the Western Front – initial striking success followed by the onset of the law of diminishing returns – was beginning to reassert itself, Haig, Horne and Plumer could draw little comfort from the situation confronting them as the second day of the battle drew to a close. Foch however was finally persuaded of the seriousness of the threat to the British. He ordered a French force of four infantry and three cavalry divisions northwards, initially to provide cover for the BEF's Third and Fourth Armies. This would enable them to free units for use in the First and Second Armies' sectors. If necessary, the French could subsequently be committed to the battle itself. Whatever relief Haig may have felt at Foch's belated support was insufficient to stop him issuing his uncharacteristic and famous 'Backs to the Wall' Order of the Day on 11 April. The fact that the normally reserved Haig could be driven to such a pitch of eloquence reflected his belief that a major crisis of the war for the Allied cause was being fought out by First and Second Armies.[16]

Whatever disappointment the Germans may have felt in their achievements of the first two days of the battle was not reflected in their plans for the third. They were to exploit their successes in the direction of Hazebrouck and Calais. The day's fighting made it clear that a serious threat to the vital town of Hazebrouck was developing, but the following day the Germans made no serious attacks, contenting themselves with probing which paid off at several points because of the exhaustion and weakness of the British defenders. The following day, they threw three fresh divisions into the battle in an attempt to reach Hazebrouck. But the timely arrival of 1st Australian Division effectively blocked any prospect the Germans might have had of reaching the French town.[17]

The next three days were to be comparatively quiet on the First Army front, but less so for Plumer's army which lost Bailleul on 15 April and Meteren, Wytschaete and Spanbroekmoelen the following day. Counterattacks succeeded in stabilising the situation without recovering any of these places. [18]

The next two days were to see the resumption of furious German assaults which were to prove both expensive and largely unsuccessful. The following day, attacks were launched aimed at capturing Givenchy, Festubert and Béthune in First Army's sector, and Mount Kemmel in Second Army's. The attack had been anticipated by First Army intelligence and, in fierce fighting, was largely repulsed. The Second Army and French troops also turned back the German assault on Mount Kemmel.[19]

When the fighting on 18 April died down it was not to be renewed at anything like the same level of intensity for several days. Day succeeded day without a major renewal of the German offensive. In point of fact there was to be no further serious German attack against First Army before the Battle of the Lys was officially suspended by General Ludendorff on 29 April. Second Army were less fortunate; on 25 April, the Germans once again assaulted Second Army and this time were successful in taking Mount Kemmel from the French 28th Division.[20] The previous day, the Germans had also renewed their ultimately unsuccessful attempt to break through the allied defences at Villers Bretonneux which were blocking the enemy's road to Amiens.

For much of the late spring and early summer of 1918 there was a recurrent expectation that the Germans would mount a further offensive on the First Army's section of the line and possibly Third Army's too. The intelligence came largely from prisoners. On 14 May First Army Intelligence thought that the Germans were ready to attack in their sector. Four days later, GHQ Intelligence concluded an enemy attack astride the Scarpe was probable but that the main blow would fall against Third Army.[21]

In the event, when the German blow was launched on 27 May it fell on the French in what was to become known as the Third Battle of the Aisne. Over the next 11 days, until the offensive petered out, the Germans were to make striking gains and inflict severe losses on the Allies (4 tired British divisions sent to the French area for rest and recuperation were severely mauled in the initial German assault and suffered 29,000 casualties). But once again the offensive was ultimately a German failure as no decisive breakthrough was achieved and a salient vulnerable to counterattack had been created.[22]

The switch of German attentions to the French sector did nothing to diminish Haig's belief that the British sector was still clearly in the German sights, if not in the immediate future. They still had enough troops in reserve to put in another heavy attack somewhere but the odds were growing that it would seek to exploit their current success against the French, as Paris was a tempting target. But prisoners continued to insist that an attack against First Army was coming and the build up of enemy activity in the area seemed to back up their claims.

By mid June two new factors were beginning to have an impact on the Western Front. The first was the steady arrival of British reinforcements which had been denied to Haig until the authorities in Britain had been galvanised into response by the German spring offensive. The second was the availability of artillery ammunition in almost unlimited quantities.

Although there was a continuing expectation that it was only a matter of time before the Germans launched an attack, Haig was increasingly thinking in terms of taking the battle to the enemy.

On 15 July the Germans struck once again against the French in Champagne. There was a general belief in the allied camp that this was a last desperate gamble on the part of the Germans and that if it could be defeated it would extinguish any lingering German hopes that they could win the war. French Intelligence had learned what the Germans were planning. They were thus able to limit the normal initial success which surprise would have gained as well as plan a counterattack. Three days later the French Tenth Army of General Mangin launched this counterattack against the German right flank and transformed the situation.[23] General Ludendorff was forced to postpone the offensive he had been planning against the British in Flanders which Haig had been expecting, The German postponement was to prove permanent even though it would be some days before Haig could be certain that the initiative had passed firmly to the Allies.

By late July it was becoming possible to believe that the greatly overstretched Germans were losing the capacity to mount large-scale offensive operations. The initiative was once more passing back to the Allies whose thoughts could increasingly concentrate on going over to the offensive.

Chapter XIV

The Campaign of 100 Days: August-November 1918

Field Marshal Haig was well to the fore of his senior colleagues, both British and allied, in concluding in late July that the overall situation on the Western Front had moved, possibly decisively, in favour of the Allies. He even dared to think that it might be possible to win the war before the end of 1918. This at a time when virtually everyone else, including General Ferdinand Foch, thought that it would drag on into 1919.

Haig could not be immediately certain that the successful French counterattack of 18 July in Champagne would spell the end of the German capacity to mount offensives and would entail the postponement and subsequent cancellation of Ludendorff's planned attack on the BEF in Flanders. But there was growing evidence that the enemy's offensives from 21 March onwards had resulted in huge losses to them in men and equipment which they no longer had the resources to replace. The Allies too had lost heavily but, unlike the Germans, the BEF could now count on a regular flow of reinforcements. In addition the American build-up on the Western Front was proceeding and could continue *ad infinitum* if necessary. A major plus to emerge from the German *Kaiserschlacht* had been the appointment of General Foch as overall co-ordinator (*Generalissimo*) of the allied armies. In addition to putting forward his own proposals for attacks to the national army commanders, he was able to ensure that their plans were synchronised or staggered in such a way as to keep the Germans constantly on the back foot.

There were other events which were to set the scene for the allied return to major offensive operations in August. Following the dismissal of Sir Hubert Gough as Fifth Army Commander he was replaced on 28 March by Sir Henry Rawlinson. On 2 April the Army was renamed the Fourth Army.[1] Rawlinson's immediate task had been to preserve Amiens. His substantial reinforcements included the Australian Corps who played a major part in driving the Germans back from Villers Bretonneux, the nearest point they had reached to Amiens.[2]

With the threat to the French city removed Rawlinson was keen to go on to the offensive. In a series of minor actions in April-June the Australians had successfully attacked and pinched out small German salients, demonstrating German weakness in the sector. On 4 July, three Australian brigades, incorporating four American companies and supported by 600 guns and 60 tanks, attacked a small German salient on the Fourth Army front. Dispensing with a preliminary bombardment the operation achieved complete surprise and was a total success. It demonstrated how much the BEF had learned over the past four years and was now ready to put into practice. The Battle of Hamel, as the operation was called, though small-scale, was to be used as a model for future operations by Fourth Army, who were to be at the forefront of much that was to follow for the Allies.[3]

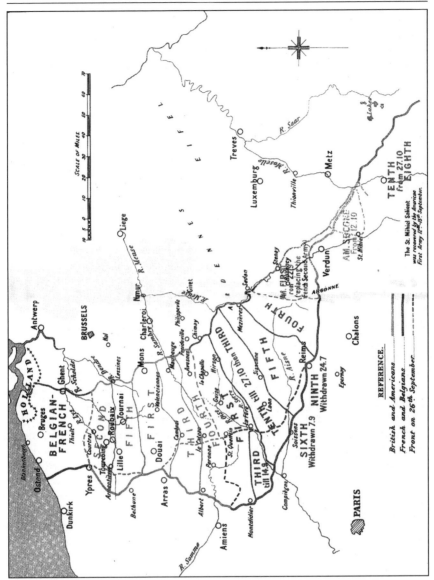

Map 8: The Campaign of 100 Days

On 15 July Haig instructed Rawlinson to plan a major attack to start on 8 August. In addition to his Australian and III British Corps, Rawlinson would be given the Canadian Corps. The attack would be supported by the French First Army on the Fourth Army's right. The Battle of Amiens began as planned on 8 August and lasted until the 11th. The first day of this battle, was described by Ludendorff as, 'the black day of the German Army. It put the decline of our fighting powers beyond all doubt'. The three Fourth Army corps and the French

First Army attacked at 04h20 achieving complete surprise. Most of the damage was done on the first day but in all the Germans lost just under 30,000 as prisoners out of total losses of around 75,000 and between 400 and 500 guns.[4]

The Battle of Amiens ushered in what became known as the Campaign of 100 Days (a deliberate allusion to Napoleon Bonaparte's 100 days between his escape from Elba and the Battle of Waterloo; there were in fact only 96 days between 8 August and the Armistice). In terms of sheer scale the Campaign was the greatest in British military history. Yet it is relatively little known even though it was the major contribution to the final defeat of the German Army on the Western Front and its, in effect, unconditional surrender with the signing of the Armistice. From 'the black day of the German Army' until the end, the BEF and, to a lesser extent its Allies, recorded a series of victories as the German Army was pushed back towards its own frontiers. The Campaign took the form of a series of large scale battles of short duration, by Western Front standards, interspersed with gaps for pursuit and deciding on and planning the next moves.

With the Battle of Amiens over the Canadian Corps began its return, division by division, to Sir Henry Horne's First Army where it would remain right through to the liberation of Mons on the last night of the war. Since June 1917 the Corps had been commanded by a Canadian, Lt General Sir Arthur Currie, who would prove to be an, and arguably the, outstanding corps commander of the BEF.[5] Since the Battle of Vimy Ridge the four Canadian divisions had always remained brigaded together as a Corps and it became a political necessity in the eyes of the Canadian government for this to remain the case. The Canadians were looking towards the creation of a national army, hence their reluctance to contemplate the breaking up of the Corps other than in the most critical circumstances. Haig was to come under constant and unwelcome pressure, emanating from the politicians in Ottawa and London and from Sir Arthur Currie, not to break it up. This particularly rankled during the German offensives of the first half of 1918 when, in effect, the Canadians could not be called on to play their part because of the insistence that they not be used piecemeal.[6] However unwelcome this insistence was at the time, in the event it did mean that when the BEF went over to the offensive Haig could call on the Canadian Corps, who were brilliant shock troops, were relatively fresh and had not been obliged to reduce their divisional size from 12 battalions, to play a leading part. Hence their transfer to Fourth Army for the Battle of Amiens.

In pursuit of the strategy of maintaining the pressure on the enemy created by the battle of Amiens, Haig initially wanted the Fourth Army to resume its offensive after a minimal pause. He was dissuaded from this course of action by the shared opinion of Rawlinson and Currie that such a resumption would come up against a fully alerted and very strong German defence, which would make success problematic and, whatever the outcome, certainly result in unacceptably heavy casualties.[7] Instead, Haig ordered the Commander of the Third Army, Sir Julian Byng, to prepare an attack across the old Arras and Somme battlefields eastwards towards Bapaume. Relying heavily on surprise Byng's plan called for an advance on a three corps front. The battle was opened on 21 August and made steady, if unspectacular, progress. On 22 August, while Third Army remained on the defensive and coped successfully with a series of German counterattacks,

Fourth Army attacked again. Albert was recaptured and gave its name to the battle. On the following day both armies resumed their attacks and made some progress, capturing a number of villages. On the right 1st Australian Division of Fourth Army joined in and succeeded in shattering three German divisions opposite them despite lack of surprise. In all the Germans lost well over 10,000 in prisoners alone and had suffered their second serious defeat at the hands of the BEF in little more than a fortnight.[8]

Over the ensuing days Third and Fourth Armies kept up the pressure on the Germans with night attacks and daylight advances which included the occupation of Bapaume by the New Zealand Division on 29 August, and the Australians reaching the Somme opposite Mont St Quentin and Péronne on the same day.[9]

The clearest reflection yet of the changed situation since 8 August was the telegram which Haig addressed to all his army commanders on 22 August. Its obvious purpose was to make things crystal clear to his subordinates but it may also also have been prompted by his disappointment at the lack of ambition there had been in Byng's plans for the offensive of 21-23 August. Haig made it clear that such irresolution was no longer appropriate.

> I request that Army Commanders will, without delay, bring to the notice of all subordinate leaders the changed conditions under which operations are now being carried on.
>
> The methods which we have followed hitherto in our battles with limited objectives when the enemy was strong, are no longer suited to his present condition.
>
> The enemy has not the means to deliver counter-attacks on an extended scale, nor has he the numbers to hold a position against the very extended advance which is now being directed upon him.
>
> To turn the present situation to account the most resolute offensive is everywhere desirable. Risks which a month ago would have been criminal to incur, ought now to be incurred as a duty......
>
> The situation is most favourable; let each one of us act energetically, and without hesitation push forward to our objective.'[10]

It was Sir Henry Horne's First Army that would be the first to operate within the Commander-in-Chief's new framework. He was given the formidable assignment of advancing to the Drocourt-Quéant Switch (or 'Line') and assaulting and breaking through that heavily defended line before moving southeast against the Germans facing Third Army. Horne selected the Canadian Corps, two of whose divisions had already returned in full from Fourth Army, for the task. With the other two divisions still on their way back, 51st Highland and 4th British Divisions were placed at the disposition of Canadian Corps.

In expectation of making an attack south of the River Scarpe Horne had set in train an elaborate deception plan. It was aimed at persuading the Germans that his main assault would be north of the river, not easy to achieve if the presence of the Canadians south of the river were detected. Horne employed a mixture of artillery bombardments, combined tank and infantry training which it was made sure the enemy would observe, the establishment of dummy ammunition dumps and casualty clearing stations and an intensification of wireless traffic. The enemy were so far persuaded that the attack would take place north of the river, that they kept their reserves in position to intervene there. When the attack was launched, complete surprise was achieved.

The assault began at 03h00 on 26 August. The Canadians, supported by accurate artillery and machine gun barrages, initially carried all before them. Chapel Hill, Orange Hill, Monchy-le-Preux, Wancourt and Guémappe were taken. A heavy German counterattack was successfully broken up by artillery. There were however some problems for the attackers. Their first attempt to carry the ridge between the Scarpe and the Cojeul rivers was stopped by machine gun fire and uncut wire. The attack was renewed that night without artillery support and was successful. The 51st Highland Division, north of the Scarpe, reached the outskirts of Roeux and the western slopes of Greenland Hill, and captured the chemical works north of the town.

Overall, the day was a great success for First Army. The Canadians had advanced about three miles and called into question the viability of the German Lys salient to the north. That very night the Germans decided to retire from it voluntarily, beginning three nights later.

The weather on the 27th was to prove a great handicap for the attackers. The rain and low cloud badly affected the RAF's operations and artillery counterbattery work. Nevertheless Vis-en-Artois, Chérisy, Bois du Sart and Bois du Vert were captured in the face of stiffening German resistance. Lt General Currie had hoped that the day would end with the German Fresnes-Rouvroy Line, about a mile in front of the Drocourt-Quéant Line, in First Army hands. But it was not even to be reached despite savage fighting.

Horne instructed the Canadians to be ready to attack the Drocourt-Quéant Line on 30 August. Currie ordered his attacking divisions to advance to within two miles of the Line on the 28th and capture the enemy trenches at the limit of this advance. It was to prove a day of mixed fortunes. The Canadian 2nd Division managed to advance about 1,000 yards but still failed to reach the German positions. The 3rd Division took Pelves, Boiry-Notre Dame and Jigsaw Wood.

After three days of often ferocious fighting, Currie felt obliged to relieve his 2nd and 3rd Divisions. Between them they had suffered nearly 6,000 casualties. The relief was effected by 1st Canadian and 4th (British) Divisions. Along with 51st Highland Division, their initial task was to prepare for the assault on the Drocourt-Quéant Line by mounting local attacks to improve their positions and close up to the Line. The Highlanders completed the capture of Greenland Hill. The 4th Division crossed the Sensée river and took the villages of Rémy and Haucourt.

The following day, the 30th, 1st Canadian Division successfully attacked the Vis-en-Artois Switch, the German defence line linking the Fresnes-Rouvroy Line with the Drocourt-Quéant Line. They advanced an average of two miles and came up level with 57th Division of Third Army on their right. The 4th Division also made progress and took the village of Eterpigny in front of the Drocourt-Quéant Line. In the meantime the artillery were carrying out a programme of wire-cutting.

The next day the Canadians advanced further, capturing some German trenches. The 4th Division took St Servin's Farm. On what was to prove to be the last day before the actual assault on the German Line proper, the Canadians on 1 September captured Hendecourt Château and the Crows Nest, a strongpoint on a prominent knoll north of the Château. The 57th Division took Hendecourt village.[11]

By the evening of 1 September the stage was set for the breaking of the Drocourt-Quéant Line, the most formidable defensive system to have confronted the BEF thus far. The assault would take place simultaneously with major attacks by Third and Fourth Armies.

General Currie's orders to his divisions envisaged a two stage assault. The first stage would be a breakthrough of the Drocourt-Quéant Line where it was crossed by the Arras-Cambrai road. Thereafter the assault would fan out, rolling up the German line to both north and south. At Zero plus three hours the second stage would start with the resumption of the advance. This stage would involve the occupation of the high ground west of, and overlooking, the Canal du Nord and the Sensée river.[12]

Zero Hour was at 05h00. It heralded a day of almost unbroken success for the Canadians. The Drocourt-Quéant Line was ruptured on a frontage of 7,000 yards and the Buissy Switch, the villages of Cagnicourt and Villers-les-Cagnicourt, as well as 8,000 prisoners, were taken before it was fully daylight. By the end of the day the Canadians had established a line well beyond the German line, except at the northern end of their attack. German opposition had been patchy but, where it was resolute, it had been very resolute indeed. The Canadians had suffered heavy casualties, opposed as they were by much of seven German divisions.[13]

The Canadian success was matched by that of the Australians of Fourth Army further south. Having crossed the Somme the Australians attacked Mont St Quentin on 31 August. In bitter fighting they captured it but were pushed out by a German counterattack. Fresh troops resumed the attack the following day and finally captured the village by mid-afternoon. Péronne was also largely taken by another Australian brigade. The effect of the Canadian and Australian successes was to make the German Winter Defence Line largely untenable. At midday on 2 September the German High Command set in motion a general withdrawal which would begin that night with the Seventeenth Army, facing the Canadians and V Corps of Third Army, retiring behind the Canal du Nord and the Sensée. The German withdrawal was completed by 10 September with the BEF in cautious pursuit once they had overcome their surprise.[14]

By 4 September the Canadians had taken Ecourt St Quentin and were in possession of the west bank of the Canal du Nord from south of Sains-lès-Marquion to Sauchy-Cauchy. The eastern bank was found to be strongly held by the enemy and all bridges blown except those at Palluel where the enemy retained a bridgehead on the western bank. A major attack in force would be required to secure a way across. Until this could be mounted, major operations on First Army's right flank would cease.[15]

The end of the first week in September ushered in a few days of relative calm as Haig and his army commanders considered how to tackle the formidable German Hindenburg Line. Haig had agreed with Foch that breaking it would be the next challenge for the BEF. All three army commanders were positive about the prospects of success. Byng considered it essential that the operation should be mounted as quickly as possible to prevent the Germans getting settled into their defensive positions. Rawlinson had identified no fewer than 6 German defensive lines or positions in front of his army, the fifth of which was the Main Hindenburg System. He was under no illusions over the size of the task. Horne focused on the crossing of the Canal du Nord, in his view a difficult but not impossible operation. The successful crossing would, in cooperation with Third Army, open up the possibility of a productive drive towards Cambrai.[16]

The relative calm came to an end on 12 September when Byng, in affirmation of his anxiety to make a breach in the Hindenburg Line before the enemy could get fully organised, launched his army in an attack which captured the villages of Havrincourt and Trescault after very hard fighting. A German counterattack on the 62nd Division in Havrincourt was smashed. Byng's attack had, however, only created a small dent, of no great strategic or operational value, in the outer defences of the Hindeburg Line.[17]

There was a much more positive outcome when Fourth Army launched its next attack on 18 September. Supported by Third Army to the north and the French First Army to the south Rawlinson's army mounted a strong assault on a 20,000 yard front against the Hindenburg Line, in the general direction of Bellicourt and the tunnel section of the St Quentin Canal, in what became known as the Battle of Epéhy. The Old British Main Line and the Old British Outpost Line were the first and second objectives, with the Advanced Hindenburg System to be seized if the other lines fell easily. As with his army's attack on 8 August Rawlinson's plan relied on surprise which excluded the possibility of a preliminary bombardment. Thereafter an elaborate artillery plan and machine gun barrages took full advantage of the British preponderance in guns and shells. Rawlinson also enjoyed a significant advantage in rifle strength over the enemy, perhaps as much as three to one. The Australians in the centre took their first two objectives and took part of the Advanced Hindenburg System. On either side of them the gains were more modest. German counterattacks were beaten back. Despite some disappointment this was a major victory with more than 9,000 Germans becoming prisoners. It instilled in Rawlinson great confidence that his army was fully capable of breaking the Hindenburg Line.[18]

During early September Foch and the commanders of the national armies had agreed on the need to maintain the pressure on the Germans by mounting broadly co-ordinated and sustained assaults. The timetable drawn up called for a joint Franco-American attack to be launched between Reims and the River Meuse on 26 September; an attack on the 27th by the British First and Third Armies across the Canal du Nord, through Bourlon Wood and towards Cambrai; an offensive eastwards in Flanders by the Belgian Army, the British Second Army and some French divisions, to start on the 28th; and the British Fourth Army and the French First Army to launch an assault on the Main Hindenburg System, crossing the St Quentin Canal, beginning on the 29th.[19]

The Argonne-Meuse Offensive, a joint Franco-American attack, began on 26 September following a day-long bombardment. Its scale and violence initially shook the Germans and advances of two to three miles were recorded on the first day. Thereafter the Americans' inexperience and logistical problems (which included 'the worst traffic jam of the war') badly affected the attack which ground to a halt on the 28th. The mess that the Americans had got into alleviated the concerns the Germans might have had after the battle's first day and did not, as a result, draw off German forces from other sectors of the front as the Allies had hoped.[20]

On 27 September the First and Third Armies began their offensive. In the preceding three weeks Horne had gone to great lengths to deceive the Germans over where his Army's blow would fall. He was understandably keen to persuade them that it would be north of the River Scarpe and not south, the true jumping-off area. Considerable effort was therefore put into persuading the enemy to keep, or move, their reserves north of the river. Horne ordered his corps, cavalry, tank and RAF commanders north of the Scarpe to prepare for a large-scale attack. Tanks and infantry were to be trained in cooperation in localities where they could be observed by enemy aircraft; additional balloons were to be put up and artillery registration set in train; wire cutting and patrolling were to be stepped up; ammunition dumps and additional casualty clearing stations were to be established; Cavalry and Tank Corps officers were ordered to reconnoitre the whole front from the Scarpe north to the La Bassée Canal as conspicuously as possible.

The Germans showed their growing nervousness by stepping up their raids and patrolling and by drenching potential forming up points for an attack with mustard gas shells. More significantly, they reinforced their front north of the Scarpe by drafting in a further 3 divisions, while at the same time doing nothing to reinforce their positions south of the river.[21]

Horne's orders initially called for the Canadian Corps to force crossings of the Canal du Nord between Moeuvres and Lock 3 before going on to attack and capture the Marquion Line and Bourlon village and Wood. The part of XXII Corps south of the Scarpe were given a supporting role aimed at keeping the enemy guessing as to the main thrust of First Army's attack. They were also to push troops across the canal to work northwards along its eastern bank to assist the operations of the Canadian left flank.

The challenge was formidable. Before Bourlon Wood could be tackled there was the matter of crossing the Canal du Nord. It presented a daunting obstacle, made more so by the measures the Germans had taken to incorporate it into their defences. The canal was approximately 40 yards wide with a western bank 10-15 feet high and an eastern bank about five feet high. Its average depth of water was about 8 feet. Behind the canal itself was the German Canal du Nord Line bristling with machine guns and covered with dense belts of barbed wire. A mile to the east was the German Marquion Line, similarly well protected by barbed wire.

The attack would need to be made over the relatively dry area between Sains-lès-Marquion and Moeuvres, on the extreme right of the new First Army front. Here the canal itself was virtually dry except for occasional shallow pools. Infantry could feasibly cross without the need for bridging equipment. The approaches were also dry and offered good concealment to attackers. The advantages of assaulting here were so manifest that it is the more surprising that the enemy allowed themselves to be persuaded that the attack would take place further north.

Z Day was set for 27 September. In total First Army would have elements of 9 divisions in the line, 1 in support and 4 in reserve. They would be facing 13 enemy divisions in the line with, in reserve, 5 divisions close by and 3 near Douai. Significantly however only three of the enemy front line divisions and 5 of those in reserve were immediately available to intervene in the area where the main assault would fall. The remaining 13 were deployed to meet an attack north of the Sensée Canal. The deception operation had worked.

The geographical and topographical constraints facing the attackers meant that although the overall frontage of the attack would ultimately expand to 15,000 yards, the crossing of the canal would take place on a frontage of only 2,700 yards. Once across the canal therefore, the attack would have to fan out to a width of 9,000 yards. Thereafter, exploitation of success would result in the frontage of 15,000 yards.

Zero Hour for the main attack was 05h20. At that hour all the guns available to First Army began the bombardment. The 1st and 4th Canadian Divisions crossed the canal under cover of the creeping barrage and quickly carried the enemy trenches and rifle pits within 500 yards of its eastern bank. Within 33 minutes of Zero Hour 1st Canadian Division had turned north and forced themselves into Sains-lès-Marquion, completing its capture in a matter of minutes.

By this time the initial advantage of surprise had been lost. The fortified quarries in Quarry Wood checked the Canadian advance. They were finally cleared and the wood surrounded and captured with the help of the tanks which had followed hard on the heels of the infantry over the canal. With Quarry Wood in Canadian hands, the Marquion Line followed suit.

With the Marquion Line secured, the barrage moved forward and 4th Canadian Division began their assault on Bourlon village. The stubborn resistance they met was once more overcome with the aid of the tanks. The attack moved on towards the western edge of Bourlon Wood. On the left 1st Canadian Division, captured a further stretch of the Marquion Line as far north as the village, and the village itself. Both divisions then paused for some 40 minutes. Meanwhile the two supporting divisions began crossing the canal and moving to the general line Quarry Wood-Keith Wood.

Shortly after 10h00 the two leading divisions resumed their advance. Protected by a barrage, the bulk of 4th Canadian Division passed north of the wood to reach its eastern edge. South of the wood were the trenches of the German Cantaing Line. The elements of 4th Canadian Division skirting the wood to the south synchronised their advance with that of 57th Division of Third Army's XVII Corps and materially assisted the latter in the capture of the village of Anneux and trenches of the German line. The 1st Canadian Division had little difficulty in clearing the crest of the ridge between Bourlon Wood and Sauchicourt Farm. This concluded the phase of the day's attack involving only two of Horne's divisions.

The attack frontage now widened to 9,000 yards with the introduction of 3rd Canadian Division on the right of 4th Canadian, and 11th British on the left of 1st Canadian. To make partial room, 1st and 4th Canadian Divisions narrowed their frontages.

With his four divisions in position and with sufficient field artillery having crossed the canal to offer support, General Currie ordered the attack to be resumed at 15h00. On the extreme right 3rd Canadian Division were quickly pinned down by heavy fire from the village of Fontaine-Notre Dame, one of the objectives of Third Army's XVII Corps. Their 57th Division were still clearing out the Cantaing Line before moving on to Fontaine. It became clear that further attempts to advance by the Canadian Division before Fontaine was taken would involve unacceptable loss. To 3rd Division's left, 4th Canadian Division also found it difficult to make progress down the bare slopes leading to the village of Raillencourt and the German Marcoing Line in the face of heavy machine gun and rifle fire. What little forward momentum they could maintain was effectively stopped by a German counterattack by the Guards Reserve Division.

In contrast with their comrades' misfortunes to their right, Canadian 1st Division found little difficulty in advancing three miles despite heavy enemy wire entanglements. They eventually established themselves on the Cambrai-Douai road, 11,000 yards from their starting point that morning.

On the left flank of the Canadian Corps attack, 11th British Division's centre and right-hand brigades attacked northeast and north, forced their way through thick enemy wire running east-west between the Marquion and Marcoing Lines and captured the village of Epinoy, thus achieving an advance of three miles. The division's left hand brigade and 169th Brigade of 56th Division were ordered to capture the commanding German position of Oisy-le-Verger and the eponymous village. The two brigades, after a further artillery bombardment of the area, completed these captures.

The results of the day were sufficiently spectacular to justify the degree of risk involved. The First Army had forced the Canal du Nord from Moeuvres in the south to Palluel in the north. Its troops had captured two powerful systems of entrenchments, the Canal and Marquion Lines, and the important tactical positions of Bourlon Wood and Oisy-le-Verger and the ridge between them. The army's line had been advanced 5 miles on a front of nearly nine miles. Favourable positions had been secured for future operations towards Cambrai and the Escaut river. A total of 4,000 prisoners and 100 guns had been captured. Three German divisions had been routed and two severely damaged. On Horne's right, Byng's Third Army had also crossed the Canal du Nord and captured Flesquières Ridge and the Hindenburg Support Line. But at the end of the day Third Army's left was lagging 3,000 yards behind the Canadians.

Both First and Third Armies resumed the offensive on the 28th. At Zero Hour 3rd Canadian Division on the right, once again in cooperation with Third Army's 57th Division advancing from the south, attacked Fontaine-Notre Dame from the north. The enemy fought well but could not withstand the joint assault and the village was taken. The Canadian Division pushed on and took the front trenches of the Marcoing Line between the Bapaume-Cambrai and Arras-Cambrai roads. On their left 4th Canadian Division took Raillencourt and Sailly and also occupied front trenches of the Marcoing Line just to the south of the Arras-Cambrai road. No further progress was possible in the face of stiffening enemy resistance in the form of heavy machine gun fire. Next in line, 1st Canadian Division, whose troops had found themselves well in advance of the divisions on their right, stood pat for the day. On their left 11th Division did push forward. Their right entered the outskirts of Aubencheul, their centre reached the Douai-Cambrai road and their left worked down the Sensée Canal and linked up with 56th Division north of the Bois de Quesnoy. The latter had pushed through Palluel and worked round the west of the wood to effect the link-up.

During the course of the day Third Army captured Cantaing, Noyelle and Marcoing and secured a footing on the eastern bank of the Escaut river. There had however been signs of a stiffening of enemy resistance with indications of increased artillery activity.[22]

The third phase of the allied offensives scheduled for late September began on the 28th when the Group of Armies in Flanders (GAF) attacked under the overall command of Albert, King of the Belgians. The attackers were the Belgian Army and Sir Herbert Plumer's Second Army, which had been released from the operational command of Sir Douglas Haig in order to serve under King Albert. Despite dismal weather and the atrocious conditions underfoot, the absence of tanks, and the lack of surprise caused by the Belgian insistence on a preparatory barrage, the offensive was universally successful. Progress on the first day was quite spectacular against relatively weak German divisions. Advances of up to 6 miles were recorded, more than had been achieved in the three months of the Battle of Passchendaele. Casualties were relatively low. The serious deterioration in the weather which set in late on the 28th and stiffening German resistance meant that progress slowed down markedly on the remaining 4 days of the offensive.[23]

The fourth phase of the series of allied offensives would involve the British Fourth Army and the French First Army making their assault on the Main Hindenburg System beginning on 29 September. In order for this operation to have a reasonable chance of success it was important that the three corps of Rawlinson's army should be as close up to the Main Hindenburg System as possible before the assault was launched. During Fourth Army's attack on 18 September only the Australian Corps had reached the desired positions; the two corps on either side had not. The days of 19-24 September saw these two corps trying to rectify their situations. This involved them in heavy and exhausting fighting against stubborn German defence and was not altogether successful. When the American II Corps entered the line on the 24th, to come under the temporary command of the Australian Corps Commander, Lt General Sir John Monash, several vital objectives were still in the hands of the Germans. One of the American divisions managed to capture those in front of it, but the other was less successful. As isolated pockets of men from this division were believed to be holding out in German positions the barrages due to be fired in support of the main attack had to be modified to the serious detriment of the attackers. By contrast with the mixed fortunes of III Corps and the Americans, IX Corps' renewed attack on the 24th and 25th was completely successful, ending with virtually the whole Advanced Hindenburg System in their possession.

On 29 September Fourth Army carried out its great assault on the Hindenburg Line. The plan adopted was largely the creation of General Monash and foresaw the Americans, followed by the Australians, crossing the Saint Quentin Canal by use of the roof of the Bellenglise Tunnel which in effect formed a long bridge across the canal. Rawlinson added in the participation of IX Corps further to the south whose Commander was confident that the canal could be crossed without the advantage of a tunnel forming a bridge. The First French Army would attack even further south on a 6 mile front. Planning of the assault was greatly helped by the Fourth Army's possession of complete details of the Main Hindenburg System.

Overall a great victory was achieved especially in the south. One American and one Australian division took heavy casualties and did not penetrate very far into the Hindenburg defences. The other American/Australian combination was more successful and captured Bellicourt and pressed on further. But the main success was achieved by 46th (North Midland) Division of IX Corps further south. Helped by mist and lavish artillery and tank support, they captured the Riqueval Bridge over the canal intact. Even so, many of the troops had to swim the canal. Overall, a wedge had been driven in the German defences between 5,000 and 6,000 yards deep on a front of 10,000 yards. 5,300 prisoners had been taken. The Germans had been driven from the Main Hindenburg System and had no hope of plugging the gap.[24]

With progress on the GAF, First and Third Armies' front largely stalled it was down to Fourth Army to maintain any sort of allied momentum. From 30 September to 6 October Rawlinson's troops pushed on as fast as their problematic communications would allow. During this period a total advance of about three miles was recorded which included the capture of the Beaurevoir Line, the last German prepared defence line in Fourth Army's path. The Australian Corps were withdrawn for rest on the night of 5 October and, although it was not known at the time, had fought their last battle of the war.[25]

On 8 October Third, Fourth and First French Army launched an attack which broke through the last defences of the Hindenburg Line between St Quentin and Cambrai. For the Germans 8 October became a day of heavy defeat. They lost 8,000 men as prisoners alone and Cambrai, although not yet captured had become untenable. They carried out a retreat to positions behind the River Selle. Cambrai was liberated by 3rd Canadian Division entering from the west and units of Third Army entering from the south.[26]

On 14 October the GAF attacked in what became known as the Battle of Courtrai. The Belgian and Second British Armies recorded six days of almost unbroken success. On the first day an advance of 4 miles was achieved and 6,000 prisoners taken. On the second day 36th (Ulster) Division liberated Courtrai and the Germans began to pull back to the River Lys. On the night of 18/19 October 35th Division crossed the Lys and 36th Division established a bridgehead on the other side. By the evening of 20 October XV Corps had established itself on the west bank of the River Scheldt.[27]

In addition to crossing the River Selle the Fourth Army's aim in the battle of that name was to capture the town of Le Cateau which had given its name to the 1914 battle. Rawlinson's army would be supported by the French First Army on its right. It had not been difficult for the Germans to deduce that this was where the next major allied attack would take place and they had brought in substantial reinforcements, a fact not picked up by Fourth Army Intelligence. The first day of this battle, 17 October, was therefore to confront Fourth Army with strong and determined German resistance. But by dusk on the first day the crust of the German defence had been broken. Le Cateau had been taken along with over 5,000 prisoners. But II American Corps had suffered severely and was no longer an effective fighting force. The attack was resumed the following day and by the end of the third day advances of up to 9,000 yards on a front of 7 miles had been achieved. The first phase of the battle was over.

The final phase of the battle fell largely to Third Army. In a night attack beginning at 0200 on 20 October the British had achieved most of their objectives by dusk and were occupying the high ground to the east of the Selle. On 23 and 24 October Third and Fourth Armies mounted concerted attacks which were generally successful.

The Battle of the Selle is now largely overlooked, unfairly so as it was a major victory in which 26 British, New Zealand and American divisions took on 31 rather weakened German divisions and took more than 20,000 prisoners and captured 474 guns while successfully crossing the River Selle and advancing towards the Escaut (Scheldt) River.[28]

Chronologically the next major action was the First Army's advance to, and capture of, the city of Valenciennes. But as this was a stepping stone on that Army's advance to Mons, it would be appropriate to deal first of all with the activities of the other armies up to the Armistice.

The Battle of the Sambre was a joint Third and Fourth Army battle intended as a grand slam blow which might succeed in knocking out the German Army. It was scheduled to take place after the First Army had secured Valenciennes; the battle was therefore timed to begin on 4 November. The Third and Fourth Armies would advance towards Maubeuge and Avesnes respectively. The Third Army would have to cope both with the town of Le Quesnoy with its formidable, even if 17th century, fortifications. and the Forêt de Mormal (which had been such a nuisance in the Retreat from Mons). Fortunately there were more west-east paths in the Forêt, suiting the direction of the advance, than there had been north-south ones at the time of the Retreat.

The Fourth Army would face the daunting challenge of strongly opposed crossings of the Sambre and Oise Canal which would have to be preceded by the elimination of the German occupants of the villages of Ors and Catillon on its western bank. Further north the Army would have to fight its way through some difficult country and capture the small town of Landrecies, the scene of Haig's rare aberrant behaviour during the Retreat from Mons over four years previously.

Zero Hour on 4 November varied slightly for the different divisions involved as did the level of opposition encountered. The battle was however characterised by much hard fighting. German resistance may have been patchy but it was very stubborn in parts. British casualties were high, notably the 700 dead suffered by 32nd Division in the capture of the village of Ors and the crossing of the Sambre-Oise Canal. A notable casualty of this Division was the War Poet, Captain

Wilfred Owen, who was killed on the towpath of the canal just north of Ors as he prepared to lead his men across. The 25th Division lost 600 dead including the divisional Commander, Major General Reginald Charles, in their successful fight to clear Landrecies. A remarkable achievement was the capture of Le Quesnoy by the New Zealand Division in a brilliant *coup de main*, which resulted in the surrender of the German garrison at a cost of negligible casualties for the New Zealanders, the defenders and the town's inhabitants.

Although by the end of the day the Forêt de Mormal had not been entirely cleared, virtually all the other objectives set for the two armies had been attained. The heavy casualties were perhaps light in relation to the size of the battle and the scale of the achievement. About 10,000 prisoners were taken and in many parts of the battlefield the Germans were in flight by the end of the day.[29]

The last week of the war was one of pursuit, punctuated by occasional forlorn German counterattacks. The main opposition came from rearguards largely composed of field artillery and machine guns, By 9 November the Germans were retreating so fast that it was becoming increasingly difficult for the allied armies to maintain contact with them. When hostilities ceased two days later the Germans were a spent force no longer capable of organised and effective resistance to the advancing allied armies.

Chapter XV

The Road Back to Mons: October-November 1918

Following the liberation of Cambrai on 9 October by First and Third Armies, First Army had continued to press eastward against stiffening German opposition. Attempts to cross the River Selle had been thwarted by strong enemy opposition and Generals Horne and Byng had concluded that a properly planned and mounted full-scale assault would be necessary to overcome German resistance.[1]

Events further north were however to make such an effort unnecessary. On 14 October the Belgian and Second Armies had launched their offensive towards Courtrai which, within three days, had outflanked Lille, Tourcoing and Roubaix from the north. The salient thus created in the German defences, when coupled with the salient which had formed in their lines to the south, threatened their entire position between Douai and Lille. The German solution was a withdrawal from their positions opposite First Army, which the latter became aware of on 17 October.[2] The Canadians immediately put pressure on the weak German rearguards, crossed the Sensée Canal and reached the Cantin-Douai road. Their presence there diminished the previously stiff enemy opposition to First Army's VIII Corps' approach to Douai from the west, which enabled units of the Corps to enter a largely burning and comprehensively looted Douai on the afternoon of the 17th.[3]

With Douai liberated the essential task of Sir Henry Horne's First Army, in association with Third Army to its south, was to give the Germans no respite and push on as hard as possible. In the three days following the capture of Douai the Canadian Corps and VIII Corps moved steadily forward against weak or non-existent German rearguards recording average daily advances of six miles or so, figures which would have been unheard of in the previous four years. On 19 October First Army's XXII Corps, south of the Canadians, joined in the general advance.[4] Such opposition as there was could easily be dealt with by the Army's cavalry and cyclists. The haste of the German departure often meant that they left behind militarily valuable equipment and failed to set their usual booby traps. But they had displayed their usual thoroughness in cratering roads and destroying bridges and railway lines, all of which would have been useful to Sir Henry Horne's troops as they confronted the main problem thrown up by the speed of their advance. This was the vital one of logistics, the need to keep the army supplied with food, equipment and ammunition as the distance from the railheads grew ever greater. The problem was compounded by the humanitarian need to get food to the near starving French inhabitants being liberated. By dint of unremitting effort Horne's staff were largely successful in keeping the supplies to the army flowing and the civilian population fed.[5]

The obstacle to the advance of Horne's army presented by the River Selle was largely overcome on 19 October when the Canadians and 51st Highland Division crossed it north of the village of Haspres without undue difficulty. It was however necessary to mount an attack involving 4th Division and XVII Corps of Third Army on the 20th to get across the river south of the village. The attack was successful and the Germans began to evacuate their bridgehead and fall back enabling the British units to move towards the next obstacle, the River Ecaillon. On the same day, despite strengthening enemy opposition, the Canadians were able to liberate the town of Denain. They found it to be bursting with over 25,000 French civilians, many of whom had been brought in from outlying villages by the Germans.

The west-east flowing River Escaut now formed the boundary between the Canadians and XXII Corps in Horne's army. Both Corps, the latter in close cooperation with XVII Corps of Third Army on the right, moved gradually eastwards over the next few days in the face of enemy opposition which varied from minimal on the left flank of the Canadian advance to very fierce opposite 51st Highland Division as they reached the confluence of the Rivers Ecaillon and Escaut. It was clear too that the Germans were very strongly entrenched on the other side of the Ecaillon. Further north the advance of VIII Corps was being held up by the Scarpe river, the bridges across which had been destroyed.[6]

A joint attack with Third Army aimed at getting get XVII and XXII Corps across the Ecaillon and onto the high ground east of the river was scheduled for 24 October. The ultimate aim for XXII Corps was to reach the Escaut River opposite Trith which was already in Canadian hands. In the meantime pressure would be maintained on the enemy by all three of Horne's corps.[7]

On 23 October VIII Corps, which had fallen somewhat behind the Canadian Corps on their right, were able to cross the river Scarpe with little difficulty. Passing through the northern part of the Forêt de Raismes they were by evening in touch with the Canadians on their right who had completed the capture of the Forêt and had pushed on to reach the Escaut. Further south the Canadians had pushed into the extreme western suburbs of Valenciennes in their efforts to reach the river.

The following day, most of VIII and Canadian Corps reached the Escaut. The XXII Corps, attacking with 4th and 51st Divisions in line, successfully crossed the Ecaillon, despite the enemy defences, a serious shortage of bridging material and the formidable nature of the river itself. It was 25 feet wide, with banks on either side that plunged 15 feet to the muddy river bottom, which contained four to five feet of water. It was heavily wired on both banks and more wire had been stretched from one bank to the other. Entrenched enemy outposts on the right bank and a trench line half way up the slope running eastwards had completed a formidable challenge. The dash with which these difficulties were rapidly overcome says much for the momentum which had been built up by First Army's recent rapid progress. Assisted by darkness, determination did the rest and at relatively light cost. By the end of the day the corps had established a new line running from Sommaing, 10 kms south of Valenciennes, to Trith-St Leger on the Escaut, five kms southwest of the city.

From 25 to 27 October XXII Corps continued to attack vigorously along the full length of their front. Advancing northeast 4th Division captured the village of Artres before pushing across the Rhonelle river to the heights beyond. To their left, 51st Division fought their way into, and cleared, Famars, less than two kilometres southeast of Mont Houy, against fierce enemy resistance. Heavy enemy fire from Mont Houy prevented any further progress northwards.[8]

Valenciennes stood firmly in the path of First Army and the task of its liberation, in an operation scheduled to be completed on 1 November, was given to Horne. The city was an important military and psychological objective. Militarily, its capture would ease the forcing of the Scheldt Line; psychologically, the loss of the last major French conurbation in their hands would deal a further blow to German morale at a time when it was already deteriorating rapidly. Haig foresaw its capture assisting materially in a complete German collapse on the Western Front.

To minimise civilian casualties in a city in which the normal population had been swelled by large numbers of refugees, Horne came up with a plan that aimed to force the enemy to evacuate the city rather than fight for it street by street. There were two serious constraints on his freedom of action. One, arising from the need to avoid civilian casualties, was the ban imposed by GHQ on the shelling of city buildings, except those overlooking the Escaut Canal which might be used by the enemy to inhibit the crossing of the waterway. (The course of the River Escaut in its passage through the centre of Valenciennes, had been diverted and canalised, hence the use of the term 'canal'.) The second constraint was that any assault from the west or north of the city was effectively precluded because both banks of the canal had been heavily wired by the Germans. They had also fortified the east bank with a well-planned trench system. As an even greater deterrent, they had cut gaps in the canal dykes and opened sluice gates, thus flooding the country on both sides of the river to a width of several hundred yards.

Horne's plan would perforce call for his army to approach and envelop the city from the south west and south. This brought into prominence a small area of partly wooded high ground, about three and a half kilometres south of the city centre, known as Mont Houy. Capture of this dominant position, nearly 290 feet high, would be a prerequisite to an entry into the city itself.

The plan therefore called for XXII Corps to capture Mont Houy and the Aulnoy-Le Poirier road just to its north on 28 October. The Canadian Corps would then take over the western part of XXII Corps' line and on the 30th the two corps would move north and northeast respectively with the latter, in tandem with the Third Army's XVII Corps, beginning a swing round the east of Valenciennes. The envelopment of the city would be completed on 1 November with XXII Corps capturing the high ground east of the city and Canadian Corps pushing into it from the west and south.

The key to Horne's plan, Mont Houy, enjoyed significant advantages as a defensive position. But it was also vulnerable to concentrated artillery fire, a flaw which would ultimately prove its undoing. The task of seizing it for XXII Corps was entrusted to 51st Highland Division who launched their attack at 05h15 on 28 October.[9] It was made by a single battalion, the 4th Seaforth Highlanders with significant artillery support. Despite strong opposition and heavy casualties (one company was reduced to 12 men) the whole of the position was taken. But an enemy counterattack launched at 14h30, with heavy artillery support, was able to force the centre of the Highlanders' line back over the summit of the hill and part way down its southern slope.[10]

The success of the enemy counterattack threw Horne's plan into some disarray. It had called for the relief of 51st Division by the Canadians to be made when the former were in full possession of Mont Houy and the Aulnoy-le Poirier road. As they were clearly not in full possession a postponement of the relief was requested by Lt General Sir Arthur Currie and agreed to by Horne, who left the final judgment on whether and when the relief should take place to the commanders of the troops on the spot. Horne later ordered that the Canadian relief of 51st Division should take place the following night. The implementation of the subsequent stages of the overall plan was deferred by 24 hours.

Although the successful conclusion of the capture of Valenciennes was thereby delayed by 24 hours it did at least have the advantage of giving the Canadians the necessary time to deploy their artillery to full advantage in support of the second attempt to take and hold Mont Houy.[11]

During the course of 29 October, the Germans made two determined attempts to complete the total reversal of 51st Division's early gains of the day before. The first attack was repulsed with heavy losses. The second was broken up by artillery fire before the enemy infantry even got underway. With the enemy's aggressive inclinations thus firmly blunted, the delayed relief of the Highlanders was carried out after dark by 4th Canadian Division on the left and 49th Division on the right.[12]

The two days prior to the planned attack saw little fighting. Zero Hour on 1 November was 05h15. Precisely on time, and from right to left, 61st Division of XVII Corps, 4th and 49th Divisions of XXII Corps and 10th Infantry Brigade of the 4th Canadian Division assaulted. The two divisions of XXII Corps got across the Rhonelle river and gained the high ground south and northwest of Préseau. In attempting to capture the village itself 4th Division were counterattacked and forced back to the edge of the village where they were able to establish touch with 61st Division on the high ground between Maresches and Préseau. This was to be the limit of the day's advance on the British right.

Further north 49th Division had a day of mixed fortunes. Having gained the spur running between Préseau and Aulnoy, they reached the Préseau-Marly road along their whole divisional front as far north as the railway immediately south of the Marly steelworks. Here they found themselves unable to advance further in the face of heavy enemy fire. Their position worsened when the enemy counterattacked their right flank with tanks. They were forced back about 1,000 yards. Under less enemy pressure, their left flank was able to make contact with the right of the Canadians on the railway immediately south of the Marly steelworks.[13]

It was 10th Canadian Infantry Brigade who were to achieve the most striking success of the day. Two battalions (the 44th and 47th) were used initially, with the 46th leapfrogging through the 47th when the first objective had been secured. The 50th Battalion were in reserve. All the battalions were by this time much under strength and could only muster 1,200 rifles for the attack, a total which included reserves. To achieve a degree of surprise no preliminary bombardment was fired; nor was there any target preregistration. But at Zero Hour a devastating, and probably unprecedented, concentration of artillery fire was unleashed which covered the infantry as they swept over Mont Houy and the open ground north of it.

Within 75 minutes of Zero Hour the Brigade's advanced troops had secured the Aulnoy-le Poirier road on their line of advance. Without pausing they continued their advance and by 07h00 had cleared Aulnoy and captured intact the town's bridge over the Rhonelle river. The infantry continued to press forward. By 12h00 they had gained the line of the railway west of the Marly steelworks and, on their left, occupied the Faubourg de Cambrai, less than two kms south of the city centre. They were prevented from making any significant further progress on their right by machine gun fire from the Marly steelworks. In the centre however, patrols were able to push on towards Marly and the southern outskirts of the city itself.[14]

Once the extent of the success of 10th Brigade on the eastern side of the Escaut became clear, the Canadian 12th Brigade, holding the western bank, began passing troops across the river from the area of the Faubourg de Paris station and, further north, across the wrecked Valenciennes-St Amand bridge. Once across however, heavy enemy fire prevented any progress beyond the railway on the western outskirts of the city before nightfall. But under cover of darkness it became possible to infiltrate patrols into the city.[15]

Thus ended a day of almost undiluted success for Horne's army and especially for the Canadian Corps. The XXII Corps and the Canadians shared a bag of 2,750 prisoners and no fewer than 800 dead Germans were counted and buried in the Canadian 10th Brigade sector. The Brigade had bought their success relatively cheaply, suffering a total of 501 casualties of whom 121 were killed or missing.[16]

Mention has been made of the effectiveness of the Canadian artillery in the events of the day. The artillery plan was drawn up by one of the most distinguished Gunners of the war, Major General Andrew McNaughton. A pioneer of scientific counter-battery techniques such as flash-spotting and sound-ranging, he was a strong believer in effective suppression of enemy guns to afford the infantry the opportunity to do its work at acceptable cost. At Valenciennes he had at his disposal almost limitless resources and a rare opportunity to deploy them on virtually three sides of the principal objective, Mount Houy. The First Army's possession of virtually all the area in their sector west of the Escaut as well as areas across the Escaut to the south and southeast of Mont Houy had left that piece of high ground particularly vulnerable to artillery fire. McNaughton was determined that German resistance would be crushed by weight of shells. Eight field and six heavy artillery brigades had been assigned to the support of 10th Brigade's attack, which initially debouched from a frontage of only 2,500 yards. In addition 12 batteries of machine guns had been employed firing in close support or in enfilade from north of the Escaut.

The devastation wrought by the Canadian artillery had a quite disproportionate effect on the enemy's morale. There is little doubt that the Canadian 10th Infantry Brigade enjoyed greater artillery support for their attack on 1 November than had ever previously been laid on in support of a single brigade action. General

McNaughton calculated that 2,149 tons of shells had been fired in support of the attack. He compared this with the 2,800 tons fired in the whole South African War by both sides.[17]

The enemy quickly recognised that the successful, if delayed, implementation of Horne's plan to envelop Valenciennes had made their continuing tenure of the city and the Scheldt Line impossible; an immediate withdrawal from both was ordered. That the Germans had recognised the danger to their overall position that the loss of the Scheldt Line would cause was evidenced by the resources they had employed, and the stubbornness and determination with which they had fought, to hold on to it. Elements of 8 German divisions were identified as having fought against the 3 divisions of First Army during the battle.[18]

Despite the German decision to withdraw, there was still to be some serious fighting on 2 November before the liberation of Valenciennes was complete. The attacks of XXII Corps and Canadian Corps went in well before daylight. By daybreak 49th Division had established themselves on the Préseau-Marly road and taken the Marly steelworks. The right of the Canadian 4th Division were able to take Marly virtually unopposed, but the left made slow progress through Valenciennes against determined German rearguards. Nevertheless, by daybreak, the Canadian 12th Infantry Brigade had reached the eastern edge of the city and were pushing out patrols further eastward. By the evening they had taken the suburb of St Saulve and patrols had advanced 4 or 5 miles east of Valenciennes against slackening opposition. North of the city however, the enemy were showing little inclination to give up their positions on the eastern side of the Escaut and the Jard canal.

The 4th Division of XXII Corps, cooperating once again with XVII Corps of Third Army on their right, launched their attack at daybreak and were soon in possession of Préseau. They pushed on against heavy opposition to occupy the high ground east and north of the village. At the same time XVII Corps took Ferme de Wult. The advance of both divisions of XXII Corps was brought to a halt by the strength of the enemy resistance.[19]

With Valenciennes fully cleared of the enemy Horne briefed his generals on Haig's plans for the immediate future. The Commander-in-Chief was looking for a general advance towards the line Avesnes-Maubeuge-Mons. The first part of this, as far as First and Third Armies were concerned, would be to attain a line from St Rémy Chaussée to the Montignies-Hensies road through Pont-sur-Sambre and Bavay. The Canadians and XXII Corps were to make a flying start to implementing their orders by setting off a day early after their patrols discovered they were only opposed by weak rearguards.[20]

The advance to Mons was on.

Chapter XVI

The Liberation of Mons: November 1918

By 3 November the First Army's advance was resembling a pursuit by advanced guards. The main problems were maintaining contact with a rapidly retreating enemy and, when achieved, stopping them settling into organised defensive positions. Horne's men were however under no illusion that the Germans were in headlong flight. By the end of the day the enemy's retreat and the pursuit by XXII and Canadian Corps had reached the Aunelle river, which marked the Franco-Belgian border on the First Army front. Their objective for the following day would be to continue their advance towards the Bavay-Hensies road.[1]

East of the Aunelle River, Horne's troops would find themselves in broken country intersected by fast-flowing streams following tortuous courses. There would be deep valleys from which would rise steep slopes covered with woods, orchards and enclosed fields. The numerous villages would be densely populated, especially those on the Belgian side of the border, where the inhabitants had never moved away. The roads would be plentiful but narrow, usually with only room for one line of traffic and often cobbled.

Such topography presented obvious difficulties to troops trying to advance rapidly, especially when coupled with an ever increasing distance from the railheads through which their supplies had to be channelled. Fortunately for the supply situation the rapid retreat of the enemy meant it was generally no longer necessary to push forward heavy artillery, with its large tractors and ammunition requirements. All that was required was for 60 pounders and 6 inch howitzers to be kept available to be called up as necessary when the infantry encountered heavy resistance.[2]

At first light on 4 November, the advanced guards of the Canadian and XXII Corps moved forward against enemy rearguards which continued to offer little resistance. The XXII Corps crossed the River Aunelle with little difficulty and managed to gain a footing on the high ground east of the river. But an enemy counterattack forced them back to the right bank of the river. Here the situation was stabilised, bridgeheads were established and bridges put in place. Supplies were brought up in anticipation of a resumption of the advance the following day.[3]

On XXII Corps' left, 4th and 3rd Canadian Divisions made some progress despite strong enemy rearguards. On the very left of First Army, VIII Corps' attempts to get patrols across the Jard Canal, north of Condé, were frustrated by heavy enemy machine gun fire.[4]

On 5 November both XXII and Canadian Corps launched attacks at 05h30. The former rapidly cleared the ridge east of the Aunelle river and, shortly afterwards, crossed into Belgium. As they approached the River Angreau,

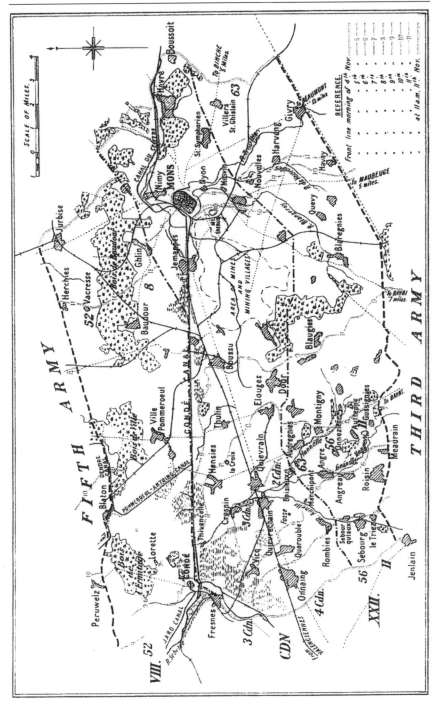

Map 9: The Liberation of Mons

capturing five ex-British tanks on the way, enemy resistance stiffened. But 11th Division secured a passage across the Angreau from which they pressed on to seize a spur overlooking the valley of the Grande Honnelle River. However, there could be no question of crossing the river itself in the face of the heavy fire the enemy were pouring across it. The 56th Division also successfully crossed the Angreau at the village of the same name. They were less successful in their attempts to cross the Grande Honnelle at Angre where the two rivers joined. The enemy had a strong bridgehead in place in the village and were not to be dislodged. In heavy fighting, all 56th Division could achieve was a foothold on the village's western edge.

The Canadian Corps also had a day of heavy fighting. The 4th Canadian Division were held up all day at Marchipont, where fighting continued into the night until the enemy evacuated. But they did clear Quarouble. To their left, 3rd Canadian Division captured Vicq. The day's fighting had been conducted in wet and cold conditions, less than conducive to successful operations. Horne was becoming worried at the potential effects of mud on the roads he badly needed to keep his troops supplied and moving forward.[5]

Both corps nevertheless resumed the attack at 05h30 on the 6th but immediately ran into heavy German resistance. The 11th Division were still unable to cross the Grande Honelle but elements of 56th Division did manage to cross just east of Angreau only to be driven back by a counterattack. Other elements of 56th Division twice managed to get across the Grande Honnelle at Angre and reach the high ground east and northeast of the village. But on both occasions they were driven back into Angre, although they did establish and maintain a bridgehead on the river's right bank.

With the help of artillery, 4th Canadian Division were able to cross the frontier, force a passage across the Grande Honnelle and take Baisieux. Its loss posed a serious threat to the line of retreat of the Germans defending the line of the Grande Honnelle against XXII Corps further south. North of the Mons-Valenciennes railway, 3rd Canadian Division continued their advance along the southern edge of floods between the River Escaut and the Mons-Condé canal and reached the western outskirts of Crespin.[6]

The overall effect of the day's fighting was to leave withdrawal as the only sensible option open to the enemy. Shortly after dark on the 6th, patrols detected the first signs of this along both corps' fronts. Advanced guards found little opposition before them. The 56th Division rapidly crossed the Grande Honnelle and occupied unopposed the high ground from which they had twice been expelled earlier.

This success was to be the precursor of a day of rapid progress on the whole First Army front south of the Mons-Condé canal; only late in the afternoon did enemy rearguards offer up more than token resistance. By dark 11th Division had reached the Bavay-Hensies road and 56th and 63rd Divisions had crossed it further north. The 2nd Canadian Division, which had relieved the 4th, had got even further ahead, their line running from Audregnies to beyond Elouges and from there north to the Mons-Valenciennes railway south of Thulin. The line of the 3rd Canadian Division faced northeast from just west of Thulin, to the Mons-Condé canal at St Aybert. North of Condé the enemy were still maintaining their positions on the Jard and Escaut canals. Further south, the Third Army had captured Bavay.[7]

By now the Germans could no longer disregard the imminent threat to Maubeuge and the effect its loss would have on their northern group of armies, which would become isolated, cut off and be forced to surrender. Accordingly, on 8 November, the enemy began a retreat from their line on the Escaut between Condé and Audenarde. The effect of this move was not immediately apparent on the First Army front along the Jard canal north of Condé. During the night of 7th/8th, First Army patrols were greeted with the heavy gunfire of an enemy seemingly determined to stay put. But the situation had changed by daylight. Patrols of VIII Corps were able to cross both the Escaut and Jard canals with no interference except from a light screen of riflemen. Against such negligible opposition the advanced troops pushed on eastwards. The main problem now confronting them was not enemy resistance, but the flooding on either side of the canals, which made bridging operations difficult. It was not until late afternoon that cavalry and cyclists were able to get across.

South of the Mons-Condé canal, both Canadian and XXII Corps were able to advance throughout the day against virtually no opposition. By nightfall they had reached a line from le Camp Perdu northwards to the western edge of Boussu, and thence westward to a link-up with VIII Corps east of Condé. The Canadians also established bridgeheads north of the Mons-Condé canal near St Aybert.[8] In a letter to his wife Sir Henry Horne expressed his satisfaction at developments.

> We continue to make progress along the road from Valenciennes to Mons
> and to the south of it. We are now 12 miles from Valenciennes and within
> 10 miles of Mons! I hope we get to Mons as it would be a great satisfaction
> to me to take Mons, as I commanded the rearguard of I Corps when we left
> it 4 years ago last August.[9]

The lines of advance of Horne's army indicated that it would be Canadian Corps, and probably 3rd Canadian Division, which would have the privilege of liberating Mons. XXII Corps and 2nd Canadian Division would probably bypass the town to the south and VIII Corps, if it could catch up, to the north.

On the night of 7/8 November the Princess Patricia's Canadian Light Infantry Battalion (PPCLI), part of 7th Canadian Infantry Brigade, joined 8th Canadian Infantry Brigade on the 3rd Canadian Division's front line. The PPCLI immediately made their presence felt by making a surprise night entry into Thulin causing the German garrison to flee in disorder. By nightfall on the 8th the Canadian Battalion had reached the outskirts of Boussu. Further north on the divisional front, the 2nd and 5th Bns Canadian Mounted Rifles had secured the south bank of the Mons-Condé canal, constructed a footbridge across it, crossed the Antoing Canal and were patrolling toward Pommeroeul.[10]

The 9th would prove to be another day of rapid progress for First Army. Resistance was light but enemy machine gunners continued to pose a problem. Advanced guards were regularly forced to deploy to outflank them. As soon as they had done so, the machine guns withdrew to renew the battle further back. The infantry nevertheless recorded an average advance of seven miles and the cavalry and cyclists no less than 13 miles. By evening, XXII Corps' infantry had reached their objective of the Maubeuge-Mons road; their cavalry were well to the east of it.

Further north, the Canadian Corps had continued to close in on Mons. The PPCLI had entered Boussu before daylight and cleared it and a machine gun nest north of the canal at St Ghislain which had been enfilading them. By mid-afternoon they had occupied Jemappes and Flénu. Cuesmes followed suit before darkness fell and the PPCLI continued their advance during the night. They were relieved by 10h00 on the 10th by the Royal Canadian Rifles (RCR). To the PPCLI's left the 49th Battalion Canadian Infantry had, on the 9th, crossed the River Haine and the Mons-Condé canal. They cleared Ville Pommeroeul and Tertre before sending out a screen of patrols which established posts from Hautrage to Ghlin through the centre of the Bois de Baudour to cover their exposed northern flank. These posts were relieved on the afternoon of the following day by 7th Bn Highland Light Infantry of VIII Corps' 52nd Division. Once the posts had been relieved 49th Battalion pulled back to Jemappes, with the RCR taking over their attacking role.

By the end of the 9th 2nd Canadian Division had established outposts on a line running from Genly to Jemappes through Frameries, with their cavalry in front of this line endeavouring to work round Mons to the south of the town. On this day, the Third Army completed the capture of the fortress city of Maubeuge.[11]

By 10 November virtually everyone was aware that an Armistice was imminent. There was nevertheless no relaxation of pressure on the enemy or in the determination to liberate Mons. From the German point of view the town might not have had the huge emotional and symbolic significance it enjoyed in British eyes, but even at this late stage it was of great tactical importance to them. While it was in their possession, the important roads leading from it to Beaumont, Charleroi, Brussels and Ath could be protected. Hence their determination to make a fight for it. On the approaches to Mons enemy rearguards were standing fast and only retiring after they had forced their opponents to deploy.

But the First Army were not to be denied. On XXII Corps' front, 11th Division drove the enemy's rearguards through Havay, south of Mons, and occupied the high ground east and northeast of the village. The 56th Division reached Harveng and the 63rd Division, Nouvelles, both villages southeast of Mons. Well ahead, and slightly to the north of the infantry, the 16th Lancers reached the Mons-Givry road east of Spiennes.

On the Canadian Corps front, 2nd Canadian Division, advancing south of Mons, captured the villages of Mesvin and Hyon and the low but important hills overlooking the town from the south. It was in front of Mons that the enemy were showing 3rd Canadian Division that they intended to resist their entry into the town to the utmost. Machine guns had been placed in houses to cover all approaches and their artillery fired barrages particularly aimed at the area immediately west of the town and north of the Mons-Condé canal.[12] The attack on the town was undertaken by the RCR (less one company) from north of the canal and 42nd Battalion (Royal Highlanders of Canada), plus one company from the RCR, under orders, from south of the canal.

During the afternoon of the 10th, one company of 42nd Battalion pushed forward a screen of scouts to reconnoitre the bridges south of the town. They met with considerable crossfire from the north side of the canal and from Mount Panisel, to the southeast of Mons. As they were under orders to avoid unnecessary destruction of property on the outskirts of town the Battalion's supporting artillery were confined to using shrapnel, a less than satisfactory response. The same objection did not apply to Mount Panisel which was adequately dealt with. The company took up concealed positions opposite the southern bridges from where they could be rushed under cover of darkness. A field gun was manhandled forward to a position from which it could engage enemy machine guns at point blank range.

A second company of the Battalion, advancing from the west, also met with stubborn resistance from enemy machine guns which controlled all the roads. The advance therefore had to be made behind the shelter afforded by houses and involved climbing over garden walls and fences. By nightfall they had reached positions close to the town and railway station. As the heaviest opposition was coming from their right it was decided to keep close to the south bank of the canal. Under cover of Lewis gun fire an entry into the town was made across the railway yards and through the station at 23h00. One platoon went through the north of the town and a second through the centre. They linked up on the eastern side of the town. A third platoon dealt with an enemy machine gun post, using Lewis guns and grenades.

The companies in position to attack from the south after nightfall discovered that the bridges had been destroyed and they were coming under heavy enemy fire. But the German defenders soon became distracted by the RCR company already in the town which was threatening to cut off their retreat. This enabled the southern companies to cobble together some makeshift bridging over which they crossed into the town at around 03h00 on 11 November.

One company of the RCR, attacking from the northwest, came under heavy machine gun fire. Nevertheless, by 02h00 they had forced their way into the town. On their left, a second company of the RCR crossed the canal by what remained of the Nimy road bridge, the scene of such heavy fighting in 1914, and fought their way southwards towards Mons, liberating the village of Nimy on the way.

By 06h00 the town had been fully secured and a line of posts established on its eastern outskirts.[13] The 5th Royal Irish Lancers, attached to 3rd Canadian Division, were sent forward on the heels of the enemy and were 5 miles east of Mons by 11h00. They joined hands with the 2nd Canadian Division on the Charleroi road.[14] It was during this action that Private George Ellison of the 5th Lancers became the last British soldier to be killed in the war.[15]

For the people of Mons the last few weeks of the war had been ones of great worry and uncertainty. Despite German censorship news had percolated through in dribs and drabs of a great allied victory on 8 August (the Battle of Amiens). The more optimistic among them interpreted this as having brought about a fundamental and probably decisive change, after the gloomy news of German victory after victory earlier in the year. But it was not until the beginning of October that the people of Mons had clear evidence that a German retreat was in full swing. From then onwards, with even the press reporting allied victories, it was possible to believe in the certainty of deliverance. The gloomy demeanour of the German soldiers in Mons added credence to this.

On 1 November German sappers began wiring bridges and the tramways for demolition. On the morning of 6 November it became evident that the Germans had conducted a large scale overnight evacuation. In front of the buildings on the *Grand-Place*, which had been requisitioned by the occupiers, were piles of papers and other rubbish giving witness to a precipitate departure. Later on that day Graf von Bernsdorff, the Head of the *Kommandantur*, and his staff left the Town Hall, to be replaced by an improvised local *Kommandantur* under a Captain Wittmer.

As his final act before leaving Mons, Graf von Bernsdorff addressed a letter to Mayor Jean Lescarts in the following terms.

> At the moment of my departure from Mons, I deem it a duty to express to *Monsieur le Bourgmestre* my thanks for the intelligent and conscientious way in which he has fulfilled his difficult functions. I thank too the population for its dignified and calm demeanour.[16]

Captain Wittmer wasted no time in spreading alarm among the people of Mons by urging each family to provide itself with from 8 to 14 days of provisions and to retire to their cellars. But as has already been noted, the First Army, whose guns could be heard getting closer and closer, had every intention of avoiding firing artillery barrages which would damage the town's buildings. Their artillery focused its efforts on silencing the German batteries.[17]

The diarist of the Sisters of the *Sacré-Coeur* recorded their growing concerns for their safety as the guns came closer and became louder. She wrote that on 8 November the cannonade had begun in the early morning and continued until nightfall. There was talk of explosions at the station and the entrances to the town, which had been mined. The Reverend Mother organised a dormitory for the Sisters in the cellars with as much as possible moved down in case the building was destroyed. The night had passed quietly and the following morning the Sisters had begun to believe that hostilities had been suspended, especially as numerous soldiers had departed and the cannons remained silent. But later on the news spread that the Allies had refused to grant the armistice so desperately sought by the Germans. The Sisters had hoped that this would be granted before the town came under bombardment. Instead the aerial dogfights had resumed and Captain Wittmer's advice had been gloomily received.

The night of 9/10 November had been frightful with the German guns firing continuously. They did not stop with the coming of the day although the Sisters managed to celebrate two masses with much diminished congregations. As they waited for what providence would bring they were joyously calm. If God has chosen some of them to be victims for Mons and the Motherland the lot of those chosen would be enviable.[18]

On 12 November the Sister diarist described the events of the previous day.

Did we really live yesterday? Everything now is so different from what it was two days ago that one believes oneself to be dreaming. Happy dream succeeding the most frightful nightmare!

Sunday finished in a racket of cannons ... M le Directeur who returned to us at around 11 am and with whom we cheerfully spent the midday recreation period (exhibition of Boche souvenirs brought back from rue Ferrer, and a public burning of some pictures of the Kaiser on the orders of our guest) ... We were all convinced that staying on the ground floor was becoming dangerous as the noise doubled in intensity. (Only today do we know that danger surrounded us for more than 24 hours and that the cannon fire was reaching the suburbs of Mons, that the shells were sweeping the boulevards and causing some damage there! Knowledge of this danger would have been terrible for several of us!)

We hurried through supper and spent a few moments of recreation in the common room without any notion of peril. Then after prayers we went down into the cellar where, despite the noise of the shelling, we fell asleep immediately after our previous sleepless nights.

The shelling continued; after midnight there were some even stronger explosions the echoes of which were prolonged by the arched ceiling of our cellar. Then nothing. I left our retreat for a moment to go and breathe the air of outside on the staircase leading from the cellar to the courtyard. There was an extraordinary calm. One could believe that the war had never existed here, or at least that it had well and truly finished ... At 5.30 am the Sisters got up. The silence gave us enough of a sense of security to make our toilet in our rooms upstairs. While I was dressing I heard a loud shout, 'The Germans have left!' It was too good to be believed. In the street someone cried, 'The English have arrived!' One hears, above all feels, that the whole population is on the streets; gradually there are cries, singing and clamours of all kinds ...We notice the chimes soon followed by the sound of the bells: we are free, our torturers have disappeared, our liberators are here! It is with tears of emotion and gratitude that we take part in our devotions; unforgettable moments that we will never experience a second time!

Our first care is to go up to raise the national flag. And there is another scene: the streets are decked with the flags of all the allied nations; it is magnificent! We feel moved and unable to utter a word. Then from the square we see an English battalion marching towards us, accompanied by a delirious crowd. The whole day will be like this, marching troops, Canadians and Scottish; a parade on the square in the presence of the Canadian Commander-in-Chief. There was talk of visits by the Prince of Wales, Marshal Foch, even our own beloved King; alas, also the arrest and locking up of some miserable German soldiers who had hidden themselves in suburban houses out of cowardice or treachery.

We have had a visit from brave Englishmen; we would have liked to have understood their language, but that privilege is only granted to few. We contented ourselves with shaking their hands, looking at them with emotion and gratitude and wishing them a happy return to their homes, which no doubt will not be long in coming. For the Germans, with men, reserves, munitions and money exhausted, have accepted all the conditions that the Allies put to them at the Armistice talks; the Armistice was signed in the morning and came into effect at 11am. So that is the end of all fighting and, in all probability, the end of the war. (And also the end of the Empire, be assured!) It is the glory of our dear town of Mons to have been the last to be recaptured by force of arms. It was at Mons that the English intervention in the war began on 23 August 1914; at Mons it finished gloriously on 11 November 1918. Glory to our heroic defenders! And glory above all to the heart of Jesus![19]

Even though the village of Givry-lez-Mons is ten kilometres southeast of Mons it is worth recording the experiences of the Brothers of the *Pensionnat Saint-Joseph* in the last couple of weeks of the war. They found themselves having to cope with many hundreds of refugees driven away by the Germans from their homes in the Cambrai area of France. There was not only the question of feeding them, but also of offering medical care to the many debilitated among them. The Spanish 'flu was also rife and the Fathers had to allocate two dormitories, one for each sex, to the refugees who had come down with it. At the same time they were under pressure from the Germans to keep the refugees moving eastward so that the *Pensionnat* could be used as a casualty station for wounded German troops as the front moved ever closer. Although some refugees were moved on, events overtook the Germans and led on 8 November to the shutting down of their medical facilities. The main danger now for the Fathers and their refugee guests was the close proximity of German guns which inevitably invited British counterbattery fire. As far as possible everyone moved down to the cellars.

After days of incessant noise from the guns and aircraft the Brothers awoke to quiet on the morning of 11 November. At 07h30 British troops arrived in the village to the delirious joy of the inhabitants. As the soldiers marched by the Brothers and evacuees sang the British national anthem. At 09h30 a British officer paused on his gallop at the *Pensionnat* and announced. 'From 11 o'clock there is an Armistice along the whole front. The Kaiser has abdicated. Germany is a republic.' Fifteen minutes later the officer returned. He was asked to sign a sheet of paper, which he did. He was Lieutenant Hopkinson, Intelligence Officer, 63rd (RN) Division.[20]

By 05h00 on the morning of 11 November Mons had been sufficiently cleared of enemy soldiers to enable the notables of the town to assemble at the Town Hall to meet the first Canadian officers to arrive there. The latter were invited to sign the *Livre d'Or* in recognition of their part in the deliverance of Mons from German occupation. Just after daybreak the pipe band of the Royal Highlanders of Canada marched through the town unleashing an outpouring of joy and happiness from the people, including many French refugees, emerging from shelter. Everyone seemed to be dancing, or singing allied national anthems including *It's a long way to Tipperary*, which many seemed to think was the British anthem. Every available allied soldier was enthusiastically embraced. In no time at all every vantage point was decorated with the flags of allied nations.[21]

The notification that the Armistice had been signed reached First Army headquarters at 06h20 on 11 November. A message was immediately sent to all three corps that hostilities were to cease at 11h00 that morning. The Canadian Corps HQ reported that they were temporarily out of touch with their leading divisions, by now 5 miles east of Mons, as the telephone lines had been cut. But the message nevertheless got through to the front line troops in sufficient time to ensure full observance of the end of the fighting.[22] Sadly the Armistice came just a bit too late for one Canadian soldier. Private George Price was with his unit in the village of Ville-sur-Haine, east of Mons, awaiting the Armistice when at 10h58 a German sniper shot rang out and he fell dead. He was the last Canadian, and probably the last BEF, casualty of the war. He was killed only a short distance from where Corporal Thomas of the 4th Royal Irish Dragoon Guards had fired the first shot of the BEF's war more than fifteen hundred days previously.[23]

In reaching the point it had, the First Army had had a remarkable final week of the war. During it, XXII and Canadian Corps had advanced an average of 25 miles, distances which would have been inconceivable at earlier stages of the war. They had fought their way forward against resistance which might best be described as patchy. At times the German rearguards had given up or vanished very quickly. But on other occasions both corps had had to deal with determined opposition from forces much stronger than rearguards, who were not only ready to stand and fight, but also to deliver counterattacks. The country through which they had advanced had not been conducive to ease of movement. The XXII Corps had frequently been confronted with broken and enclosed ground. The Canadian Corps had had to put up with marshy conditions on either side of the Mons-Condé canal as well as fighting through a succession of large mining villages and towns which offered ideal conditions for the enemy's defensive tactics.

The VIII Corps had covered a similar distance to the other 2 corps, but in only the last 4 days. They had met little resistance after the Germans had retreated from the Jard canal, but they had still had to cross the wide flooded areas on the eastern banks of the Jard and Antoing-Pommeroeul canals. Their line of advance had lain through low-lying wet country studded with woods which had inevitably put a brake on the pace of their pursuit.

A further major contribution to the speed of advance of Horne's troops had been their morale. This had understandably risen as the realisation had grown that, after the dark and difficult days of spring, the tide had finally and irrevocably turned in the Allies' favour. It was boosted by the troops' reaction to the stories that they heard from the French and Belgian inhabitants of the areas occupied by the enemy since 1914, especially those relating to the ill-treatment that had sometimes been meted out to British prisoners of war. These had made them even more determined to continue to press forward and drive the enemy back to their own territory. It might have been expected that, as the prospect of an armistice being signed very soon looked like becoming a reality, a certain amount of circumspection would have begun to permeate throughout Horne's Army. But the apparently commonly shared view remained that the enemy should be driven back as far and as fast as possible before the armistice was signed, to leave as little doubt as possible in their minds that they were a defeated army. An additional incentive for Horne's army had been that they had had in their sights the town of Mons where it had all begun for the BEF more than 4 years previously. How gratifying it would be to conclude proceedings with the town wrested from the enemy and firmly back in First Army hands. In these circumstances, therefore, it is hardly surprising that there had been no relaxation of the vigour and determination of Horne's army's pursuit of what had by now become a manifestly beaten enemy.[24]

Horne recorded his own pleasure at the final turn of events.

At 11h00 today hostilities ceased! We took Mons. We were well round it last night and early this morning we disposed of the Germans who made an attempt to hold it, and occupied the town. I am so pleased. I began at Mons and I end the fighting at Mons! The C-in-C was very pleased, I saw him today and told him.[25]

Chapter XVII

Epilogue

The Armistice had come into effect at 11h00 on 11 November and, as far as could be seen, was being universally observed. The rest of that momentous day would be devoted to celebrations of the allied victory and the liberation of Mons, some formal and others less so.

The 3rd Canadian Division would have Mons as its base for the immediate future. Accordingly it set up its headquarters and residence for the GOC, Major General Loomis, in the house of Madame Amory in the Place du Parc. It was in this house that General Ludendorff had chaired the fateful meeting exactly a year previously which had determined the German strategy for the spring and summer of 1918. The 7th Infantry Brigade established its headquarters in the Maison Losseau, 37 rue de Nimy, which, for much of the last 18 months of the war, had been the headquarters of Prince Rupprecht of Bavaria, Commander of the German Northern Group of Armies.[1]

The GOC-in-C of the Canadian Corps, Lt General Sir Arthur Currie, made his formal entry into Mons at 15h30. Currie's escort was furnished by an officer and men of the 5th Royal Irish Lancers who had taken part in the fighting around Mons with the Regiment in August 1914. On the *Grand-Place* were drawn up representatives of all units which had participated in the liberation of Mons. The Corps Commander was received by Mayor Jean Lescarts and other notables. The Mayor delivered an address expressing the citizens' thanks and joy at having been delivered from the German tyranny after four years of war, and their satisfaction and relief at the complete victory gained by allied arms. General Currie replied and presented his pennant to the town of Mons as a token that would always serve to remind the people of Mons of the arrival of Canada in their midst on 11 November 1918. He concluded with a call for three cheers for the King of the Belgians.[2]

The population of Mons, swelled by large numbers of refugees from France and other parts of Belgium, thronged the streets throughout the day to greet and lionise the Canadians. The whole town seemed to be *en fête*, bedecked, as it was, with the flags of the allied nations, for so long banned.

On the afternoon of the following day the streets were once again crowded with people, but this time in solemn mood. They were there to pay homage to eight Canadian soldiers who had been killed in Mons during the operations to liberate the town. Their funeral cortege began its journey at the Town Hall and concluded at the Mons Communal cemetery around which there had been so much fighting on 23 August 1914. The coffins were carried on gun carriages each drawn by four horses; they were almost hidden by the huge numbers of wreaths and flowers placed on them. They were escorted by troops of Canadian soldiers and a regimental band playing solemn music. Local dignitaries and representatives of the Belgian national government accompanied the cortege.[3]

Following the Armistice, casualty clearing stations were posted to Mons, as a consequence of which these 8 Canadians were not the last BEF soldiers to be buried in Mons Communal Cemetery. Nor were they the first, as the Germans had extended the communal cemetery to accommodate their own and allied dead after occupying Mons. There are now 393 BEF burials in the cemetery.

A perhaps better known cemetery in the Mons area is the St. Symphorien Military Cemetery, situated about five kms east of the town. It was started by the Germans in 1914 as a burial place for their and the British dead of the Battle of Mons. The cemetery can lay plausible claim to being the most beautiful on the Western Front and it is the resting place for a number of remarkable casualties. Here are buried the first British fatality (Private J Parr), the first VC (Lieutenant Maurice Dease), the first British officer to die (Major William Abell), the first RE officer to die (Lieutenant H Wilfred Holt), the last Canadian to be killed (Private George Price) and the last British soldier to die (Private George Ellison). The cemetery is also interesting for the memorials erected by the Germans to honour their enemy. The inscription on the one dedicated to 4th Bn Middlesex Regt incorrectly contains the prefix 'Royal' as the Germans could not apparently believe that a battalion that had fought so courageously could be other than 'Royal'. A second German memorial is jointly dedicated to 4th Bn Royal Fusiliers and 2nd Bn Royal Irish Regt. A third is a memorial to the men of both armies who died on 23-24 August 1914. In total the cemetery has 229 Commonwealth and 284 German graves.[4]

Over the years a number of memorials have been erected in and around Mons testifying to the events of the First World War. There are a number of plaques under the entrance porch to Mons Town Hall. One of them commemorates the 5th Royal Irish Lancers and their presence in Mons in both 1914 and 1918. A second commemorates the liberation of Mons by 3rd Canadian Division.[5] There is a third plaque put up by the Town Council of the French town of Douai in recognition of the hospitality and kindness their fellow citizens received when they were forcibly evacuated to Mons. At the Place des Martyrs/rue de la Trouille on the south side of the town there is a plaque recording the names of the 5 citizens of Mons who were killed when forming part of the human shield on 23 August 1914.

Outside Mons, on the N6 heading towards Casteau there are two memorials almost opposite one another on either side of the road. The one on the left, a free-standing stone memorial, marks the firing of the first British shot in anger of the war by Corporal E Thomas of the 4th Royal Irish Dragoon Guards. The one on the right, a wall plaque, indicates the point which the 116th Canadian Infantry Battalion had reached when the Armistice came into effect. Around five kms southeast, in the village of Ville-sur-Haine is a plaque commemorating the death of Pte George Price, the last Canadian to be killed in the war. Southwest of Ville-sur-Haine is Obourg. The village railway station was the centre of 4th Bn Middlesex Regt's defences and a plaque there records the fact. The main station building on which it was originally placed no longer exists and the plaque in now affixed to a specially built brick memorial. Further to the west a street has been named for 4th Bn Middlesex near L'Hermite Farm which was defended by the

English regiment and where the first British officer fatality, that of Major William Abell, occurred.[6]

The railway bridge at Nimy, which has replaced the one so tenaciously defended by 4th Bn Royal Fusiliers on 23 August 1914, shelters at its southern end a wall plaque dedicated to the Regiment and to its two members, Lieutenant Maurice Dease and Private Sidney Godley, who won the first two Victoria Crosses of the war there, the former posthumously.[7]

Outside Mons and due east of the town is the La Bascule crossroads on which stand two conspicuous monuments. The first, on the southwestern side of the crossroads commemorates the fact that the BEF fought its first and last battles of the war at Mons. It was originally situated close to the Belfry in the centre of Mons but was moved to its present site when the original one became unsafe in 1986. The second, on the northwestern side, is a celtic cross dedicated to the Royal Irish Regiment, whose 2nd Battalion mounted such a strong defence at the crossroads during the Battle of Mons.[8]

The fortunes of war were to mark the futures and reputations of the main protagonists of the Battles of Mons in 1914 and 1918 and the years in between in many different ways.

Field Marshal Sir John French had essentially left the fighting of the 1914 Battle to Sir Horace Smith-Dorrien and never really showed much grasp or grip of what was required of the BEF Commander-in-Chief during the battle or the subsequent Retreat from Mons. His belated belief that Smith-Dorrien had betrayed him by fighting the Battle of Le Cateau and his unfair dismissal of him at the first perceived opportunity in April 1915 undermined his own position and left him vulnerable to recall by a government annoyed at his tactics in exposing the Shell Scandal and his contribution to the failure of the Battle of Loos. Duly recalled in December 1915 to become C-in-C Home Forces and an Earl, his effort to impose his own version of the events of 1914 in the book of the same name led to further public airing of his relationship with Smith-Dorrien, more to the detriment of his reputation than to that of his erstwhile subordinate. Field Marshal the Earl of Ypres, as he had become, died in 1925.[9]

Following Sir Horace Smith-Dorrien's dismissal from command of the BEF's Second Army for advocating a tactical withdrawal in the Ypres Salient during Second Ypres, which was subsequently implemented by his successor, he was never to hold a senior appointment again. He was supposed to have taken over as Commander-in-Chief in East Africa but a bout of pneumonia put paid to that. Smith-Dorrien is generally credited with having saved the BEF by fighting the Battle of Le Cateau and was arguably the most competent commander in the British Army during the early part of the war. Had he not fallen foul of Sir John French's malevolence he might have succeeded him as C-in-C BEF instead of Sir Douglas Haig. General Sir Horace Smith-Dorrien died in 1930.[10]

The principal beneficiary of Sir John French's shortcomings and Sir Horace Smith-Dorrien's departure from the Western Front was undoubtedly General (later Field Marshal) Sir Douglas Haig. As Commander of I Corps he played only a peripheral role in the Battle of Mons and the Retreat. Having succeeded French as C-in-C BEF in December 1915, he retained that position for the rest of the war. Whatever may be thought of his strategy in 1916 and 1917 which let to the appalling casualty lists on the Somme and at Third Ypres (Passchendaele) there can be no question that he was virtually the only military leader who believed, as early as July 1918, that the war could be won that year. It was his strategy, more or less readily accepted by the Supreme Allied Commander, General Foch, that was implemented in the Campaign of 100 Days and forced the Germans to surrender unconditionally (in effect if not in name) on 11 November 1918.

The successes of the latter half of 1918 were insufficient to redeem Haig in the eyes of his political masters, especially Prime Minister David Lloyd George. With the war ended he remained C-in-C BEF until April 1919, then served briefly as C-in-C Home Forces. It soon became apparent that Haig would not be given any further employment in the Government's gift. He was awarded an Earldom and a grant of £100,000 and devoted the rest of his life to furthering the interests of his former comrades in arms. He founded the British Legion and instituted its well-known Poppy Fund. Much mourned by the country, if not by Lloyd George, he died at the age of 67 in early 1928.

Major General Henry Wilson (later Field Marshal Sir Henry Wilson Bt) began the war as Sir John French's Vice Chief of Staff and ended it as Chief of the Imperial General Staff. Thanks largely to his pre-war tenure of the jobs of Commandant of the Staff College at Camberley and Director of Military Operations at the War Office, Wilson, probably more than any other individual, was responsible for the BEF finding itself fighting the battle of Mons. His close professional relationship and personal friendship with General Ferdinand Foch led him to exceed his authority in committing the British to come to the aid of France in the event of a German attack and in determining the form this aid would take. As his was the only fully formulated plan it was largely accepted by a government completely unprepared for the crisis which had hit it in the summer of 1914. Hence the BEF's conformity with the French Plan XVII which saw it advancing into Belgium to confront a supposedly weak German right wing. Wilson's insistence until the very last moment that the French intelligence was right, and that being provided by the RFC and the BEF's cavalry screen was wrong, almost resulted in complete disaster which was only retrieved by the Battle of Mons and the subsequent Retreat.

When General Sir 'Wully' Robertson was preferred to Wilson as General Murray's replacement as Sir John French's Chief of Staff, Wilson became Principal Liaison Officer with the French Army. This was followed by an undistinguished period in command of IV Corps on the Western Front. In February 1918 Wilson was appointed British Representative at the Inter-Allied Supreme War Council at Versailles. But very shortly thereafter he succeeded Robertson as CIGS which he remained until his retirement from the Army in 1922. In the same year he was assassinated by IRA terrorists on the doorstep of his London home.[11]

Two other BEF generals who had a direct impact on Mons were the Commander of First Army 1916-19, General Sir Henry Horne, and his immediate subordinate, Lt General Sir Arthur Currie, the Commander of the Canadian Corps. Brigadier General Horne was Haig's Commander Royal Artillery at I Corps during the Battle of Mons, but can have had little direct involvement in a battle in which I Corps played virtually no part. Horne was to distinguish himself in the Retreat from Mons, at stages of which he commanded the I Corps rearguard and flankguard. In 1915 he commanded 2nd Division and was Commander of XV Corps on the Somme. In late September 1916 he took over First Army where he remained until March 1919. He proved an effective army commander both offensively at Vimy Ridge in 1917 and during the Campaign of 100 Days in 1918 and defensively during the German *Georgette* offensive earlier the same year. He owed much of his offensive success to the fact that the Canadian Corps was for most of the time part of his Army. Unlike some other British generals he proved himself tactful in handling the sensitivities of the Canadians and achieved a generally harmonious working relationship with General Currie, with strikingly positive results, one being the liberation of Mons by the Canadians. Horne took immense pleasure and pride in his association with the liberation, recalling, 'I began at Mons and I end the fighting at Mons.'

Horne remained in the army after the war becoming GOC Eastern Command based at Horse Guards, London. In 1923 he went on to half pay and retired three years later. He died in 1929.[12]

The Canadian Lieutenant General Sir Arthur Currie was in no sense a typical senior army officer. He did not even sport a moustache, an almost unheard of omission in military circles of the time. Before the war Currie had been an insurance broker, estate agent and militia officer. His business activities looked like ending in embezzlement charges from which he was only saved by friends coming to his rescue. He arrived in France as a Brigade Commander in the first Canadian division to reach the Western Front. He was subsequently promoted to the command of a division and when General Sir Julian Byng relinquished command of the Canadian Corps in June 1917, Currie was the obvious choice to succeed him as the first Canadian commander of the Corps. He was to prove himself one of the outstanding BEF corps commanders of the war. Under his leadership the Corps became superlative shock troops. Currie's forte was detailed and careful planning of his battles and painstaking analysis subsequently of what had gone wrong and right. He was to be regularly accused by an implacable enemy, Sir Sam Hughes, who had been sacked in 1916 from his position as Canadian War Minister, of repeatedly sacrificing his troops in hazardous missions in pursuit of personal glory. A case in point, it was claimed, was pressing the Germans to the very end at Mons, and taking casualties in doing so, when it would have been sensible to have held back and waited for the Armistice. Hughes invariably made his accusations under the protection of Parliamentary privilege.

Currie returned to Canada after the war. He was promoted to General but retired from the army in 1920. He became Principal and Vice-Chancellor of McGill University in Montreal, positions he successfully held for the rest of his life. But even though Sir Sam Hughes had died in 1921, Currie continued to be haunted by his accusations. In 1928 an Ottawa newspaper reprinted them and Currie sued for libel. After a two week-long trial during which his pre-war, and entirely irrelevant, peculations were given an unwelcome airing, Currie won his case. But the stresses and strains of the long drawn out legal battle may have contributed to his premature death in 1933 at the age of only 57.[13]

The French officer most closely involved in the fate of Mons in 1914 was the Commander of the Fifth French Army, General Charles Lanrezac. He realised probably earlier than anyone else on the allied side that the German thrust through Belgium was a great deal more powerful than General Joffre had reckoned and that if he carried out the deployment he had been ordered to make, his army and the BEF on its left would come under attack from vastly superior forces on ground unsuited for defensive operations. He persuaded Joffre to allow him to halt his advance south of the Sambre River between Charleroi and Namur. Even so he was forced into retreat by the onslaught of the German Second Army. He subsequently went over to the attack at Guise and, although again forced to retreat, his attack was responsible for beginning the opening of a gap between the German First and Second Armies which ultimately was to give Joffre the opportunity to launch the Battle of the Marne.

Lanrezac's contempt for the BEF and its Commander-in-Chief led to unforgivable failures to keep the BEF informed of his intentions at vital moments, notably his decision not to attack on 23 August and instead, shortly thereafter, to retire. These decisions were to leave the BEF's right flank open and precipitate the Retreat from Mons. Lanrezac's conduct was to lead to a breakdown of mutual trust between the Allies which, had in not been for high level political intervention, could have led to the BEF refusing to participate in the Battle of the Marne. As it was Sir John French ordered Sir Douglas Haig not to get involved in Lanrezac's Battle of Guise, which may well have spelt the difference between defeat and victory.

It is rare for a subordinate commander to survive long when he has shown his superior to be wrong and himself right. Despite the skill with which he fought the Battle of Guise, Lanrezac was dismissed very soon thereafter on the grounds of his alleged defeatism and inability to get on with his British allies. He was never reemployed and died in 1925.[14]

It was General Alexander von Kluck's First German Army which took possession of Mons during the course of 23-24 August. Although 68 years old at the time von Kluck was a general of great energy who had been given the largest of the German armies to carry out the most crucial part of the Schlieffen Plan, the wide sweep through Belgium and northern France round the west and south of Paris. The Battles of Mons and Le Cateau were two early hitches which, with others, would lead von Kluck and the German Second Army Commander, General Karl von Bülow, to modify the Plan, effectively sowing the seeds of its failure.

If von Kluck had had any accurate ideas of the strength, deployment and whereabouts of the BEF in the early days of the war he would have been saved a lot of uncertainty and would probably have been able to bring about its destruction. But his intelligence was persistently sketchy and inaccurate, partially reflecting the mastery the BEF's cavalry had gained over their German counterparts.

Von Kluck did not see eye to eye with his equally elderly neighbouring army commander, von Bülow, who was as cautious and pessimistic as von Kluck was energetic and thrustful. When von Bülow became alarmed at the gap opening up between their two armies, largely as a result of the Battle of Guise and von Kluck's continuation on the southwesterly course called for by Schlieffen, he asked von Kluck to turn his army southeastward to close the gap. Probably because of a mistaken belief on his part that the French armies facing him and the BEF had ceased to be effective fighting forces, von Kluck agreed. He thereby offered his army's flank and rear to the counterattack that became known as the Battle of the Marne.

Von Kluck remained in command of the German First Army throughout the first winter of trench warfare. In March 1915 he was badly wounded in the leg by shrapnel when visiting the trenches. He never returned to active service and was retired from the army in October 1916. He died in 1934. Von Bülow also remained in command of his army through that first winter. In January 1915 he was promoted to Field Marshal, but two months later suffered a heart attack. Although he recovered and tried to return to active duty he did not succeed and resigned from the army in 1916. He died in 1921.[15]

The name of Jean Lescarts has been mentioned on several occasions in this narrative. In having him as their Mayor throughout the war the people of Mons were fortunate in having the right man in the right place at the right time. Jean Lescarts was born in Mons in 1861 making him 53 at the outbreak of war. He trained and practised as a barrister and became a Liberal politician. His father had briefly been Mayor of the town in the 1880s. Jean Lescarts became an alderman and in 1905 was elected Mayor, an office he was to hold until his death in 1925.

Much the greatest challenge of his tenure of office was that presented by the German occupation. He showed a degree of foresight and a grasp of reality in preparing for a German occupation when he ordered the *Garde Civique* to deposit their arms at the railway station and remove their uniforms, and called on his fellow citizens to hand in any arms in their possession. His intention was to avoid anything which the Germans might construe as provocation and use as an excuse to unleash reprisals. His measures had the desired effect and Mons was spared the reprisals visited on Nimy by the same German troops who occupied Mons.[16] Some of its senior citizens, including Mayor Lescarts, were not however spared the human shield which the Germans had been driving before them since leaving Nimy.

When the Germans arrived in the *Grand-Place* they were told by Mayor Lescarts that Mons was an open town without defences and that he would answer for the maintenance of order. He was peremptorily told to join the human shield and it was only by good fortune that he escaped with his life when the shield was caught in crossfire in the southern part of the town.[17]

On the day following the Mayor's lucky escape a proclamation was put up over his signature which read in translation as follows.

To the Population of Mons

The territory of our country is occupied by foreign armies. We must observe the sacred laws of hospitality towards them all. The safety of the town and the lives of its representatives will answer for it. The population should remain calm and offer a good welcome to everyone and lavish their devotion on the victims of the war, whoever they may be. All acts of ill-will will be a betrayal of the town and the members of the Communal Council.

(The concern shown in this proclamation for the town's representatives no doubt reflected the German decision to hold senior citizens, four at a time, as hostages for the population's good behaviour.)[18]

For the rest of the war Mayor Lescarts was to act as a channel of communication between the German administrators of Mons and its people. A whole raft of communiqués, orders, instructions and threats were conveyed to the citizenry by poster, many of which contained the signature of Mayor Lescarts. But the Mayor did not see this as a rubber stamp operation. Inevitably, as many of the posters dealt with subjects with unwelcome implications for the people, Mayor Lescarts found himself protesting and making representations to the German authorities designed to mitigate the harm the proposed measures would do. If his advice was sought by the Germans, which it sometimes was, the Mayor did not shirk from giving what he knew would be unwelcome counsel. The Mayor also declined to provide the Germans with any information that would help them carry out schemes detrimental to the local population, such as identifying suitable candidates for deportation. But he was unable to do anything about the swingeing fines which the Germans imposed on the town from time to time, as much for revenue raising reasons as for punishment. Mayor Lescarts was lucky that ill-health prevented him from attending a council meeting in late October 1917 which decided to refuse a German demand that the Belfry bells should be rung to celebrate their victory at Caporetto. Those present were fined amounts ranging from 500 to 3,000 Marks. As an absentee the Mayor got away with a token fine of 20 Marks.

Mayor Lescarts, who was to die in office in 1925, also played a leading role in the charitable and governmental projects to keep the people fed and clothed. His success in keeping on at least tolerable terms with the German occupying authorities, in order to try to protect his fellow citizens from their worst excesses, was recognised in the message Graf von Bernsdorff addressed to him as he was leaving Mons.[19] No such letter would have been written to Fulgence Masson, one of Mayor Lescarts' close colleagues on the Communal Council for much of the war. Like the Mayor a lawyer and Liberal MP Masson did not see his role in the emollient terms that the Mayor saw his. At the beginning of the war he was appointed President of the *Comité Provincial de Secours et d'Alimentation*, based in Mons. His strong protests at the deportations made him a marked man. He was fined for disclosing to a worker threatened with deportation that the Germans had agreed to discontinue the practice, something which manifestly they were not doing. Later the Germans saw him as being the leading light behind the Communal Council's refusal to ring the Belfry bells in celebration of Caporetto; he was fined 3,000 Marks. In early 1918 he was identified as being behind a secretly drafted law on future relations with Germany after an allied victory and this, coupled with the discovery in his waste paper basket of a list of persons who had contributed money to the families of the three *Montois* shot for espionage in 1915, led to his being sentenced to 6 months jail in Germany in April 1918. He was in Germany until the end of the war. Immediately on his return to Belgium he was appointed Minister of War, then Minister of Justice and finally Minister of State. He retired from Parliament in 1939, and died in Mons in 1942, no doubt greatly saddened that his home town was once more occupied by the Germans.[20]

With the war over Mons and the rest of Belgium could try to revert to peacetime concerns. The Treaty of Versailles was territorially kind to Belgium; it gained Eupen, Malmédy, Moresnet and St.-Vith at Germany's expense. Despite the experience of 1914 the country clung to its treaty-backed status of perpetual neutrality.

In 1934 the popular warrior King Albert I was killed in a climbing accident near Namur. He was succeeded by his son, who became Leopold III.

The rise of Hitler to power in Germany was a source of great concern to the Belgian government. He had made no secret of his views on pan-Germanism and the need to dismantle the Treaty of Versailles where he perceived it to have been inimical to Germany. Belgium would be an obvious target with its recent acquisition of former German territory. But still they clung to neutrality although they did agree that Britain and France could come to their aid if Germany attacked them.

The attack duly came on 10 May 1940. The allied defence of Belgium was markedly less effective even than it had been in 1914 thanks to the German *Blitzkrieg* tactics. Along with other parts of Belgium, Mons suffered heavily from German aerial bombardment in the first few days before it found itself once more in German hands after only about a week of hostilities. This time there was no BEF to fight a Battle of Mons; its area of deployment was further north. Also in contrast to 1914, when the Belgians had refused to give in, King Leopold III surrendered his country and armed forces on 28 May. The fissures in Belgian society, which would see many more Belgians killed wearing German uniforms than those killed fighting alongside the Allies, quickly surfaced. Not all of the former were willing adherents to the Nazi cause, but many were.

The next 4 years were to be ones of great hardship and misery for the people of Mons. To the harshness of the German occupation was added the threat from allied aerial bombardments which were to cause about 13,000 civilian deaths in Belgium. But on 2 September 1944 reconnaissance tanks of the United States' 3rd Armored Division reached the outskirts of Mons. The town was occupied in force the following day by 3rd Armored and 1st US Infantry Divisions. There was serious fighting in the area until the 5th which ended with the taking of nearly 30,000 German prisoners. The strong German counterattack, known as the Battle of the Bulge, which was launched on 16 December 1944, was successfully contained well before it could threaten Mons. The German presence had therefore ended for the town on 3 September.

Since the war the political scene has been transformed by the succession of moves towards closer European integration which now go under the name European Union. It is no longer conceivable that there can ever be a military threat to Belgium from Germany. Twice bitten, Belgium renounced neutrality in favour of membership of the North Atlantic Treaty Organisation (NATO) when it was established in 1949 before the future political geography of Europe had become foreseeable. The establishment of the precursor of the European Union, the Common Market, improved immeasurably Belgian economic prosperity. It has helped Mons to cope with dramatic change as the coalfields, which once were one of the bedrocks of its prosperity, became exhausted and shut down. Chalk and limestone continue to be quarried locally, to fuel a healthy local cement industry. The town has also become a flourishing centre of higher education with several centres of excellence attracting a large student and academic population. Perhaps a tinge ironically Mons has also sheltered since 1967 the headquarters of the military arm of NATO, the Supreme Headquarters Allied Powers Europe (SHAPE). Here British, Belgian and German officers (among others of many nationalities) make contingency plans for military operations, which happily do not include operations against each other!

In Britain the name of Mons lingers on in the public consciousness with several towns boasting a Mons Square or Road or Street. Perhaps the best known reminder of the Belgian town in Britain is the British Army's Mons Barracks in Aldershot. Recently refurbished, it now houses the Army's First Mechanical Brigade. But it is undoubtedly best remembered as the place where around 50,000 National Servicemen were turned from privates into officers in the years prior to the abolition of National Service in the early 1960s. The Barracks were for many years bestrode by the formidable figure and voice of Regimental Sergeant Major Ronald Brittain, a Coldstream Guardsman and senior non-commissioned officer in the British Army, whose main function seemed to be to instil terror in the hearts of the officer cadets in his charge, a role which he appears to have fulfilled to perfection.

The most enduring way in which the Battles of Mons and Le Cateau, the Retreat from Mons and the Pursuit to Mons (the 1918 campaign culminating in the liberation) are recalled is through their display as battle honours on the colours of some of the regiments concerned. Although the battle honour for a particular engagement or campaign may be awarded to many regiments only a certain number are permitted to add it to their colours. In the case of 'Mons' that permission was granted to 11 cavalry and 31 infantry regiments. In the case of 'Le Cateau' the figures were 10 and 12. In both these cases the regiments concerned were virtually entirely from II Corps.

In appearance today the town of Mons looks prosperous and attractive, especially the striking *Grand-Place*, which those Old Contemptibles who passed through it in August 1914 would readily recognise if they were still alive and able to return. The flourishing Mons tourist industry reaps a great bonus from the large numbers of British visitors who come to see the places where the British Army came to grips with a Continental enemy for the first time since Waterloo. The visitors are seldom disappointed. There is much to see and to reflect on, perhaps thanking providence that those tragic events of more than ninety years ago are almost certainly never to be repeated.

Appendix A

The Political Road to Mons

The political circumstances and events which brought about a war involving the five great empires of Europe – Germany, Austria-Hungary, Russia, France and Great Britain – were of a complexity beyond the scope of this book to analyse in detail. The aim of this and the next appendix is to explain how a British expeditionary force found itself confronting a German army at Mons in August 1914. This chapter will deal largely with the political background and developments which affected Britain and Germany and, to a lesser extent, France, the three main future combatants on the Western Front. It will focus on the establishment of Belgium as an independent country whose perpetual neutrality was guaranteed by treaty; on the events, largely of the third quarter of the nineteenth century which were to result in the unification of Germany under Prussian hegemony, and the resultant increased assertiveness and bellicosity of the German Confederation and its successor, the Second German Empire; and finally on the system of alliances entered into by the future belligerents in the last decade of the nineteenth century and the first decade of the twentieth.

The German violation of Belgium's neutrality on 4 August 1914 was the immediate cause of Britain's declaration of war. Other considerations, such as a growing national sentiment that Germany was getting above itself and needed to be taken down a peg or two, and a sense of a moral obligation to France, might have led to the same outcome. But it was the German assault on Belgium that eased the British government's task in persuading itself and public opinion in general that a declaration of war was both right and unavoidable.

From at least the time of the Spanish Armada, when a Spanish army had assembled on the Belgian coast in preparation for an invasion of England, it had been one of England's major foreign policy aims to ensure as far as possible that the Low Countries should not fall under the control of a European power strong enough to pose a threat of invasion. Not for nothing had Antwerp, for many years the principal port of the Low Countries, been described as 'a dagger pointed at the heart of England'. In pursuit of this foreign policy aim (and in religious solidarity) England was strongly supportive of the successful Dutch attempt to throw off the Spanish yoke, formalised by treaty in 1648. The Spanish, by now perceived as in decline and less of a threat, remained in control of their Belgian provinces until 1713 when, under the terms of the Treaty of Utrecht, the Austrian branch of the Hapsburgs took over. The Austrian Netherlands survived until the revolutionary French armies overran and took control of the Low Countries in 1795. The Congress of Vienna, charged with drawing up a peace settlement following the defeat of Napoleonic France, reaffirmed the independence of the Netherlands and extended the nation's area to cover the whole of the Low Countries.

In 1830 the discontented Belgian provinces rebelled against Dutch control. The British Foreign Secretary, Lord Palmerston, saw that British interests would best be served by the establishment of an independent Belgium. Despite strenuous opposition from the Netherlands and France, Palmerston finally had his way when the Treaty of London, affirming Belgian independence and its perpetual neutrality, was signed in 1839 by Britain, France, Prussia, Russia and Austria. It was the violation of this treaty by Prussia's successor, the German Empire, that was Britain's *casus belli* in 1914. That Britain attached rather more significance to the treaty than Germany can be inferred from German Chancellor Bethmann Hollweg's contemptuous reference to it as 'a scrap of paper' as he remonstrated with the British Ambassador over what, in his view, were the wholly inadequate reasons for Britain's imminent declaration of war.[1]

Although it was Germany which took the ultimate step of violating the Treaty, it was not only they who had considered setting it aside in a perceived national interest. Napoleon III of France, in a revival of his uncle's policy of 'natural frontiers' had sought Prussian agreement, in the immediate aftermath of that country's victory over Austria at Sadowa in 1866, to a treaty under the terms of which France would be allowed to take over Luxembourg and Belgium. The latter occupation would be backed by a promise of Prussian military intervention on France's side, should a third country, presumably Britain, oppose the French move. The German Chancellor Bismarck procrastinated and when the Franco-Prussian War broke out in 1870 he had the French draft of the treaty published. The international outrage this provoked helped dissipate any international sympathy there might have been for France in its struggle with Prussia. It may also have contributed to a determination by the French, as they drew up their strategy for the next war with Germany, that if and when Belgian neutrality was violated it would not be by them, at least in the first instance.

The unification of Germany, in a process completed by the proclamation of the Second German Empire in the Hall of Mirrors at Versailles on 18 January 1871, had begun at the Congress of Vienna over half a century earlier. There a German Confederation of 39 states, which included Prussia, was formed under the overall suzerainty of Austria. The growing economic and military strength of Prussia put this arrangement under increasing strain but Austria remained at least nominally dominant until the two countries fell out over Schleswig-Holstein. Lord Palmerston had waggishly claimed of the Schleswig-Holstein problem that, 'There are only three men who have ever understood it: one was Prince Albert, who is dead; the second was a German professor, who became mad. I am the third – and I have forgotten all about it.'[2] Ownership of the two provinces had long festered relations between Denmark, in possession, and Prussia and in 1863 war broke out once again between Denmark and an alliance of Prussia and Austria. Unsurprisingly the Danes were defeated and under the terms of the Treaty of Vienna, signed in 1864, surrendered Schleswig-Holstein to the Prussians and Austrians.

It did not take long for the victorious allies to fall out over the post-war arrangements for Schleswig-Holstein's governance. The falling out soon led to all-out war which the relatively new Prussian Chancellor, Otto von Bismarck, for long resentful of Austrian preeminence in the German Confederation, did little to avoid. The result was a spectacular defeat for Austria at the Battle of Sadowa and the loss of that country's role in North German affairs. The German

Confederation was replaced by a North German Confederation which excluded Austria and was completely dominated by Prussia.

It was the North German Confederation under Bismarck's political, and von Moltke the Elder's military, leadership that was to provoke Napoleon III's France into ill-advised aggression, thus beginning the Franco-Prussian War of 1870-1. The French had belatedly begun to realise that the new Prussian dominance in Northern Germany was leading to a relative decline in their own standing as a European power. This relative decline was to become painfully apparent on the battlefields of the war in which the French were to suffer comprehensive defeat. The Prussian victory brought into being the Second German Empire under the sovereignty of the King of Prussia (now crowned additionally Emperor (*Kaiser*)), and the further extension of his domains by the addition of the south German provinces, which included Bavaria and Württemberg. The harsh peace terms dictated to the prostrate French included the annexation by the victors of Alsace and part of Lorraine, of itself an almost certain guarantee that there would be a future confrontation between the two powers. *Revanche* was to be a word never far from the thoughts of Frenchmen over the next half century as the country, once more a Republic (the Third), made a hugely impressive and rapid recovery from the nadir of its defeat.

In the meantime the German Empire had reached the apogee of its territorial extent in Europe. Despite the awesome and forbidding reputation of its 'Iron Chancellor', as Bismarck was known, there was never any serious suggestion that Germany harboured any further territorial ambitions in Europe. Such aspirations would be directed at the acquisition of colonies overseas as its *Weltpolitik*[3] was pursued. In Europe Bismarck focused his efforts on persuading the other powers to accept the new reality of a powerful and dominant Germany in their midst, without their forming defensive alliances between themselves to contain it. Bismarck reinforced this approach with alliances of his own. In 1879 the Austro-German Treaty which essentially gave Austria a German guarantee should it be attacked by Russia, was signed. Despite the implicit hostility towards them in this treaty, Bismarck prevailed on the Russians to sign a secret Reinsurance Treaty in 1887 which committed Germany to neutrality if Austria were to attack Russia, and Russia to neutrality if France were to attack Germany. Unsurprisingly both signatories were keen to keep the existence of this treaty from the Austrians. Both of these treaties were to play a role in bringing about the conditions for war.

Bismarck's European policy received the acquiescence, albeit sometimes reluctant, of Kaisers Wilhelm I and Friedrich III, whose reign sadly was to last only 99 days. But the succession of Wilhelm II on the premature death of his father from throat cancer in 1888 signalled a departure from the Chancellor's carefully crafted policies. The changed situation was ushered in by the dismissal from office of Bismarck himself by the new Emperor in 1890.

It was to be the world's misfortune that its leading military power, and one of increasing economic strength, should find itself under the rule of an individual like Kaiser Wilhelm II. His power was virtually untrammelled despite the theoretical constraints of a parliamentary system. Once the restraining hand of Bismarck had been removed, and he had surrounded himself with sycophantic politicians and officers, he chose to exercise it largely in the area of foreign policy.

The complexities of Wilhelm's character began their build-up at birth. He was born with a withered left arm which seems to have led his mother, Princess Victoria, a daughter of Prince Albert and Queen Victoria, to withhold the normal maternal love and affection he might have expected. In return he grew up to hate his mother and the country of her birth, Britain. But his anglophobia was as convoluted as his character as a whole. He was devoted to his maternal grandmother, Queen Victoria, and inordinately proud of his appointment as a Royal Navy Admiral of the Fleet. But he strongly resented what he took to be, not without some reason, the patronising manner of his uncle, Edward VII, who, even when only Prince of Wales, disdained to accord his nephew the esteem he thought his due as the absolute ruler of a powerful state. The Kaiser saw his uncle as the architect of the encirclement of Germany by potentially hostile states. He was blind to the fact that it was mainly his own actions, which often seemed designed to give the impression of a Germany only too ready to resort to war, that had the effect of bringing together traditional enemies such as France and Britain and countries with diametrically opposed systems of government such as autocratic Russia and democratic Britain.

As Britain was forced by the realities of developments in Europe to abandon the 'splendid isolation' which had served it so well for many years, it was able to sign an 'Entente Cordiale' with France in 1904 only 6 years after the two countries had come close to war over a colonial dispute involving possession of the settlement of Fashoda on the upper White Nile in Sudan. The Entente was in fact drawn up principally to settle outstanding colonial differences, but it is difficult to believe that it would have been signed other than as a means of clearing up these differences in the light of the growing belligerence of Germany.

For Britain there were two major issues involving Germany which made a rapprochement with France not only prudent but desirable. The first, and the lesser of the two, had arisen out of the ill-starred Jameson Raid in 1895. This had been a half-baked attempt, in which Cecil Rhodes among others had been involved, to engineer a coup d'état in the Transvaal in Southern Africa. Following its failure the Kaiser sent a telegram to the Transvaal's President Kruger congratulating him on his escape. However shady and dubious the whole enterprise had been, and it was both, the Kaiser's intervention produced a storm of self-righteous indignation from the British government and public at his interference in a British sphere of influence. Even the Fleet was mobilised before tempers cooled and the incident faded from the headlines. But it had confirmed suspicions that the Kaiser was no friend of Britain.

Much more significant however as a source of friction with Britain were the naval ambitions of the Kaiser. These were to lead to a naval arms race with Britain which will be dealt with in detail in the next appendix. Suffice it to say at this stage that the undoubted threat to Royal Navy supremacy was to be a major cause of Britain's abandonment of its 'splendid isolation' in favour of ties with France and Russia.

The transformation of British foreign policy was justified by the increasingly aberrant behaviour of the Kaiser on the world stage in the early years of the new century. There had been warning signs. After an auspicious start in 1890 in which the British government readily assented to Wilhelm's wish to exchange

British Heligoland for German Zanzibar, future events involving Wilhelm were almost invariably to lead to a ratcheting up of tension and a fraying of nerves. The first instance of this was the notorious Kruger telegram, already described. It marked the end of an era in which Britain and Germany had been generally comfortably at ease with each other (even if the Germans were never as well-disposed towards them as the British complacently assumed). It was replaced with a nascent antagonism on the British side which was to grow with each incident.

By the time of the second critical episode to be intensified into a crisis by the Kaiser's intrusion, the Morocco Crisis of 1905, there had been a seismic shift in the political geography of Europe with the signature of the Anglo-French Convention, more popularly known as the Entente Cordiale, on 7 April 1904. Not even the signatories, still less Germany, realised at the time what momentous and mould-breaking changes would follow from it. It was to prove to be a second major example of Germany shooting itself in the foot diplomatically with consequences even more serious than the first, the unilateral decision not to renew the German-Russian Reinsurance Treaty in 1890, immediately following the dismissal of its architect, Bismarck.

The German decision appears to have stemmed from a fear that it could only be a matter of time before the Austrians learned of the treaty's existence with resultant damage to Austro-German relations. Be that as it may, the mortified Russians immediately sought consolation in the arms of France. The Military Convention, signed in 1894, committed both these countries to come to the aid of the other in the event of an attack by Germany. So, through their own actions, the Germans had brought a step closer what they feared most – encirclement by potential enemies. It was further failures in German diplomacy which had led to France and Britain coming together to sign the Entente,

As the end of the nineteenth century approached it was becoming increasingly apparent to the British government of Lord Salisbury that the 'splendid isolation' which had for so long formed the basis of British foreign policy was rapidly losing its practicality. Added impetus was given to this realisation by the Boer War and the almost universal foreign support and sympathy it evoked for the Boer republics. Britain discovered to her consternation that she had no friends in the world beyond her Empire – just rivals and potential enemies.

Even though he held the scarcely relevant Cabinet post of Colonial Secretary it was the dynamic Joseph Chamberlain who took the initiative in advocating an alliance with a European power, specifically Germany. His choice of Germany was based on the appeal of shared blood and the assumption that an alliance with either of the other two main candidates, France and Russia, was inconceivable. Such an alliance would however ride roughshod over another basic tenet of British foreign policy, the desirability of maintaining the balance of power in Europe by the formation if necessary of close relations with the second strongest power against the strongest. This would clearly not be the case in an alliance with Germany. When the Germans received Chamberlain's overtures they took the view that Britain had nowhere else to go; the longer they kept her waiting, the better the bargain they would ultimately secure. The Germans would persist in this assessment of Britain's options right up to the signature of the Entente Cordiale. They failed to see that Chamberlain's advocacy of a German alliance had not persuaded all his Cabinet colleagues. Nor had the case for it been helped by the changing British perceptions of Germany induced by the Kruger telegram and the growing threat of its naval challenge.

With the Germans playing hard to get and in any case looking increasingly undesirable as a partner, the scarcely conceivable possibility of an accommodation with France began to be considered seriously by men of influence on both sides of the Channel, including Chamberlain, by now thoroughly disillusioned with his erstwhile favourites. The most significant roles in bringing it about were however to be played by Foreign Minister Théophile Delcassé and President Emile Loubet on the French side, and Foreign Secretary Lord Lansdowne and King Edward VII on the British.

Despite the ministerial musical chairs which were a characteristic of French governments of the Third Republic, Théophilé Delcassé enjoyed a long unbroken run (1898-1905) as Foreign Minister. From its outset he recognised that Germany was the main threat to France and harboured the hope that he could bring about an alliance with Britain. In pursuit of this he was prepared to swallow the humiliation of Fashoda and play down French delight at British ineptitude in the Boer War, not popular attitudes to espouse in anglophobe France. He was able to override opponents to his hope of Anglo-French rapprochement through the steadfast support of French President (1899-1906) Emile Loubet, and push it towards fruition through the masterful diplomacy of the French Ambassador in London, Paul Cambon.[4]

Through the inevitable ups and downs inherent in international relations, Delcassé never deviated from his ultimate aim. He took encouragement from the British government's decision in early 1901 not to pursue the possibility of an alliance with Germany. The inferences to be drawn from Britain's signature of an alliance with Japan the following year were more ambivalent. It was intended to curb Russian expansionist ambitions in the Far East but might have conceivably opened the way to conflict between France, as an ally of Russia, and Britain, as an ally of Japan. But Delcassé chose to take comfort from the fact that the alliance was concrete proof that Britain had at long last abandoned splendid isolation.

The Anglo-Japanese Alliance was the first significant contribution to his country's foreign policy of the new British Foreign Secretary, the Marquess of Lansdowne, who succeeded Lord Salisbury at the Foreign Office in 1900. In the early months of his tenure the new incumbent had to play second fiddle to Joseph Chamberlain, still meddling in British foreign policy from the Colonial Office. Delcassé's hope that Lord Lansdowne's possession of a French mother would predispose him in favour of a French alliance could only be put to the test once the Foreign Secretary had emerged from the shadow of the Colonial Secretary, or if the latter were to change his stance to one in favour of an Anglo-French Entente. This in fact was what happened. Chamberlain made it clear in late 1902 that he now favoured coming to an understanding with France.

What the nascent sentiment in favour of an Anglo-French rapprochement could now benefit from was the impulsion that could be supplied by a pivotal figure. This would be provided by none other than King Edward VII. Edward is popularly and exaggeratedly credited with being the architect and prime mover of the Entente Cordiale. What he in fact contributed was the bringing about of an atmosphere of mutual diminution of mistrust which would enable the politicians to sign the Entente without bringing the opprobrium of their respective peoples down upon their heads. Edward was well placed to play such a role, but it would not be easy to bring off. In French eyes, he had been transformed from the popular playboy Prince who had somehow personified the *Belle Epoque* into the sovereign and personification of a nation which, at the best of times, the French loved to hate; and these were not the best of times. But in early 1903, getting well ahead of his government, Edward proposed to President Loubet that he should be invited to visit Paris and that the visit should be attended with as much pomp and public exposure as possible.

President Loubet responded enthusiastically and on 1 May greeted his guest at the start of a hectic four day visit during which Edward did not put a foot wrong. By the time of his departure Parisian sentiment had been transformed from sullenness or vocal hostility to his presence to something approaching enthusiasm. The way was now clear for the politicians to capitalize on the opening fashioned by the King. It was to take nearly a year of detailed talks which focused almost entirely on colonial disputes and spheres of influence before agreement was reached and the two could sign the Entente, more formally known as the Anglo-French Convention, on 7 April 1904. Ratification followed without undue delay.

The main losers in this new development, Germany, reacted with remarkable complacency, appearing to believe that it was inconceivable that such a rapprochement could last and that it would disintegrate at the first sign of pressure. They were more than willing to be the appliers of the pressure required and an opportunity appeared to present itself in the Morocco Crisis of 1905.

France had long harboured ambitions to incorporate the Sultanate of Morocco into a North African empire already consisting of Algeria and Tunisia. It had been inhibited from doing so by Britain's dominant economic and political role in the Sultanate and the Treaty of Madrid of 1880 under which the five signatories, France, Britain, Spain, Germany and Italy, undertook to consult the other signatories before making any move which would affect Moroccan political or economic independence. In 1904 two developments led France to believe that the opportunity existed to fulfil its ambition of taking control of the Sultanate. The first was the signature of the Entente Cordiale by which Britain conceded that Morocco should be in the French sphere of influence, in return for France conceding similar status to the British in Egypt. The second was the increasing chaos into which Morocco seemed to be descending, as exemplified by a recent kidnapping and holding to ransom of one British and one American national by a rebellious local chieftain.

Using the pretext of the need for Morocco to be pacified France presented a series of unacceptable demands to the Sultan who, aware that Britain had distanced herself from the affairs of the Sultanate, appealed to Germany to intervene. The Germans, only a few months previously, had expressed indifference to the fate of Morocco, but having belatedly woken up to the possible adverse implications for them of the Entente Cordiale, now saw in France's failure to observe the stipulations of the Treaty of Madrid the opportunity to humiliate that country and probably do irreparable harm to the burgeoning Anglo-French rapprochement.

In taking this approach the Germans were to overplay their hand. The German Chancellor, Bernhard von Bülow, planned to make it clear to the French that their behaviour in not consulting Germany as required under the terms of the Treaty of Madrid was provocative, and that Germany had political and economic interests in the Sultanate which were at variance with French ambitions there. The German Chancellor did not hesitate to reinforce his démarches with some sabre rattling at a time when France was ill-prepared for war and its main partner, Russia, was suffering military and naval humiliation in its war with Japan.

Had it been left there the French might well have been forced to abandon their ambitions in Morocco and the Germans would have emerged from the crisis with credit. But von Bülow chose to exploit the crisis further by directly involving the Kaiser. To be fair to the Kaiser, after early enthusiasm he began to have considerable reservations about the role assigned to him by his Chancellor, not only on grounds of its likely political effectiveness, but also over a natural concern for his personal safety. For von Bülow wanted Wilhelm to pay a triumphant visit to Tangier, not a place renowned for a deep attachment to law and order. When the visit was made it was brief, largely devoid of content, and sometimes teetered on the edge of farce. But the fact that it had taken place reinforced French government concerns that they had overstepped the mark in Morocco. The Germans maintained the diplomatic pressure on them. It paid off with the enforced resignation of their arch-enemy, Théophilé Delcassé, and the convening of an international conference to consider the Moroccan problem. But their crude attempts to humiliate the French further finally brought about a stiffening of French resolve.

The British government had from the outset of the crisis concluded that Germany's principal aim in all that it did was to undermine the Anglo-French alliance. They had seen nothing wrong with French actions in Morocco as they were within the terms of the Entente Cordiale. For his part, King Edward had found the involvement of his nephew at Tangier 'mischievous and uncalled-for'. Although, to their great regret, they were unable to prevent the resignation of Delcassé, the British government did offer the French their full diplomatic backing at the Morocco Conference. In the face of this the Germans could draw little comfort from the meagre concessions they were able to wring from the French. In exchange for these they were reluctantly to accept that the Anglo-French alliance had not only not been undermined; it had been greatly strengthened. A further consequence of the Morocco crisis was that it was to leave a growing fear that Germany was becoming unpredictably aggressive.

The advent of a Liberal government in 1905 led to a smooth transition from the Conservatives and Unionists as far as British foreign policy was concerned. The new Foreign Secretary, Sir Edward Grey, had fully supported his predecessor's negotiation and signature of the Entente Cordiale and had deplored the German attempts to derail it on the pretext of Morocco. As Foreign Secretary, Grey enjoyed a freedom of action which must be the envy of more recent holders of that office, used to having to cope with interventionist Prime Ministers. Grey recognised earlier than most that the new circumstances brought about by the

Entente Cordiale might put Britain in a quandary if Germany were to attack France. With the growing likelihood of such an event, the French were keen to conclude a defensive alliance. In response to French diplomatic pressure the new War Minister, Richard Haldane, and Grey agreed that bilateral military staff talks could be conducted on the strict understanding that they did not constitute a guarantee of a British declaration of war in support of France in the event of a German attack. The staff talks, and where they almost ineluctably led, will be dealt with in the next appendix.

A significant aim of the new government's foreign policy was to conclude an agreement with the Russians on broadly similar lines to the Entente Cordiale. Such a transformation of the bilateral relationship could only be born out of a perceived need strong enough to overcome the historic antipathy the two countries had for each other. In Britain's case the need was to protect its Indian empire from Russian incursion and to curtail German influence with Russia. In Russia's case the need was for a period of stability following the disastrous war with Japan and the Revolution of 1905. As long as an entente could be concluded with Britain without giving offence to Germany they were keen to press on. Once again failing to pick up on the long term implications for them, the Germans gave the Russian government a green light.

The Anglo-Russian Entente which was duly signed on 31 August 1907 focused. like its Anglo-Frrench predecessor, on the settlement of colonial issues. There were no clauses relating to military or defence matters. The Russian government had at all stages of the negotiations kept the Germans informed. They looked at its terms, and in another failure of their diplomacy, concluded that there was nothing in it inimical to their interests. But the mere conclusion of an Anglo-Russian entente ran counter to a long-held principle of German policy; that Anglo-Russian friendship should be actively discouraged. Even the Kaiser, not always the most percipient analyst of the nuances of foreign policy, concluded that the Entente was, when taken all round, aimed at Germany.

The Russian Foreign Minister who had negotiated the Entente, Alexander Isvolsky, nearly brought about its early demise when he intrigued with his Austrian opposite number to secure the right of passage through the Dardanelles for Russian warships. A démarche seeking this would be synchronised with an Austrian announcement of their annexation of Bosnia and Herzegovina, still nominally under Turkish sovereignty. The two Foreign Ministers reckoned that the support each would give to the other's move would ensure the resigned consent of the other Powers. In the event the Austrian Minister acted unilaterally and, with reluctant German support, successfully. Isvolsky's subsequent attempts to achieve his Dardanelles ambition met with hostility from the other Powers, including Britain, for the manner in which he had sought to realize his aim. An enduring consequence of this experience was a Russian determination that never again would they emerge humiliated from a Balkan crisis. In 1914 this resolution would be put to the test.

The political leverage that the German Naval Programme might give them was shown in the talks that went on from 1909 to 1911 between Britain and Germany about the possibility of a naval agreement that would, through an agreed mechanism, limit the size of both fleets. The German side thought that in exchange for such an agreement they might secure a guarantee of British neutrality in any future German conflict with France and Russia. They would require the neutrality commitment to be firmly nailed down before the naval agreement was signed and sealed. The British side could see the obvious objections to this. They would in effect be giving Germany a free hand in Europe which could well result in German hegemony on the Continent and leave them free, subsequently, to turn their probably less than benevolent attentions to Britain. The talks nevertheless dragged on until a further Moroccan crisis was precipitated by Germany.

Since the first Moroccan crisis the French had continued to seek ways of extending their influence in the Sultanate with a view to its ultimate annexation. Britain had no objections. The Germans might have been content if the French had fulfilled their undertakings to protect German commercial interests in the Sultanate. They had not, at least in the eyes of some German businesses trying to operate in Morocco. The French had informed the Germans that they were sending a military column from Casablanca to the capital, Fez, to protect European lives in the latest eruption of unrest, verging on civil war, that was convulsing the country. The Germans declined to accept there was any danger to Europeans and warned the French that complications would arise from their move. These complications proved to be a decision to send a German gunboat to the southern Moroccan port of Agadir, ostensibly to rescue German citizens in danger in the south of the country. A problem with this scenario was that no such Germans existed. A German businessman was ordered to make his way from 75 miles away to Agadir to become 'the endangered German'.

The German gunboat *Panther* duly arrived and dropped anchor at Agadir on 1 July 1911 and was followed 3 days later by the light cruiser *Berlin*. The German businessman was taken under the protection of the Imperial German Navy. If Germany had been able to confine the subsequent diplomatic manoeuvrings to bilateral exchanges with France, they might well have been able to achieve what apparently they were looking for, possession of the southern half of Morocco. But the Germans had reckoned without the new imperative in British foreign policy, the maintenance of close relations with France and a concern to see that that country was not bullied or humiliated by Germany as a stepping stone to that country's hegemony in Europe. The Germans learned of the depth of British concerns through a speech delivered by David Lloyd George on 21 July. The then Chancellor of the Exchequer was known to be a pacifist and a Germanophile in favour of an Anglo-German understanding. But he had become concerned, even angry, at Germany's discourtesy in not answering Foreign Secretary Grey's repeated requests for clarification of their intentions over Morocco. Without mentioning Germany by name Lloyd George's speech made it quite clear that Britain would fight in defence of its vital national interests and its prestige.

Germany's initial reaction was one of outrage which soon gave way to a realisation that if the Moroccan dispute came to war with France, Britain would be at France's side. Morocco was not worth such an outcome. The Germans therefore gave an undertaking to Britain that the Franco-German talks would have no outcome inimical to British interests. Britain then indicated to France that a conciliatory attitude would be helpful but that if she found German demands excessive, Britain would support her. The difficulty for both France and Germany, was the belligerence of public opinion in both countries which made reaching a settlement, still less making concessions, very difficult. The negotiations in Berlin lasted over three months, often coming to the brink of breakdown. But on 4 November an agreement was signed under which Germany recognised a French protectorate over Morocco in return for a pledge to safeguard the principle of the Open Door in the Sultanate and the cession of 100,000 square miles of territory in the French Congo to the German colony of the Cameroons. There was no question that the French had emerged triumphant. The German press and public were unforgiving. A popular sentiment in Germany was that if the country's foreign policy aims could not be secured by diplomacy then it should fall back on the tried and trusted one of military might.

The last strenuous attempt to reach an Anglo-German understanding, based on a reduction of the planned German naval shipbuilding programme in exchange for some form of British neutrality in the event of Germany becoming involved in hostilities, dragged on through the first half of 1912. The secret negotiations were started when the British War Minister, Richard Haldane[5], visited Berlin for discussions which involved the Kaiser, the German Chancellor and Admiral von Tirpitz, the Navy Minister. Haldane appeared to have secured a reduction in the rate of German construction of new capital ships, but when the full draft German naval law was read in London, it became clear that the Germans also had grandiose plans for the construction of destroyers and submarines and for a large increase in naval personnel. British insistence on these programmes being cut back might have been very reluctantly agreed by the Germans had the British been prepared to offer in return their unconditional neutrality should Germany become embroiled in war. But such an offer would clearly have been incompatible with Britain's commitments to France and Russia. All that could be offered to Germany was an undertaking to stand aside should Germany be attacked. This was insufficient for the German Chancellor to have any hope of forcing through changes in the draft German Naval Law. The bilateral talks were abandoned.

Considering that it was to be a Balkan episode that precipitated the First World War it is perhaps surprising that the three Balkan wars which took place between October 1912 and August 1913 did not become *casus belli* for any of the great European powers. A spirit of conciliation, born of a determination not to see little wars spread, seemed to permeate their negotiating stances at the Conference of London called and chaired by Foreign Secretary Grey. The Conference and the wars ended with the signature of the Treaty of Bucharest in August 1913.

The details of the crisis that erupted in the summer of 1914 and bought about the First World War are sufficiently well known to require only a brief description here. In annexing Bosnia and Herzegovina in 1908, the Austro-Hungarian Empire had increased the size of its Slav population to three-fifths of the Empire's total. The more nationalistically inclined of these hankered for a nation of free Slavs centred on the Kingdom of Serbia. The Austrian attitude towards Serbia had gradually hardened until, by 1914, it was intent on crushing that country when the opportunity arose. It received full support for this attitude from some intemperate remarks by the Kaiser and the German Chief of the General Staff, von Moltke, even though it was clear that any such move would involve a strong response from Serbia's ally Russia, which was not in the mood to countenance a further international humiliation.

Ironically the only senior member of the Austrian hierarchy in favour of conciliating the Serbs was the heir to the Austro-Hungarian throne, Archduke Franz-Ferdinand. This would not save him and his wife from assassination by a Bosnian nationalist on that fateful day of 28 June 1914 in Sarajevo, the Bosnian capital. As soon as the funeral obsequies were over the Austrian Emperor sought the Kaiser's confirmation that Germany would fully support any measures taken against Serbia even if these would provoke a Russian response. The fact that there was no evidence of Serbian government involvement in the assassination did not worry the Austrians, who had no doubt that Serbian support for pan-Slavism was sufficient guilt of itself. After very little reflection the Kaiser offered his full support, a decision which was unhesitatingly endorsed by his Chancellor and senior military and naval advisers.

The Austrian ultimatum was delivered in Belgrade at 17h00 on 23 July. It was deliberately couched in terms which were assumed to be unacceptable to the Serbs. A reply was demanded within 48 hours. Its delivery ended nearly three weeks of prevarication and bland reassurances to the Entente Powers by both Vienna and Berlin about its likely contents. They came as a bombshell to the appalled Serbs. But when they replied they accepted 9 of the 10 demands in the Austrian ultimatum even though every one of them constituted an infringement of Serbian sovereignty. At this stage neither Serbia nor any of the European powers not directly involved, such as Britain and France, had realized that Austria and Germany were intent on war. When the Austrians received the Serb reply it was deemed unacceptable and they broke off diplomatic relations. The Entente powers' attempts at mediation went into overdrive to try to prevent the next step, an Austrian declaration of war. But to no avail; this came on 28 July. On the following day Austrian artillery began bombarding Belgrade and Czar Nicholas of Russia ordered partial mobilisation.

The next couple of days saw desperate attempts by the German Chancellor to avoid the descent into general European war. Shaken by a telegram from the German Ambassador in London warning that British neutrality in the event of German involvement was very unlikely, the Chancellor strove to pull back. But it was all too late; the generals were now in the driving seat. On 30 July Austria ordered total mobilisation. The Russians responded immediately with full mobilisation. As soon as the news reached Berlin the Germans decreed a state of *Kriegsgefahr* (Danger of War) and sent an ultimatum to Russia demanding their demobilisation. Although the French had not at any stage been involved and were certainly not seeking war, they were also the recipients of a German ultimatum demanding to know whether they would remain neutral in the event of a Russo-German war. If the answer was yes they would be required to hand over the fortresses of Toul and Verdun as guarantees of their neutrality.

On 1 August Germany mobilised and declared war on Russia, which had disdained to reply to the ultimatum to demobilise. On the same day the French rejected the German ultimatum and decreed mobilisation. Two days later, the Germans declared war. Ironically it was only the German declaration of war on Russia that forced Austria to follow suit. Until that point Austro-

Russian negotiations to resolve the Serbian problem had been proceeding quite promisingly.

By the end of 3 August the only one of the great European powers not fully mobilised and at war was Britain. Since the situation had reached critical level when the text of the Austrian note was circulated, Britain had been working hard to defuse the situation on the basis of an assumption that Germany was equally keen to achieve a peaceful outcome. The scales slowly fell from British eyes when the emollient Serbian reply to the Austrian note was received. It made no difference to the Austrians, and the Germans clearly approved of their intransigence. While the British continued to make strenuous efforts to resolve the situation they, at the same time, were confronted with the problem of what they should do in the event of a European war. While there was little doubt among the senior Government ministers who had been involved in foreign affairs that Britain had moral, if not treaty, obligations to France, and France was clearly an innocent party in the present crisis, these sentiments were not shared by a significant number of members of the Liberal Cabinet and party as well as large segments of public opinion. It is arguable that, if it had not been for the German violation of Belgian neutrality and the Belgian decision to fight rather than acquiesce, the British government would not have been able to carry its own party and the country with it into a war simply on the basis of a moral obligation to France.

The Germans were to solve the British government's problem. On 2 August, news of a German ultimatum to Belgium was received in London. This was followed during the night of 2nd/3rd by an appeal from King Albert of the Belgians asking Britain to redeem her treaty obligation to defend Belgian neutrality. With Parliament and public opinion now rallied to Belgium's and the Government's side, Britain sent Germany an ultimatum to quit Belgium. When Germany failed to respond or acquiesce Britain and Germany found themselves at war with effect from midnight on 4 August. Within days the British Expeditionary Force was *en route* to Mons.

Appendix B

The Military Build-up to the War

The nineteenth century had been a period in world history in which *Pax Britannica* had been imposed on the seas and littorals of the world by a largely beneficent, and totally dominant, Royal Navy. Germany itself had benefited, with its merchant ships and colonies able to call on the protection of Royal Navy vessels in time of need. But, probably inevitably, the increasing economic and military strength of unified Germany would call into question this dependence for maritime protection on a foreign navy even though it might be difficult to envisage circumstances in which it would be withheld, still less wielded hostilely. The issue was not to remain on the back burner for long once Wilhelm II had succeeded to the throne as Kaiser.

Should a decision be taken in favour of creating a significant German navy, its planned configuration would play a large part in determining how it would be perceived outside Germany, especially in Britain. Given the Kaiser's determination to strut the world stage, his passion for naval matters and his grudging admiration of the Royal Navy it was unlikely that a decision on a future German navy would come down in favour of maintaining the *status quo*. So it proved. Wilhelm initially favoured the construction of a navy based on cruisers, which would have been a fit with his country's colonial ambitions. But when a strategy for the navy was finally agreed it was to build a High Seas fleet of capital ships strong enough to present a serious challenge to British maritime supremacy.

The Kaiser was nine years into his reign before the decisions were finally taken that committed the navy to its new strategy. Wilhelm himself had gradually been won over to the concept of a High Seas battle fleet by the persuasive advocacy of Alfred Tirpitz. Grand Admiral Alfred von Tirpitz, as he was later to become, had first gained the Kaiser's ear as a relatively junior navy captain. In 1897 he was appointed Minister for the Navy and soon afterwards presented his proposals for a total of 19 battleships to be in service by 1905. Such proposals could only gain credence on the basis of Britain being the enemy; no such naval strength would be necessary to confront and defeat Russia or France. In order to get his proposals accepted, therefore, Tirpitz had to paint Britain as the future enemy. A self-fulfilling exercise, as it was tragically to prove.[1]

Tirpitz shared his master's ambivalent attitudes to England. He was a fluent English speaker and had his daughters educated at Cheltenham Ladies' College. He was a great admirer of the Royal Navy. Yet he is perceived to have shared Wilhelm's anglophobia. In his case it probably stemmed from his suffering from, and resentment of, the patronising attitudes which appear to have been one of the less attractive character traits of the nineteenth-century Englishman.[2]

Only a year after Tirpitz's initial naval construction programme had been approved it was replaced by one twice as large. He was able to secure approval for this on the crest of a national wave of hostility to Britain induced by sympathy with the Boers, now at war with the British Empire, and some high handedness by

Royal Navy vessels seeking to blockade the Boer Republics. Three supplementary Naval Laws were to follow in 1906, 1908 and 1912, their passages through the Reichstag having been eased by international crises, such as the Moroccan episodes, from which Germany had emerged with a sense of national humiliation. When the construction programmes approved under these laws were completed, which would not be until 1920, Germany would have a fleet of 41 capital ships.[3]

Since the Reichstag debate which ended in the passing of the Second Naval Law in 1900, Britain could have been under no illusion that Tirpitz had assigned them the role of Germany's future enemy. But it was not until the signing of the Entente Cordiale that Britain began to see Germany in a similar light. Until that point Britain's naval construction programmes were maintained at more than adequately high rates without reference to those of Germany. The revolution in naval capital ship design ushered in by HMS *Dreadnought*, which was commissioned in December 1906, left the German construction programme in disarray for a complete year, the time it took to absorb the lessons of *Dreadnought* and design similar vessels. From the British point of view, the problem was that *Dreadnought* made all previous warships obsolete. It would be difficult to recreate the preponderance that the Royal Navy had enjoyed in the pre-Dreadnought era now that all naval powers would be starting virtually simultaneously from scratch. Specifically a post-Dreadnought Anglo-German naval race would begin on more or less equal terms.

In the four years 1905-08 the British government had been content to authorise a Dreadnought building programme of four ships a year. But in response to the pressures that Liberal governments are always under, to direct their money to social programmes and not armaments, four of the authorised vessels had been cancelled. In 1909 this rather laid-back approach to the defence of the Realm was called into question with a vengeance. The German Naval Law of 1908 had made even clearer the extent of German ambitions to rival the Royal Navy in northern European waters. The Admiralty also suspected that the Naval Law did not truly reflect the size and speed of the German construction programme. They feared that keels were being laid down sooner than programmed and that essential equipment, such as guns and gun mountings, was being manufactured and stockpiled ready for instant installation in launched vessels. A further cause for concern was that Italy and Austria-Hungary, both members with Germany of the Triple Alliance, were also building Dreadnoughts.

When all this information had been digested, the response of the Admiralty was to confront a shocked Government in December 1908 with a request that the laying down of six Dreadnoughts in each of the years 1909, 1910 and 1911 should be approved. A month later the Admiralty increased its request for 1909 to eight vessels. With threats of resignation from senior Cabinet colleagues and admirals who were either strongly in favour or equally strongly opposed to granting the Admiralty's request, Prime Minister Asquith came up with a generally acceptable compromise that four keels should be laid in 1909. If by 1910 the situation could be shown to be as serious as the Admiralty believed four more keels would be laid down in addition to that year's planned four keels. But a groundswell of public opinion orchestrated by the Conservative Opposition built up which was strongly supportive of the Admiralty's case. The slogan 'We want eight and we won't wait!' was frequently heard. But the Prime Minister stood his ground and a Conservative censure motion was defeated. This did not however silence the furore in the country. In the end the growing evidence that Germany was indeed accelerating its construction programme, and the Italian and Austro-Hungarian Dreadnought programmes, forced the government to authorise the laying down of the four extra keels in 1910. In addition a further two, paid for by the governments of Australia and New Zealand, were laid down in the same year.[4]

After the failure of the Anglo-German naval talks in 1912 to come up with an agreed formula to limit the construction programmes of both countries, the war began with Britain's fleet consisting of 42 post-Dreadnought capital ships and Germany's 21, with four more completed in the early months of the war. The Royal Navy had succeeded in maintaining an adequate superiority over the German High Seas Fleet.

The main reason for Britain's entry into the war on the side of France was Germany's violation of Belgian neutrality in complete disregard of its obligations under the Treaty of London of 1839. That Germany acted in a manner completely at odds with its own self-interest – it hardly needed a belligerent British Empire to add to its list of enemies – may be ascribed to the imperatives of the Schlieffen Plan.

Field Marshal Graf Alfred von Schlieffen became the German Army Chief of Staff in 1891 and remained in that position until his retirement in 1906. The Franco-Russian Military Convention, signed on 18 August 1892, confirmed von Schlieffen's belief that the next war would see Germany assailed from both sides. His period in office would be largely spent in devising and then refining a strategy to deal with this eventuality. The Schlieffen Plan, as handed over to his successor, General von Moltke, determined that the greater and most immediate of the two threats would come from France. The vast bulk of the German Army should therefore be deployed against the French, and whatever British forces may have joined them, in order to achieve a victory within 6 weeks, leaving only a small screen on the Eastern Front. With victory in the west secured the main German armies could be transferred to the Eastern Front to deal with Russian offensives, which were unlikely to be mounted before the German redeployments were completed because of the slowness of Russian mobilisation. Von Schlieffen calculated that 48 and a half infantry corps and 11 cavalry divisions would assault the French and only ten divisions be made available to cover the Eastern Front. These latter would be drawn proportionately from the corps attacking France should Russia have declared war.

On the detail of the assault on France, von Schlieffen decreed that seven armies would be deployed from the First in the north to the Seventh in the south. The vast bulk of the troops would be allocated to the armies situated north of Metz-Thionville. While the northern armies would make a gigantic left wheel through Belgium and south Holland and into France, which would take the strongest First Army to the west and south of Paris, those south of Metz, where French assaults could be confidently expected, would stand on the defensive. If they were forced to give ground so much the better as the French would fall further into the trap which would be completed by the arrival of the northern armies by now moving eastwards towards Alsace-Lorraine.

Von Schlieffen planned to overcome the tricky problem of the violation of Belgian and Dutch neutrality by massing the right of the German Armies on the Belgian and Dutch borders and leaving no doubt as to their intentions. He assumed that the French would take countermeasures which would entail their being the first to violate Belgian neutrality. He did not in any case believe that the Belgians would offer any more than token objections to the Germans crossing their territory and that the then King, Leopold II, would acquiesce in return for money. He thought too that the Dutch, at that time going through a bout of anti-Britishness in sympathy with the Boer Republics, would not object, if Britain had allied herself with France.

Von Schlieffen's constant themes, as he entrusted his Plan to his successor, were, 'Keep the right wing strong' and 'Let the last man on the right brush the Channel with his sleeve'.

In the period between his inheriting the Plan and the outbreak of the war, the new Chief of the General Staff, General Helmuth von Moltke, deemed it necessary to tinker with it in the light of changing circumstances and broader political considerations. An important change was the decision not to violate Dutch neutrality; on military grounds out of a wish not to add another country to the list of enemies; on political grounds out of a wish to keep the Dutch ports available as points of entry for supplies from the outside world. There was however a tactical military price to pay for this decision. Not being able to cross the Dutch province of Limburg, which bordered on Germany and Belgium, the German army would not be able to invade Belgium on the route passing north of the fortress city of Liège which would have enabled them to bypass it and take it from the rear. At the same time the rapid capture of Liège would become even more important to free up the route between Aachen and Limburg for the invaders.

Von Moltke also felt obliged to alter the planned troop dispositions. He transferred three corps from the army's right wing to the left. He calculated that once the French First and Second Armies had been dealt with in Alsace-Lorraine he could transfer the three corps back to the right wing. (This was to be frustrated by the Belgian destruction of the Meuse railway bridges and other demolitions. Von Moltke was also to weaken the right wing further, after battle was joined, when the Russians mobilised much quicker than expected and invaded East Prussia. Troops were transferred to the east to deal with this threat.)[5]

In the event no serious attempt was made to trick France into violating Belgian neutrality first. Knowing what was at stake, France had in any case given Britain a solemn undertaking that they would not do so, something which the Germans had failed to give.[6]

The tragedy of the Schlieffen Plan was that it was so predicated on defeating France first that once war was declared on Russia there was no alternative but to declare war on France. Even the Kaiser's belated pious hope that the war could be confined to Germany and Austria versus Russia and Serbia was of no avail once Germany and Russia were at war and the imperatives of Schlieffen took over. In any case the French would almost certainly have honoured their longstanding commitment to Russia by declaring war on Germany.

The French Army's plan of campaign in the event of war with Germany was enshrined in Plan XVII. The old saw that plans never last beyond first contact with the enemy was to prove to be all too true in the case of this plan. The development of the philosophy behind it can be traced back to the humiliation suffered by France at the hands of the Prussians in 1870-1. With the latter having taken possession of Alsace and much of Lorraine, France's first post-war reaction was to construct a fortress system along the new common boundary. This despite the fact that France's main military disasters during the war had come about by allowing their armies to be trapped in the fortresses of Sedan and Metz.

By around the turn of the century the new generation of senior French officers had tired of the defensive frame of mind exemplified by the reliance on fortress systems. The new attitude that was to emerge was given its philosophical underpinning by the French philosopher, Henri Bergson, who was born in 1859. His concept of *élan vital* (the all-conquering will) was seen in military terms as being the spirit of the offensive. This doctrine was given a great boost when General Ferdinand Foch was appointed Director of the *Ecole Supérieure de la Guerre*, the French equivalent of the Staff College at Camberley. Although Foch preached the doctrine of the offensive in such aphorisms as 'The will to conquer is the first condition of victory' he was not as singleminded or lacking in a grasp of reality as the interpretations put on his words by others would seem to indicate. One of these others was Colonel Louis Loyseau de Grandmaison, the Director of Military Operations on the French General Staff. In 1911 he delivered two lectures at the *Ecole Supérieure* in which he advocated *attaque à outrance* (attack to the limit). This doctrine of all-out attack was enthusiastically adopted by GQG and permeated Plan XVII which was finalised over the following two years. Foch's more realistic approach recognised that all-out attack had to take account of, and if necessary be modified by, the arrival of the machine gun and quick-firing field artillery, two potent weapons in the hands of a well-organised defence. But the Grandmaison doctrine carried all before it. Even suggestions that the army's battledress should be changed from its red pantaloons and képis to something less conspicuous were rejected on the grounds that, '*Le pantalon rouge c'est la France!*'[7]

The Plan XVII's commitment to attack meant that it mainly focused on the area in which the attacks would be mounted and the ways and means of carrying them out. Disdaining subtlety, the main attacks would be carried out by First and Second French Armies, on the right of the French line opposite Alsace-Lorraine. The other three French armies, strung out along the borders with Luxembourg and Belgium, would, assuming a German violation of the neutrality of those two countries, prepare to advance up to the River Meuse with a view to taking the offensive against a presumed weak German right wing. No mention was made of the BEF in Plan XVII. But if it arrived in France it would be deployed on the left of the French Fifth Army.

The almost criminal deficiency in Plan XVII was the sweeping assumptions it made about German intentions. It is difficult to believe that the French were unaware of the Schlieffen Plan and the strategy it advocated. Yet they managed to persuade themselves that the Germans would attack through Lorraine, only just encroaching on Belgian territory in the corner east of the Meuse. When they gave consideration to the possibility of a large German sweeping movement through Belgium they discounted it on the grounds that the Germans did not have sufficient first line troops to do this and operate effectively further south. The French calculations were based on an assumption that the Germans would not commit reserves as active troops, even though they must have known that the Germans were planning to do just that. Finally, the French persuaded themselves that even if the German right wing was sufficiently strong to pose a major threat, it would very rapidly have to be shorn of its strength which would be needed in Alsace-Lorraine to counter the French offensives. This farrago of wishful thinking was to govern French strategy for the first three weeks of the war. It was only reluctantly, almost disbelievingly, abandoned when the accumulating evidence of Germany's real strategy became too clear to be discounted. The revelation came too late to prevent the BEF, not backward themselves in discounting evidence that did not fit with GQG preconceptions, arriving at Mons with little inkling of what they were about to face.[8]

Britain's involvement in what were essentially French plans for the conduct of military operations against Germany had begun soon after the signature of the Entente Cordiale. The Entente may have been a purely colonial agreement; the British government were indeed at pains to emphasise there was no suggestion that it was, or would become, a military alliance when they sought its ratification. But the French would never be content to leave it there. In response to pressure from them during the latter stages of the Moroccan crisis of 1905, the new Foreign Secretary Sir Edward Grey and the War Minister, Richard Haldane, agreed that secret bilateral military staff talks could begin in January 1906. They would focus on plans to send 100,000 British soldiers to the Continent within two weeks of an outbreak of war with Germany. The talks began when the threat of imminent war was very real. They were to continue even when the threat receded. Although the new Prime Minister, Sir Henry Campbell-Bannerman, was told, and approved of the initiative of his two Ministers, the Cabinet was not to learn of the talks until six years later.

Given that Foreign Secretary Grey had no Parliamentary endorsement for the talks, he had to be sure that the French clearly understood that they implied no commitment on the part of Britain that it would ally itself with France in the event of hostilities with Germany. While the French paid lip-service to this understanding their intention was clearly to get Britain so closely interwoven into their war plans that a British decision not to declare war when the time came would reek of betrayal. The new Prime Minister, Herbert Asquith, was not quite clear to what extent the talks committed Britain to France and he was not happy at the drift towards commitment which seemed to be happening. Grey tried to reassure him while admitting that ministerial speeches and the talks themselves had raised French expectations. All that seems to have been done to counter any drift towards commitment was to reiterate at every opportunity that no such commitment existed.

In the early stages of the talks the British assumption was that they were aiming to land their troops at Belgian ports from where they would operate quite separately from the French. This notion was dropped, partly at the behest of the French but mainly because the Royal Navy made it quite clear that they could not guarantee the safe transportation and resupply of an expeditionary force if it were landed any further north than the Straits of Dover. Thereafter planning went ahead on the basis of using the French ports of Le Havre, Boulogne and Rouen.[9]

With international tensions having died down with the solution of the first Moroccan crisis, so did the tempo of the bilateral staff talks. It was to take the appointment of Brigadier General Henry Wilson to the War Office post of Director of Military Operations (DMO) and another international crisis to restore a sense of urgency to them. Prior to becoming DMO Wilson had spent the 4 years 1907–10 as Commandant of the Staff College at Camberley. In late 1909 he conceived the idea of calling on his French opposite number, the Director of the *Ecole Supérieure de la Guerre*, General Ferdinand Foch. The arrangements were quickly made through the British Military Attaché and General Wilson duly arrived at the *Ecole* on the morning of 2 December 1909. Having spent the morning with Wilson during which they attended several lectures, Foch bad Wilson a pleasant farewell on the assumption that the visit was over. Wilson quickly made it clear that he wished to return in the afternoon. In the evening Foch again made his farewells, only to discover that Wilson was planning to return the following day, which he duly did. During the course of that second day, what had been a professional relationship became a personal friendship, in which the two officers could relax and unburden themselves concerning their professional preoccupations. Wilson returned to Paris for a second visit to the *Ecole* in January 1910 and in June of the same year Foch paid an official visit to England as Wilson's guest. During this visit Wilson prophetically described Foch to those who were about to meet him as the French general who would 'command the allied armies when the big war comes on'.[10] It was probably during one of these early meetings of the two officers that, in reply to a question from Wilson asking what would be the smallest British military force that would be of any practical assistance to the French in the event of war, Foch replied, 'One single private soldier, and we would take good care that he was killed'.[11]

There was a limit to what Wilson, as Commandant of the Staff College, could do to help bring about a stronger British commitment to the French than that represented by the desultory staff talks. He would have more scope as Director of Military Operations, which he became on 1 August 1910. One of the first people to call on him at the War Office was the French Military Attaché in London, Major Huguet. When the latter bewailed the lack of progress in the staff talks he must have been reassured by Wilson's insistence that Anglo-French military cooperation was vital and all-important.[12]

Wilson was appalled at the state of the Army's plans to get an expeditionary force of six divisions over to the Continent. The men may have been earmarked and satisfactorily trained for their role, but the arrangements to get them into place on schedule with all their equipment were virtually non-existent. Wilson noted that there were no train arrangements in place to get the men to the embarkation ports, no staff in place at the ports to ensure problem-free embarkation, no medical arrangements, no arrangements for troopships and naval escorts and, perhaps most serious of all, no plans to procure and feed the many thousands of horses the expeditionary force would require.

It says much for Wilson's energy and drive that a meeting under his chairmanship only 8 months into his tenure of office was able to agree that planning would proceed on the basis of the six infantry divisions embarking four days after mobilisation, the cavalry seven days and the artillery nine days. By the time of this meeting the deficiencies he had identified on taking over were well on the way to being rectified if they had not been already. Less than 4 months later the Germans precipitated the Agadir crisis.

Within days Wilson was in Paris for discussions with the French Chief of Staff, General Dubail. On 20 July they jointly signed a memorandum which provided that, in the event of British intervention in hostilities, the British would ship 150,000 men and 67,000 horses to France between the 4th and 12th days of mobilisation. They would be transported by rail from their disembarkation ports to a concentration area near Maubeuge so as to be ready for action on the 13th day of mobilisation. The choice of Maubeuge envisaged that the BEF would in effect prolong the French line northwestwards and offer protection against its envelopment. The French were delighted at the Memorandum's implicit acceptance that the British had abandoned an independent role in favour of joint action with them. In signing it, Wilson had gone well beyond anything that had been agreed in London about the role of the BEF.[13] He was soon to have the opportunity to persuade the Committee of Imperial Defence (CID) to see things his way.

The CID meeting took place on 23 August with the Agadir crisis rumbling on. It was convened by Prime Minister Asquith to hear a presentation of the Army and Navy's war plans. Henry Wilson spoke for the Army. Using a large scale map of northwestern Europe he told his audience that the joint assessment of the British and French staffs was that the Germans could mobilise 110 divisions, more than three quarters of which would be hurled against France which would mobilise 85 divisions. The right wing of the German offensive would wheel through Belgium to bypass the French fortress system, but only four divisions would be committed west of the Meuse. As it was by no means certain that the Belgians would fight, it was essential that 6 British infantry and one cavalry divisions should be placed as soon as possible after the outbreak of war on the left of the French line. It was important that British mobilisation should take place on the same day as the French. Wilson revealed that the British and French had carefully worked out plans to carry the expeditionary force across the Channel and through France, even allowing for ten minute tea breaks for the troops. The War Office had already printed thousands of maps of Belgium and northern France. The only major fault in Wilson's presentation was in the calculation of probable German strength west of the Meuse. This indicates that French wishful-thinking was already well underway and had permeated Wilson's thinking, almost certainly against his better judgment.

Before sitting down Wilson sought an assurance from the Royal Navy that it could guarantee the transport of the expeditionary force across the Channel. The Navy's presentation was given by the First Sea Lord, Admiral Sir Arthur Wilson. The disadvantage of the Navy not having a General Staff soon became apparent; the presentation was a disaster. He described the Navy's role as one of blockade, to bring the German fleet to battle and defeat it, and to land an, of necessity, small army on Germany's Baltic coast in East Prussia. As for escorting troopships to France, the Navy was not prepared to offer any guarantees until the seas had been swept clear of enemy ships. It was clear to the listening members of the Committee that there had been little or no consultation between the Services and that of the two presentations they had heard, the army's was much the more impressive. No final decisions were taken, but only a few weeks later Winston Churchill was appointed First Lord of the Admiralty. He soon put in hand studies to determine how the Navy could transport an expeditionary force to France in safety and keep it supplied.[14]

Although there would be ups and down over the next two and a half years before war finally broke out, the form British military participation would take when it did was essentially that agreed between Generals Wilson and Dubail in July 1911 (except, of course, in the size of the BEF, which lost two of its infantry divisions). Wilson was to suffer immense frustration in the last few days of peace as the British government delayed its decision on a declaration of war. He believed that Germany's declaration of war on France was all the reason Britain needed to enter the fray. The violation of Belgium's neutrality was not a *sine qua non*. Wilson had virtually promised the French, on his own authority, that British mobilisation would be synchronised with theirs. The delay in declaring war prevented this. But in the end, no great harm was done, except to shredded nerves. Wilson's carefully crafted plans to get the BEF to its concentration area near Maubeuge worked without a hitch and made up any lost time there may have been.

Appendix C

Order of Battle

THE BRITISH EXPEDITIONARY FORCE
AUGUST 1914

Commander-in-Chief: Field-Marshal Sir J.D.P French, GCB, GCVO, KCMG
Chief of the General Staff: Lieutenant Genera Sir A.J. Murray, KCB, CVO, DSO
Major-General, General Staff: Major General H.H. Wilson, CB, DSO
GSOi (Intelligence): Colonel G.M.W. Macdonogh
Quartermaster-General: Major-General Sir W.R. Robertson, KCVO, CB, DSO

THE CAVALRY DIVISION
Major General E.H. Allenby, CB

1ST CAVALRY BRIGADE
Brigadier-General C J Briggs, CB
2nd Dragoon Guards (Queen's Bays)
5th (Princess Charlotte of Wales') Dragoon Guards
11th (Prince Albert's Own) Hussars

2ND CAVALRY BRIGADE
Brigadier General H. de B. de Lisle, CB, DSO
4th (Royal Irish) Dragoon Guards
9th (Queen's Royal) Lancers
18th (Queen Mary's Own) Hussars

3RD CAVALRY BRIGADE
Brigadier-General H. de la P. Gough, CB
4th (Queen's Own) Hussars
5th (Royal Irish) Lancers
16th (The Queen's) Lancers

4TH CAVALRY BRIGADE
Brigadier General Hon. C.E. Bingham, CVO, CB
Composite Regiment of Household Cavalry
6th Dragoon Guards (Carabiniers)
3rd (King's Own) Hussars

5TH CAVALRY BRIGADE
GOC: Brigadier General Sir P.W. Chetwode, Bart., DSO
2nd Dragoons (Royal Scots Greys)
12th Lancers
20th Hussars
'D', 'E', 'I', 'J', 'L' Batteries, RHA

I CORPS
GOC: Lieutenant General Sir D. Haig, KCB, KCIE, KCVO, ADC-Gen.
BGGS: Brigadier-General J.E. Gough, VC, CMG, ADC

1ST DIVISION
Major-General S.H. Lomax

2ND DIVISION
Major-General C.C. Monro, CB

1st (Guards) Brigade
Brigadier General F.l. Maxse, CVO, CB, DSO
1/Coldstream Guards
1/Scots Guards
1/Black Watch
2/Royal Munster Fusiliers

4th (Guards) Brigade
Brigadier-General R. Scott-Kerr, CB, MVO, DSO
2/Grenadier Guards
2/Coldstream Guards
3/Coldstream Guards
l/Irish Guards

I CORPS continued

2nd Brigade
Brigadier-General E.S. Bulfin, CVO, CB
2/Royal Sussex Regiment
1/Loyal North Lancashire Regiment
1 /Northamptonshire Regiment
2/King's Royal Rifle Corps

3rd Brigade
Brigadier-General H.J.S. Landon, CB
1/Queen's (Royal West Surrey Regiment)
1/South Wales Borderers
1 /Gloucester Regiment
2/Welch Regiment
'A' Squadron, 15th Hussars
XXV (113th, 114th, 115th Batteries)
XXVI (116th, 117th, 118th Batteries)
XXXIX (46th, 51st, 54th Batteries)
XLIII (30th, 40th, 57th (How) Batteries)
Brigades RFA
26th Heavy Battery, RGA
23rd, 26th Field Companies, RE

5th Brigade
Brigadier-General R.C.B. Haking, CB
2/Oxfordshire & Buckinghamshire Light Infantry
2/Worcester Regiment
2/Highland Light Infantry
2/Connaught Rangers

6th Brigade
Brigadier-General R.H. Davies, CB (NZ Staff Corps)
1/King's (Liverpool Regiment)
2/South Staffordshire Regiment
1/Royal Berkshire Regiment
1/King's Royal Rifle Corps
'B' Squadron, 15th Hussars
XXXIV (22nd, 50th, 70th Batteries)
XXXVI (15th, 48th, 71st Batteries)
XLI (9th, 16th, 17th Batteries)
XLIV (47th, 56th, 60th (Howitzer) Batteries)
Brigades RFA
35th Heavy Battery, RGA
5th, 11th Field Companies RE

II CORPS

GOC: Lieutenant-General Sir J.M. Grierson, KCB, CVO, CMG, ADC-Gen. (died 17 August 1914)
General Sir H.L. Smith-Dorrien, GCB, DSO (assumed command 21 August)
BGGS: Brigadier-General G.T. Forestier-Walker, ADC

3RD DIVISION
Major-General H.I.W. Hamilton, CVO, CB, DSO

7th Brigade
Brigadier-General F.W.N. McCracken, CB, DSO
3/Worcester Regiment
2/South Lancashire Regiment
1/Wiltshire Regiment
2/Royal Irish Rifles

8th Brigade
Brigadier-General B.J.C. Doran
2/Royal Scots
2/Royal Irish Regiment
4/Middlesex Regiment
1/Gordon Highlanders

9th Brigade
Brigadier-General F.C. Shaw, CB
1/Northumberland Fusiliers
4/Royal Fusiliers
1/Lincolnshire Regiment
1/Royal Scots Fusiliers
'C' Squadron, 15th Hussars
XXIII (107th, 108th, 109th Batteries)
XL (6th, 23rd, 49th Batteries)
XLII (29th, 41st, 45th Batteries)
⟨XX (Howitzer) (128th, 129th, 130th (Howitzer)
Batteries) Brigades, RFA
48th Heavy Battery, RGA
56th, 57th Field Companies, RE

5TH DIVISION
Maj.-General Sir C. Fergusson, Bart., CB, MVO, DSO

13th Brigade
Brigadier General G.J. Cuthbert, CB
2/King's Own Scottish Borderers
2/Duke of Wellington's (West Riding Regiment)
1/Queen's Own (Royal West Kent Regiment)
2/King's Own (Yorkshire Light Infantry)

14th Brigade
Brigadier-General S.P. Rolt, CB
2/Suffolk Regiment
1/East Surrey Regiment
1/Duke of Cornwall's Light Infantry
2/Manchester Regiment

15th Brigade
Brigadier-General A.E.W. Count Gleichen, KCVO, CB, CMG, DSO
1 /Norfolk Regiment
1/Bedfordshire Regiment
1/Cheshire Regiment
Dorsetshire Regiment
'A' Squadron, 19th Hussars
XV (11th, 52nd, 80th Batteries)
XXVII (119th, 120th, 121st Batteries)
XXVIII (122nd, 123rd, 124th Batteries)
VIII (Howitzer) (37th, 61st, 65th (Howitzer)
Batteries) Brigades, RGA
108th Heavy Battery, RGA
17th, 59th Field Companies, RE

III CORPS
GOC: Major-General W.P. Pulteney, CB, DSO
BGGS: Brigadier-General J.P. Du Cane, CB

4TH DIVISION
GOC: Major-General T.D'O. Snow, CB

10th Brigade
Brigadier-General J.A.L. Haldane, CB, DSO
1/Royal Warwickshire Regiment
2/Seaforth Highlanders
1/Irish Fusiliers
2/Royal Dublin Fusiliers

12th Brigade
Brigadier-General H.F.M. Wilson, CB
1/King's Own (Royal Lancaster Regiment)
2/Lancashire Fusiliers
2/Royal Inniskilling Fusiliers
2/Essex Regiment
'B' Squadron, 19th Hussars
XIV (39th, 68th, 88th Batteries)
XXIX (1/25th, 126th, 127th Batteries)
XXXII (27th, 134th, 135th Batteries)
XXXVII (Howitzer) (31st, 35th, 55th Howitzer
Batteries) Brigades, RFA
31st Heavy Battery, RGA
7th, 9th Field Companies, RE

11th Brigade
Brigadier-General A.G. Hunter-Weston, CB, DSO
1/Somerset Light Infantry
1/East Lancashire Regiment
1/Hampshire Regiment
1/Rifle Brigade

19th Brigade
Major-General L.G. Drummond, CB, MVO
2/Royal Welch Fusiliers
1/Cameronians
1/Middlesex Regiment
2/Argyll & Sutherland Highlanders

ROYAL FLYING CORPS
Brigadier General Sir D. Henderson, KCB, DSO

2nd Aeroplane Squadron
3rd Aeroplane Squadron
4th Aeroplane Squadron
5th Aeroplane Squadron
1st Aircraft Park

Illustrations

1. Field Marshal Sir John French
(Q28858 Photograph courtesy
of The Imperial War Museum,
London)

2. General Sir Horace Smith-
Dorrien (Q70056 Photograph
courtesy of The Imperial War
Museum, London)

3. General Alexander von Kluck
(Q45327 Photograph courtesy of The
Imperial War Museum, London)

4. Firm friends: Generals Ferdinand Foch
and Henry Wilson

5. Generals Joseph Joffre, Sir Douglas Haig and Ferdinand Foch
(Q951 Photograph courtesy of The Imperial War Museum, London)

6. Army Group Commander Crown
Prince Rupprecht (Q45320 Photograph
courtesy of The Imperial War
Museum, London)

7. General Sir Henry Horne
(Portrait by Sir Oswald Birley
courtesy of Mrs Maive Impey)

8. Lt General Sir Arthur Currie
(CO1539 Photograph courtesy of The
Imperial War Museum, London)

9. Mayor (Bourgmestre) Jean Lescarts
(Courtesy of Mons Tourist Office)

10. The Mons Garde Civique just prior to demobilisation 21.8.1914
(Photograph courtesy of the Mons Musée de Guerre 1914/18 et 1940/45)

11. The 4th Bn Royal Fusiliers resting on arrival in Mons 22.8.1914
(Q70071 Photograph courtesy of The Imperial War Museum, London)

12. A German parade in the Grand-Place
(Photograph courtesy of the Mons Musée de Guerre 1914/18 et 1940/45)

A LA POPULATION
de Mons

Le territoire de notre pays est occupé par des armées étrangères.

Nous devons observer envers les uns et les autres les lois sacrées de l'hospitalité.

La sécurité de la ville et la vie de ses mandataires en répondent.

Que la population garde tout son sang-froid, qu'elle fasse bon accueil à tous, qu'elle prodigue aux victimes de la guerre, quelles qu'elles soient, tout son dévoûment.

Tout acte de malveillance serait une trahison envers la Ville et les membres du Conseil communal.

Mons, le 24 Août 1914.
Le Bourgmestre,
Jean LESCARTS.

Imprimerie Gottigny-Thiemann, Mons.

13. Mayor Jean Lescarts' first Proclamation after the German capture of Mons (Courtesy of the Mons Musée de Guerre 1914/18 et 1940/45)

VILLE DE MONS
INSTRUCTIONS
CONCERNANT
L'Examen des Chevaux

ordonné par l'Arrêté de l'Inspection d'Étape du 19 Décembre 1916, N° 11.

Par ordre de la Kommandanture d'Étape les instructions suivantes sont données :

1) Les chevaux seront présentés à l'examen bien nettoyés, bien ferrés, nus et bridés convenablement par le propriétaire ou un délégué de celui-ci. Au côté droit de la bête, mettre une étiquette signalant le nom du propriétaire et de la commune du domicile. Ensuite, chaque commune devra fournir un écriteau portant le nom de la localité et à placer à l'aile droite de chaque groupe de chevaux.

2) Tous les chevaux, à l'exception des chevaux malades, incapables d'être transportés ou se trouvant en traitement, devront être présentés. Comme preuves pour les chevaux manquant à l'appel, seuls les certificats des vétérinaires traitants, et signalant la maladie de la bête, seront reconnus valables.

3) Les bourgmestres ou leur remplaçant apporteront la liste complète des chevaux, lors de l'examen de ceux-ci.

4) Les vétérinaires belges seront convoqués en temps voulu.

Les examens auront lieu :

a) Le mardi 20 février, à 9 heures du matin (H. A.), à Mons, boulevard Baudouin, pour Mons et les communes de l'étape situées au Nord de la ligne du chemin de fer de Saint-Ghislain-Mons, Mons-Havré, cette dernière localité comprise. Les vétérinaires belges de Mons, Harmignies et St-Symphorien assisteront à l'examen.

b) Le jeudi 22 février, à 9 h. 1/2 du matin, (H. A.) à Harmignies, au croisement de la route vers Givry, pour toutes les communes situées à l'Est de la Chaussée Mons-Maubeuge. Les vétérinaires belges de Mons, Warquignies, St-Symphorien et Givry devront être présents.

c) Le samedi 24 février, à 8 heures 1/2, (H. A.) à Genly (sortie Genly-Ciply), pour toutes les communes situées à l'Ouest de la Chaussée Mons-Maubeuge et au sud de la ligne de chemin de fer St-Ghislain-Mons. Les vétérinaires de Frameries, Pâturages, Givry et Gœgnies-Chaussée seront présents.

d) Le mardi 27 février, à 9 h. 3/4 (H. A.), à Boussu (sortie de la route vers Hornu). Les vétérinaires de Pâturages et Frameries devront y assister.

Mons, le 17 février 1917.

Le Bourgmestre,
Jean LESCARTS.

N° 8. Imprimerie provinciale du Hainaut, Léon LAMBERT, rue de Houdain, 19, Mons.

14. A typical poster of the Occupation Years (Courtesy of the Mons Musée de Guerre 1914/18 et 1940/45)

15. 'The Angel of Mons', painting by Marcel Gillis
(Courtesy of the Mons Musée de Guerre 1914/18 et 1940/45)

16. 'The 5th Lancers re-enter Mons, November 1918', painting by Richard Caton
Woodville (By kind permission of the Queen's Royal Lancers Museum)

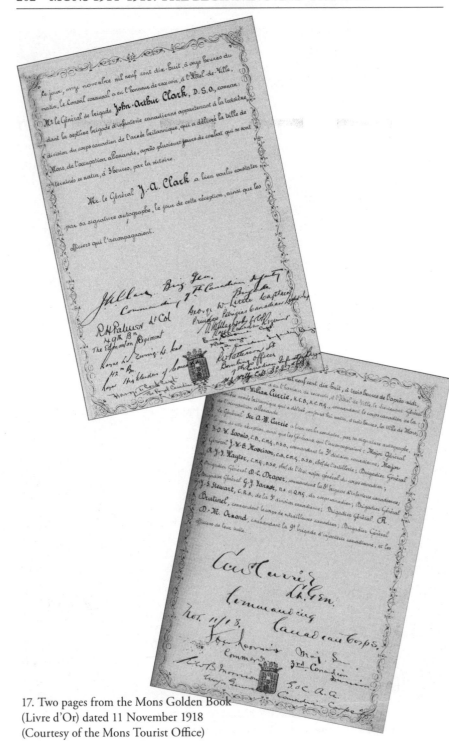

17. Two pages from the Mons Golden Book
(Livre d'Or) dated 11 November 1918
(Courtesy of the Mons Tourist Office)

18. Official entry of Lt General Sir Arthur Currie into Mons, 11 November 1918
(CO3619 Photograph courtesy of the Imperial War Museum, London)

19. General Sir Henry Horne taking the Salute of the 7th Canadian Infantry Brigade at
Mons, 15 November 1918
(CO3672 Photograph courtesy of the Imperial War Museum, London)

20. St Symphorien Military Cemetery
Background: The German Memorial to the 4th 'Royal' Middlesex Regiment
First and last graves:
Private J Parr, first British fatality 21.8.1914
Lieutenant M. Dease, first Victoria Cross winner 23.8.1914
Major W Abell, first British Officer fatality 23.8.1914
2nd Lieutenant H. Holt, first RE Officer fatality 23.8.1914
Private G Price, last Canadian fatality 11.11.1918
Private G Ellison, last British fatality 11.11.1918
(Photographs: Ann Farr)

21. The memorial to the BEF at Mons 1914 and 1918, La Bascule crossroads (inset: inscription on memorial) (Photograph: Ann Farr)

Notes

Chapter I

1. OH 1914, Vol I, Appendix 9.
2. Ibid, pp.56-61.
3. Ibid, pp.29-31. B. Collier, *Brasshat*, pp.162-3.
4. The so-called Curragh Mutiny of 1914 arose from the British government's commitment to grant Home Rule to Ireland. In anticipation that they might be ordered to Ulster to coerce the largely Protestant population of the Province into accepting a united Ireland governed from Dublin, officers of Brigadier General Hubert Gough's Third Cavalry Brigade, and others, notified the War Office that they would resign their commissions rather than obey. They secured a written guarantee from the Secretary of State for War, the Rt Hon Sir John (Jack) Seeley, backed by the Chief of the Imperial General Staff, FM Sir John French, that no such order would be issued. Although this was in fact no more than an affirmation of the government's decision on the issue, Seeley's letter was leaked to the press who made it seem like a government climbdown in the face of army pressure. The government then partly repudiated Seeley's action and he and FM French were forced to resign.
5. W. Reid, *Douglas Haig: Architect of Victory*, p.182
6. Although Haig's criticisms of FM French were largely if not entirely justified, there was a large element of self serving at work too, even if he did not see it that way. Haig unquestionably saw himself as a much more suitable choice for the role of C-in-C BEF and did not scruple in using his access to the King and Prime Minister Asquith to denigrate French and, by implication, boost his own candidacy. Haig had served as French's Chief of Staff in South Africa and his admiration for his boss at that stage appeared uncritical. It was only when French's appointment to command the BEF was confirmed that a degree of hindsight seemed to creep in. On 11 August 1914 he told the King that his doubts about French dated back to South Africa and that he was convinced that French was quite unfit for 'this great command at a time of crisis in our Nation's history'. Over the first year or so of the war French was to offer up plenty of evidence to confirm Haig in his negative opinion of him. The last straw was the handling of the reserves on the first two days of the Battle of Loos in September 1915. Within 3 months French had been recalled and Haig moved up to replace him.
7. R. Holmes, *The Little Field Marshal*, pp.208-9.
8. B. Tuchman, *The Guns of August*, pp.236-40.
9. OH, op.cit.,Appendix 10.
10. J. Terraine, *Mons: the Retreat to Victory*, pp.72-5.
11. J. Terraine, *Douglas Haig: the Educated Soldier*, p.53. Reid, op.cit., pp.159-60.
12. Terraine, *Mons: the Retreat to Victory*, p.73. OH, op.cit., p.66.
13. Ibid, p.73.
14. Ibid, pp.76-7. OH, 1914, op.cit., pp.62-3.

15. Terraine, *Mons: the Retreat to Victory*, pp.82-3.
16. Holmes, op.cit., pp.132-3.
17. Terraine, *Mons: the Retreat to Victory*, pp.83-5.

Chapter II

1 The origin of the word *Borinage* is uncertain. The best guess is that it derives from the German verb *bohren*, which means to bore or to drill. Perhaps appropriate given the main economic activity of the area to which it refers.
2. J. Terraine, *Mons: the Retreat to Victory*, p.86.

Chapter III

1. OH 1914, Vol I, p.68. J. Terraine, *Mons: the Retreat to Victory*, pp.84-5.
2. Terraine, op.cit., pp.88-9.
3. Ibid, p.86.
4. Ibid, p.85. R. Holmes, *The Little Field Marshal*, pp.214-5.
5. Terraine, op.cit., p.88.
6. Holmes, op.cit., pp.216-7.
7. OH, op.cit., pp.68-70.
8. Ibid, pp.72-6.
9. Ibid, p.76.
10. Ibid, pp.73,76.
11. The more or less discredited versions of the circumstances of Private Parr's death have him as being a victim of the early exchanges between the 4th Middlesex in Obourg station and the Germans firing across the canal from Obourg village. These versions have him dying on either 22 or 23 August. Earlier versions of his headstone in Saint Symphorien cemetery had one or other of these dates on it. But his current headstone records his date of death, presumably accurately, as 21 August.
12. OH, op.cit., pp.73-4.
13. Ibid, pp.77,82-5.
14. J. Horsfall and N. Cave, *Mons 1914*, p.60.
15. Ibid. pp.76-7.
16. OH, op.cit., p.85. H. O'Neill, *The Royal Fusiliers in the Great War.* pp.39-40. Horsfall, op.cit., p.75.
17. O'Neill, op.cit., p.40.
18. The numbers of houses destroyed and Belgian civilians shot vary widely in different accounts. Between 30 and 108 houses are claimed to have been destroyed and between 13 and 22 civilians shot. What is undisputable is that a serious and unjustified atrocity befell the people of Nimy. O. Lhoir, *La Vie Quotidienne à Mons durant le Première Guerre Mondiale*, p.3.
19. OH, op.cit., p.85.
20. Horsfall, op.cit., pp.48-9.
21. Ibid, pp.65,80-7.
22. Captain Wright was killed on the Aisne on 14 September, 3 weeks after winning his VC.

Chapter IV

1. J. Horsfall and N. Cave, *Mons 1914*, p.51.
2. OH 1914, Vol I, p.76.
3. Ibid, pp.78-80. Horsfall, op.cit., p.67. Major C. Molony, *Invicta: With the Queen's Own Royal West Kent Regiment in the Great War*, pp.7-11.
4. W. Bloem, *The Advance from Mons 1914*, pp.48-9.
5. Horsfall, op.cit., pp.52-54,91-93. OH, op.cit., pp.80,86-7.
6. Horsfall, op.cit., pp.52-55. OH, op.cit., p.74.
7. Horsfall, op.cit., pp.93-6,103. OH, op.cit., pp.81,87.
8. Horsfall, op.cit., pp 56-7,96-7. OH, op.cit., pp.74-5,90.
9. Horsfall, op.cit., pp.97-8.
10. OH, op.cit., p.87.
11. Ibid, p.90.

Chapter V

1. R. Holmes, *The Little Field Marshal*. p.217.
2. OH 1914, Vol I, pp.91-4.
3. Ibid, p.97. Holmes, op.cit., p.218.
4. B. Collier, *Brasshat*, p.179.
5. OH, op.cit., p.98.
6. Major General C. Simpson, *The History of the Lincolnshire Regiment 1914-1919*, pp.12-14.
7. OH, op.cit., pp.99-100.
8. Ibid, pp.101-7 passim.
9. Ibid, pp.107-112 passim.
10. Ibid, p.112.

Chapter VI

1. R. Holmes, *The Little Field Marshal*. p.218.
2. Ibid, pp.228-9.
3. W. Reid, *Douglas Haig: Architect of Victory*, pp.188-9.
4. Holmes, op.cit., pp.231-5.
5. OH 1914, Vol I, pp.119-20.
6. Ibid, p.122.
7. Ibid, pp.133-4.
8. Ibid, pp.135-6. Reid, op.cit., pp.185-7.
9. OH, op.cit., p.135.
10. I. Cull, *The China Dragon's Tales: the 1st Battalion of the Royal Berkshire Regiment in the Great War*, pp.9-11. OH, op.cit., pp.132-3.
11. OH, op.cit., p.201.
12. Ibid, pp.220-6. There was to be a grim postscript to the gallant sacrifice of 2nd Royal Munster Fusiliers. Six of their number and one 15th Hussar managed to elude capture by the Germans and took cover in nearby woodland. Here they were joined by two Connaught Rangers. Leading a precarious existence in the

woods they made their way south without ever managing to catch up with the retreating BEF. Near the village of Iron, about 5 miles north of Guise, they were spotted by a M. Chalandre, a retired cloth manufacturer. He resolved to help them with the aid of his wife and daughter, Germaine, and a Mme Logez, who ran the local mill and a farm. Over the course of the next 6 months the soldiers were given food and shelter, regularly moving from building to building to avoid detection by the Germans, who were frequent visitors to the village. After two months a further two Connaught Rangers were found and added to the group. Remarkably in such a small community the secret of the group's existence was known to but a few. Unfortunately, an elderly friend of both families involved, feeling himself slighted by them in favour of a younger man in his pursuit of a local girl, betrayed the families and the group to the German commandant at Guise on 22 February 1915. The British soldiers were arrested and brutally manhandled before being taken to Guise. The Chalandres' house was burnt down and all members of the two families were arrested and also taken to Guise where they were all brutally treated, Mme Logez especially so. For good measure the Germans returned to Iron and burnt down her mill. Early on 25 February the 11 British soldiers and M. Chalandre were taken up to Guise fortress, beaten up and shot. After the war the bodies were dug up from their mass grave and reinterred in Guise Communal Cemetery. The suffering of the remaining civilians was more prolonged. Mme Chalandre was sentenced to 4 years imprisonment in Germany; she died there. Daughter Germaine received two years which she survived to return to care for her younger siblings. Mme Logez narrowly escaped the death penalty and was sentenced to 5 years. She served three and a half years in appalling conditions before regaining her freedom at war's end. Her son and daughter also underwent shorter stretches of prison which they survived. (H. Walton, *The Secret of the Mill*. 'The Poppy' (the Newsletter of Thames Valley Branch, Western Front Association), Issue 8, March 2005.)

13. OH, op.cit., pp.228-9.
14. Ibid, pp.231-2,241.
15. Ibid, pp 241-7 passim.
16. Ibid, pp.260-2.
17. Ibid, p.243.
18. Ibid, p.268-72.
19. Ibid, pp.273-83 passim.

Chapter VII

1. OH 1914, Vol I. p.113.
2. Ibid, pp.119-121.
3. Ibid, pp.123-9 passim,136-9 passim.
4. Ibid, p.139.
5. Ibid, pp.140-1. R. Holmes, *The Little Field Marshal*, p.222.
6. OH, op.cit., pp.142-3. C. Calwell, *Field Marshal Sir Henry Wilson: His Life and Diaries*, p.169.
7. OH, op.cit., p.128.

8. Ibid, pp.152-197 passim.
9. Ibid, pp.198-9.

Chapter VIII

1.J. Terraine, *Mons: the Retreat to Victory*, p.142.
2. OH 1914, Vol I, pp.142-3. C. Calwell, *Field Marshal Sir Henry Wilson: His Life and Diaries*, p.169.
3. Terraine, op.cit., p.143.
4. OH, op.cit., pp.191-2.
5. Ibid, p.199. R. Holmes, *The Little Field Marshal*, p.226.
6. Terraine, op.cit., p.154.
7. Holmes, op.cit., p.224.
8. Ibid, pp.224-5. Terraine, op.cit., pp.154-55.
9. Holmes, op.cit., pp.223-4.
10. Ibid, pp.283-4.
11. OH, op.cit., pp.199-200.
12. Ibid, pp.212-5.
13. Ibid. pp.217,230.
14. Ibid, pp.232,242-3.
15. Ibid, pp.255-8. P.Takle, *The Affair at Néry*, pp.31-138 passim.
16. OH, op.cit., p.262.
17. Ibid, p.259-60.
18. Ibid, p.263-4.
19. Ibid, pp.281-4.

Chapter IX

1. Shakespeare, *Henry V*, Act III, Scene I.
2. M. Gilbert, *First World War*, pp.63-4.
3. D. Clarke, *The Angel of Mons*, pp.96-7,247-50.
4. Ibid, pp.62-3.
5. Ibid, pp.160-3. H. Begbie, *On the Side of the Angels*.
6. Ibid, pp.136-9.
7. Joan was canonised in 1920 nearly 500 years after she was burned at the stake in Rouen in 1431 at the age of 19 on charges of witchcraft and heresy.
8. Mons Tourist Office *Battlefield Guide, August 1914*.
9. Clarke, op.cit., pp.41-2.

Chapter X

1. See Appendix B.
2. See Appendix B.
3. OH 1914, Vol I, p.277.
4. P. Warner, *The Battle of Loos*, p.6.
5. G. Sheffield and J.   Bourne, *Douglas Haig: War Diaries and Letters*. pp.86-7.
6. OH 1915, Vol I, p.70.

7. Ibid, p.72.
8. R. Holmes, *The Little Field Marshal*, pp.283-5.
9. OH 1915, Vol II, p.80.
10. Ibid, pp.19-39 passim.
11. Ibid, pp.56-76 passim.
12. J. Terraine, *Douglas Haig: the Educated Soldier*, pp.153-6. Warner, op.cit., pp.6-7.
13. OH 1915, Vol II, pp.148-158.
14. Holmes, op.cit., pp 303-5.
15. B. Liddell Hart, *The Real War*, p.392.
16. OH 1916, Vol I, p.26.
17. Ibid, p.52-3.
18. M. Brown, *Verdun 1916*, pp.43-55 passim.
19. Ibid, pp.63-90 passim, 130. C. Williams, *Pétain*, pp.119-140 passim.
20. Brown, op.cit., pp.127-60 passim.
21. OH 1916, Vol I, pp.46-9.
22. Ibid, p.38.
23. Ibid, p.193, footnote 1.
24. Ibid, pp.251-6.
25. Ibid, pp.288-94.
26. Ibid, pp.483-93.
27. M. Brown, *The Imperial War Museum Book of the Somme*, pp.251-9.

Chapter XI

1. E. Lebas, *Journal de Guerre*, vendredi 21 aôut 1914.
2. *Montois* means a citizen of Mons. (Masculine singular and plural: *Montois*. Feminine singular: *Montoise*. Feminine plural: *Montoises*.)
3. But see Chapter III, Note 18.
4. J. Destrée, *Mons et les Montois*, pp.253-4. O. Lhoir, *La Vie Quotidienne à Mons Durant la Première Guerre Mondiale*, p.3.
5. Congrégation des Filles du Sacré-Coeur de Jésus, *Souvenir du Premier Centenaire de sa Fondation*, pp.88-9.
6. Lhoir, op.cit., p.4.
7. Congrégation des Filles du Sacré-Coeur, op.cit., p.93.
8. Lebas, op.cit.,jeudi 3 septembre 1914. Lhoir, op.cit., pp.43-4.
9. Congrégation des Filles du Sacré-Coeur, op.cit., pp.94-5.
10. Lebas, op.cit.,vendredi 11 septembre 1914. Lhoir, op.cit., p.4.
11. J. Horne and A. Kramer, *German Atrocities 1914: A History of Denial*.
12. Lhoir, op.cit., pp.60-1.
13. Ibid, pp.7-8.
14. Congrégation des Filles du Sacré-Coeur, op.cit., p.134.
15. C. Barnett, *The Swordbearers*, pp.306-7.
16. Lhoir, op.cit., pp.9-11.
17. Congrégation des Filles du Sacré-Coeur, op.cit., p.186.
18. Lhoir, op.cit., p.10.
19. Ibid, p.10.

20. Ibid, pp.11-16.
21. Ibid, pp.18-27.
22. Ibid, pp.52-4.
23. Congrégation des Filles du Sacré-Coeur, op.cit., p.163.
24. Lhoir, op.cit., pp.58-9.
25. Ibid, pp.59-60.
26. Ibid, pp.44-6.
27. Ibid, pp.46-7.
28. Ibid, pp.47-9.
29. Ibid, pp.49-51.
30. Ibid, pp 57-8. Congrégation des Filles du Sacré-Coeur, op.cit., pp.161-2.
31. Lhoir, op.cit., pp.67-8.
32. Ibid, pp.126-31.
33. Ibid, pp.131-2.
34. Ibid, pp.132-5.
35. Congrégation des Filles du Sacré-Coeur, op.cit., pp.132-3.
36. Lhoir, op.cit., p.136.
37. Ibid.
38. Ibid, pp.136-8.
39. Ibid, pp.138-9.
40. Ibid, pp.139-41.
41. Ibid, pp.141-2.
42. Ibid, pp.142-3.
43. Ibid, pp.143-4.

Chapter XII

1. O. Lhoir, *La Vie Quotidienne à Mons durant la Première Guerre Mondiale*, pp.76-9.
2. Ibid, pp.79-83.
3. Ibid, pp.83-4.
4. Ibid, pp.45-6,84.
5. Ibid, p.85.
6. Ibid, p.92
7. Ibid, pp.90-2
8. Ibid, pp.94-5.
9. Ibid, p.96.
10. Ibid, p.93,99.
11. Ibid, p.100.
12. Ibid, pp.108-14 passim.
13. Ibid, pp.101-2.
14. Ibid, p.102.
15. Ibid, pp.118-24.
16. Ibid, pp.163-5.
17. Ibid, pp.166-7.
18. Ibid, pp.167-8.
19. Ibid, pp.168-9.

20. Congrégation des Filles du Sacré-Coeur, p.117.
21. Ibid, p.119.
22. Lhoir, op.cit., p.169.
23. Ibid, pp.169-70,196.
24. Ibid, pp.170-1.
25. Ibid, pp.171-3.
26. Ibid, pp.179-84.
27. Ibid, p.173.
28. Ibid, p.174.
29. Ibid, p.175. Quite contrary to what she would have wished, Nurse Edith Cavell has been accorded almost cult status as a result of the manner and circumstances of her death and her selfless bravery in offering shelter to British and allied soldiers seeking to escape from enemy-occupied territory. Edith Cavell was born in Norfolk in 1865 and she was there on a visit when it became clear that war was imminent. She hastened back to Brussels in anticipation that there would be many wounded to be cared for at the Berkendael Institute which was soon to be taken over by the Red Cross. Nurse Cavell was very quickly providing refuge for fugitive soldiers who, if caught, might well have been shot by the Germans. This consideration was strong enough to overcome any scruples she might have had about abusing her status as a strictly non-partisan member of the Red Cross. She knew that what she was doing was wrong in a legal sense and could have calamitous consequences for her. But her humanitarian impulses were dominant. Leaving aside questions of how she was treated by the Germans and how fair her trial was, she herself had no doubt that she merited the death penalty in German eyes for what she had done. As she was composing herself for execution she said to the Anglican chaplain, who was the last person to see her apart from her executioners, 'Standing as I do in view of God and eternity I realise that patriotism is not enough. I must have no hatred or bitterness towards anyone'. The Germans were astounded at the international outrage which their execution of Nurse Cavell unleashed. It did their cause especial harm in the still neutral United States and probably helped propel that country towards its eventual intervention in the war on the allied side.Even though the allied propogandists would have preferred Nurse Cavell's words quoted above to have been more jingoistic and less measured, her place as a martyr in the allied cause had been firmly established. Soon after the war Nurse Cavell's body was exhumed, repatriated and reinterred in Norfolk. She is memorialised by a statue on Charing Cross Road in London on which her words quoted above are inscribed.
30. Lhoir, op.cit., pp.175-6.
31. Ibid, pp.176-8. J. Destrée, *Mons et les Montois*, pp.261-3.
32. Congrégation des Filles du Sacré-Coeur, p.124
33. Ibid.
34. Ibid, pp.187-192.
35. Ibid, pp.192-5.
36. Ibid, pp.195-6.
37. Ibid, pp.183-4.
38. Lhoir, op.cit., pp.196-7.

Chapter XIII

1. OH 1917, Vol I, pp.55-7.
2. T. Wilson, *The Myriad Faces of War*, pp.439-45 passim.
3. Ibid, pp.450-6 passim.
4. J. Nicholls, *Cheerful Sacrifice*, pp.75-90 passim.
5. OH, op.cit., pp.113-5,364.
6. Ibid, pp.494-506 passim.
7. Ibid, pp.383-98,414-8,423-4,431-3.
8. Wilson, op.cit., pp 462,466,473-80 passim.
9. Ibid, pp.485,489-92.
10. OH 1918 Vol I, pp.51-5.
11. Wilson, op.cit., pp.566-8.
12. OH 1918, Vol II, pp.62-4,67-72 passim.
13. Ibid, p.149.
14. Ibid, pp.164-73 passim.
15. J. Coop, *The Story of the 55th (West Lancashire) Division*.
16. OH 1918, Vol II, pp.172-249 passim.
17. Ibid, pp.257-69 passim.
18. Ibid, pp.323-5,330-9 passim.
19. Ibid, pp.357-63.
20. Ibid, p.413.
21. War Diaries of FM Earl Haig, 18.5.18.
22. OH 1918, Vol III, p.157.
23. General Staff, First Army, *Report on First Army Operations 26 August-11 November 1918*, pp.34-5.

Chapter XIV

1. J. Harris, Amiens to the Armistice, p.59.
2. T. Wilson, The Myriad Faces of War, p.573.
3. Ibid, pp.587-8.
4. Ibid, pp.589-94.
5. G. Nicholson, *Official History of the Canadian Army in the First World War: Canadian Expeditionary Force 1914-1919*, pp.283-4.
6. D. Farr, *The Silent General: Horne of the First Army*, pp.191-2,194-5.
7. Harris, op.cit., pp.119-20.
8. Ibid, pp.121-41 passim.
9. Wilson, op.cit., pp.598-9.
10. Harris, op.cit., pp.141-6.
11. OH 1918, Vol IV, pp.337-8,347,364-6,381-3.
12. Ibid, p.397.
13. Ibid, pp.399-403.
14. Ibid, p.413.
15. General Staff, First Army, *Report on First Army Operations 26 August-11 November 1918*, p.13.
16. Harris, op.cit., pp.170-3.

17. Ibid, pp.174-5.
18. Ibid, pp.175-80.
19. Ibid, pp.182-3.
20. Ibid, pp.187-8.
21. General Staff, First Army, op.cit., pp.18-9.
22. Harris, op.cit., pp.194-7. OH 1918, Vol V, pp.21-9.
23. Harris, op.cit., pp.197-202.
24. Ibid, pp.218-25. OH 1918, Vol V, pp.99-111.
25. OH 1918, Vol V, p.178.
26. Harris, op.cit., pp.237-242. OH 1918, Vol V, pp.224-5.
27. Harris, op.cit., pp.242-4.
28. Ibid. pp.246-52, 261-3.
29. Ibid, pp.273-83. OH 1918, Vol V, pp.463-488 passim.

Chapter XV

1. General Staff, First Army, *Report on First Army Operations 26 August-11 November 1918*. pp.47-50.
2. OH 1918, Vol V, p.294.
3. Ibid, p.330. D. Farr, *The Silent General*, p.231.
4. OH, op.cit., pp.329-34.
5. General Staff, First Army, op.cit., p.52.
6. OH, op.cit., pp.333,343-9.
7. General Staff, First Army, op.cit., p.54.
8. Ibid, pp.55-7.
9. OH, op.cit., p.395.
10. Ibid. p.455. General Staff, First Army, op.cit., p.59.
11. A. McNaughton, *The Capture of Valenciennes: a Study in Coordination*, p.281.
12. Farr, op.cit., p 239.
13. General Staff, First Army, op.cit., pp.61-2.
14. J. Harris, *Amiens to the Armistice*, pp.270-1.
15. General Staff, First Army, op.cit., p.62.
16. Farr, op.cit., p.241.
17. McNaughton.,op.cit., p.293.
18. General Staff, First Army, op.cit., p.65.
19. Ibid, pp.64-5.
20. Ibid, p.65.

Chapter XVI

1. OH 1918, Vol V, p.488
2. General Staff, First Army, *Report on First Army Operations 26 August-11 November 1918*, pp.67-8.
3. OH op.cit., p.488.
4. General Staff, First Army, op.cit., p.68.
5. Ibid, p.69.
6. Ibid, pp.68-9.

7. Ibid, p.70.
8. Ibid, pp.70-1.
9. Sir H. Horne, letter dated 8.11.18.
10. 3rd Canadian Division, *Narrative of Operations 10 October-11 November 1918*, p.8.
11. Ibid, p.9. General Staff, First Army, op.cit., p.71.
12. General Staff, First Army, op.cit., p.72.
13. 3rd Canadian Division, op.cit., pp.9-10.
14. Ibid, p.12.
15. <www.cwgc.org>.
16. O. Lhoir, *La Vie Quotidienne à Mons durant la Première Guerre Mondiale*, pp.198-9.
17. Ibid, p.199.
18. Congrégation des Filles du Sacré-Coeur, Part II, pp.9-14.
19. Ibid, pp.14-19.
20. Pensionnat Saint-Joseph, *Cahiers de Guerre 1914-1919*, 3ème Cahier.
21. 3rd Canadian Division, op.cit., pp.10,14.
22. General Staff, First Army, op.cit., p.73.
23. R. Coombs, *Before Endeavours Fade*, pp.149,151.
24. General Staff, First Army, op.cit., p.74
25. Sir H. Horne, letter dated 11.11.18.

Chapter XVII

1. 3rd Canadian Division, *Narrative of Operations 10 October-11 November 1918*, p.13.
2. Ibid.
3. Congrégation des Filles du Sacré-Coeur, Part II, pp.23-4.
4. T. and V. Holt, *Battlefield Guide: The Western Front – North*, pp.25-29.
5. Ibid, p.32.
6. Ibid, pp.21-5, 31-2. R. Coombs, *Before Endeavours Fade*, pp.148-9.
7. Holt, op.cit., pp.20-2. Coombs, op.cit., p.147.
8. Holt, op.cit., pp.26-9. Coombs, op.cit., p.151.
9. R. Holmes, *The Little Field Marshal*, pp.366-7. J.Bourne, *Who's Who in World War One*, pp.98-9.
10. Bourne, op.cit., p.268. I. Beckett and S. Corvi, *Haig's Generals*, pp.203-4.
11. Bourne, op.cit., p.306. R. Neillands, *The Great War Generals on the Western Front*, pp.62-7.
12. D. Farr, *The Silent General*, pp.265-73.
13. G. Nicholson, *Official History of the Canadian Army in the First World War: Canadian Expeditionary Force 1914-1919*, pp.283-4. Farr, op.cit., pp.268-9.
14. Bourne, op.cit., p.164.
15. Ibid. pp.45,157-8.
16. E. Lebas, *Journal de Guerre*, vendredi 21 août 1914.
17. J. Destrée, *Mons et les Montois*, p.254.
18. Lebas, op.cit., p.405.
19. O. Lhoir, *La Vie Quotidienne à Mons durant la Première Guerre Mondiale*, pp.9, 13, 27 (footnotes), 61 (footnotes), 68, 74, 76 (footnotes), 93, 99 (footnote), 121, 132, 137, 140, 198-9.

20. <www.ars-moriendi.be/masson%20fr.htm>.

Appendix A

1. H. Strachan, *The First World War*, p.1126. B. Tuchman, *The Guns of August*, p.153.
2. T. Anderson (ed), *Chambers Dictionary of World History*, p.740.
3. Literally 'world policy'. In late 19th century Germany it was taken to mean the acquisition of new colonies, a greater German share in international trade and major power status. T. Anderson (ed), op.cit., p.884.
4. Despite his 23 years as French Ambassador in London, Cambon never mastered English sufficiently to be confident of conducting business in that language. As French was the accepted language of international diplomacy he was able to count on British Foreign Secretaries and senior diplomats being fluent in his native language until, that is, the advent of Sir Edward Grey. Although Sir Edward understood French well, he spoke it poorly. The two men eventually worked out a *modus operandi* whereby both spoke their own language during their meetings. They would then exchange their written records of the meetings which invariably proved to be fully accurate. R. Massie, *Dreadnought*, p.589 (footnote).
5. Richard Burdon Haldane was the obvious choice for this mission, being the only British cabinet minister who spoke German. He had studied German philosophy at the Universities of Göttingen and Dresden and acquired an abiding love for Germany which did not however extend to him sympathising with Germany in any of the crises that country fomented during his tenure of office. Even though Haldane's mission was a failure – it is difficult to see how it could ever have succeeded – his country is forever in his debt. He was an outstanding Secretary of State for War. He reformed the army after the fiasco of the South African War, established the General Staff and the Territorial Army and gave his blessing to the military staff talks with France. No less an authority than Field Marshal Earl Haig described Haldane in 1919 as 'the greatest Secretary of State for War England has ever had'.

Appendix B

1. R. Massie, *Dreadnought*, pp.180-5.
2. Ibid, pp.165-7.
3. Ibid, pp.183-5.
4. Ibid, pp.609-25 passim.
5. OH 1914, Vol I, pp.56-61.
6. Massie, op.cit., p.894.
7. B. Tuchman, *The Guns of August*, pp.50-5.
8. OH, op.cit.,Appendix 9.
9. Massie, op.cit., pp.589-93.
10. C. Callwell, *Field Marshal Sir Henry Wilson: His Life and Diaries*, pp.77-80.
11. Tuchman, op.cit., p.68.

12. B. Collier, *Brasshat*, p.111.
13. Tuchman, op.cit., p.69.
14. Massie, op.cit., pp.744-8. Tuchman, op.cit., pp.70-1. Calwell, op.cit., pp.99-101. Collier, op.cit., pp.118-9.

Bibliography

Anderson, T. and Lenman, B. (eds),*Chambers Dictionary of World History*, Edinburgh, Chambers Harrap, 2001.

Ascoli, David, *The Mons Star*, London, Harrap Ltd, 1981.

Banks, Arthur, *A Military Atlas of the First World War*, Barnsley, Leo Cooper, 1997.

Barnett, Corelli, *The Swordbearers: Studies in High Command in the First World War*, Harmondsworth, Penguin Books, 1966.

Beckett, I.F.W. and Corvi, S.J. (eds), *Haig's Generals*, Barnsley, Pen & Sword, 2006.

Begbie, Harold, *On the Side of the Angels: the Story of the Angels at Mons*. London, Hodder & Stoughton, 1915.

Bloem, Walter, *The Advance from Mons 1914*, Solihull, Helion & Company Limited, 2004.

Bourne, Dr. J, *Who's Who in World War One*, London, Routledge, 2001.

Brown, Malcolm, *The Imperial War Museum Book of 1914*, London, Sidgwick & Jackson, 2004.

Brown, Malcolm, *The Imperial War Museum Book of the Somme*, London, Pan Books, 1997.

Brown, Malcolm, *Verdun 1916*, Stroud, Tempus Publishing Ltd, 2000.

Calmes, Christian, *The Making of a Nation from 1815 to the Present Day*, Luxembourg, Imprimerie St Paul S.A, 1989.

Callwell, Major General Sir C.E., *Field Marshal Sir Henry Wilson: His Life and Diaries, Volume I*, New York, Charles Scribner's Sons, 1927.

Campbell, John, *F.E. Smith First Earl of Birkenhead*, London, Pimlico. 1991.

Charteris, Brigadier General J., *At GHQ*, London, Cassell, 1931.

Cherry, N., *Most Unfavourable Ground: The Battle of Loos 1915*, Solihull, Helion & Company Ltd, 2005.

Clarke, David, *The Angel of Mons*, Chichester, John Wiley & Sons Ltd, 2004.

Collier, Basil, *Brasshat: a Biography of Field-Marshal Sir Henry Wilson*, London, Secker & Warburg, 1961.

Congrégation des Filles du Sacré-Coeur de Jésus, *Souvenir du Premier Centenaire de sa Fondation 1814-1914*. manuscript available in University Library, Mons.

Coombs, Rose E.B., *Before Endeavours Fade*, Old Harlow, Battle of Britain International Ltd, 2006.

Coop, Rev. J.O., *The Story of the 55th (West Lancashire) Division*, Liverpool, 'Daily Post' Printers, 1919.

Dancocks, D.G., *Sir Arthur Currie, A Biography*, Toronto, Methuen, 1985.

Destrée, Jules, *Mons et les Montois*, Paris and Brussels, L'Eglantine, 1933.

Edmonds, Brigadier General Sir J.E. (ed), *History of the Great War Based on Official Documents: Military Operations, France and Belgium: 1914*, Vol I: 1915, Vols I and II: 1916, Vol I: 1917, Vol I: 1918, Vols I, II, III, IV and V,

Nashville, Imperial War Museum Dept of Printed Books in association with the Battery Press Inc, 1995.

Evans, R.J.W. (ed), *The Coming of the First World War*, Oxford, Clarendon Press, 1990.

Farr, Don, *The Silent General: Horne of the First Army*, Solihull, Helion & Company Ltd, 2007.

Gavaghan, Michael, *An Illustrated Pocket Guide to Mons 1914*, Leyland, M&L Publications, 1999.

Gavaghan, Michael, *An Illustrated Pocket Guide to the Battle of Le Cateau*, Preston, M&L Publications, 2000.

General Staff, First Army, *Report on First Army Operations, 26 August-11 November 1918*, March 1919, with Horne Private Papers, Dept of Documents, IWM, London.

Gilbert, Martin, *First World War*, London, Weidenfeld and Nicholson, 1994.

Harris, J.P., *Amiens to the Armistice*, London, Brassey's, 1998.

Holmes, Richard, *Fatal Avenue*, London, Jonathan Cape, 1992.

Holmes, Richard, *Riding the Retreat*, London, Jonathan Cape, 1995.

Holmes, Richard, *The Little Field Marshal: A Life of Sir John French*, London, Weidenfeld & Nicolson, 2004.

Holt, Tonie and Valmai, *Major and Mrs Holt's Battlefield Guide: The Western Front – North*, Barnsley, Pen & Sword Military, 2004.

Horne, General Lord (Henry), *Private Papers*, Dept of Documents, Imperial War Museum, London.

Horne, John, and Kramer, Alan, *German Atrocities 1914: a History of Denial*, New Haven CT, Yale University Press, 2004.

Horsfall, Jack and Cave, Nigel, *Mons 1914*, Barnsley, Leo Cooper, 2000.

Howard, Michael, *The Franco-Prussian War*, London, Rupert Hart-Davis, 1960.

Hyatt, A.M.J., *General Sir Arthur Currie*, Toronto, University of Toronto Press, 1987.

Lebas, Emile, *Journal de Guerre*, printed in serial form in the magazine 'Hainaut-Tourisme', issue 317 of December 1999 et seq,

Liddell Hart, B., *The Real War 1914-1918*, London, Faber and Faber, 1930.

Lhoir, Olivier, *La Vie Quotidienne à Mons durant La Première Guerre Mondiale*, Unpublished (typescript available in Univeristy Library, Mons).

Lomas, David, *Mons 1914: the BEF's Tactical Triumph*, London, Osprey, 1997.

Massie, Robert K., *Dreadnought: Britain, Germany and the Coming of the Great War*, London, Jonathan Cape, 1992.

Molony, Major C.V., *'Invicta': With the Queen's Own Royal West Kent Regiment in the Great War*, London, Nisbet & Co Ltd, 1923.

Neillands, Robin, *The Great War Generals on the Western Front 1914-1918*, London, Robinson Publishing, 1999.

Neillands, Robin, *The Old Contemptibles: The British Expeditionary Force, 1914*, London, John Murray, 2005.

Nicholls, Jonathan, *Cheerful Sacrifice: The Battle of Arras 1917*, London, Leo Cooper, 1990.

Nicholson, Colonel G.W.L., *Official History of the Canadian Army in the First World War: Canadian Expeditionary Force 1914-1919*, Ottawa, Queen's Printer, 1962.

O'Neill, H.C., *The Royal Fusiliers in the Great War*, Dallington, East Sussex, London, Heinemann, 1922.

Pakenham, Thomas, *The Boer War*, London, Weidenfeld & Nicolson, 1979.

Pensionnat Saint-Joseph de Givry-lez-Mons, *Cahier de la Guerre 1914-1919*, manuscript available at University Library, Mons.

Piérard, Clovis, *Souvenons-nous!*, Paturages, Ballez-Colmant-Wuillot,1924.

Reid, Walter, *Douglas Haig: Architect of Victory*, Edinburgh, Birlinn Ltd, 2006.

Sheffield, Gary and Bourne, John (eds), *Douglas Haig: War Diaries and Letters 1914-1918*, London, Weidenfeld and Nicholson, 2005.

Simpson, Major General C.R., *The History of the Lincolnshire Regiment 1914-18*, London, The Medici Society, 1931.

Strachan, Hew, *The First World War, Volume I: To Arms*, Oxford, Oxford University Press, 2001.

Takle. Patrick, *The Affair at Néry: 1 September 1914*, Barnsley, Leo Cooper, 2006.

Taylor, A.J.P., *The First World War: An Illustrated History*, Harmondsworth, Penguin Books Ltd, 1966.

Terraine, John, *Douglas Haig: the Educated Soldier*, London, Hutchinson & Company Ltd, 1963.

Terraine, John, *Mons: The Retreat to Victory*, London, Leo Cooper, 1991.

Third Canadian Division, *Narrative of Operations 10.10.-11.11.18*, with Horne Private Papers, Dept of Documents, IWM London.

Trainor, Luke, *The Origins of the First World War*, Auckland, Heinemann Educational Books Ltd, 1973.

Tuchman, Barbara W., *The Guns of August: August 1914*, London, Constable & Co Ltd, 1962.

Warner, Philip, *The Battle of Loos*, Ware, Wordsworth Editions Ltd., 2000.

Wilson, T., *The Myriad Faces of War*, Cambridge, Polity Press, 1986.

Index

A

Aachen 185
Abell, Major William 160
Ablain-St Nazaire 79
Admiralty 183
Agadir 178
Aisne, First Battle of the 74
Aisne, River 46
Aisne, Third Battle of the 126
Alba, Duke of 12
Alberich, Operation 118
Albert-Bapaume road 84
Aldershot Command 8
Allenby, General Sir Edmund 4, 36, 51,
    68, 118, 119
Alsace-Lorraine 171, 184, 185, 186, 187
American Expeditionary Force 122
Amfroipret 49
Angel of Mons 70
Anglo-Japanese Alliance 174
Anglo-Russian Entente 177
Angre 150
Angreau, River 148
Antoing Canal 151
Antwerp 10
Argonne-Meuse Offensive 135
Armentières 77
Armistice, The 130
Armory, Madame 92
Arras 77
Artois 77
Artois, First Battle of 79, 80
Artois, Second Battle of 80
Asquith, Rt Hon Herbert, MP 3, 117
attaque à outrance 186
Aubencheul 138
Aubers Ridge 77
Audenarde 151
Audencourt 52
Audregnies 36
Aulnoy 145
Aulnoy-Le Poirier road 144
Aunelle river 148
Australia 184
Australian/New Zealand Army Units 121,
    128–9, 131, 133–4, 139
    I ANZAC Corps 119

Australian Corps 128–9, 138–9
    1st Australian Division 126, 131
    New Zealand Division 131, 140–1
Austrian Netherlands 12, 169
Austrian ultimatum 180
Austro-German Treaty 171
Avesnes 140

B

Bailleul 126
Baisieux 36, 150
balance of power 173
Ballard, Lt Colonel C 36
Bapaume 84
Bar-le-Duc 83
Baucq, Philippe 111, 112
Baudour 28
Bavai 35
Bavay-Montay road 41
Bazentin Ridge 86
Bazuel 52
Beaurevoir 51
Beaurevoir Line 139
BEF (British Expeditionary Force) 3–9, 13,
    16–19, 32, 34, 35, 38–42, 46–49, 61,
    64, 65, 69, 70, 74–79, 82, 83, 91, 117,
    118, 122, 123, 125, 128, 130–134,
    157–167, 181, 186, 187, 189, 190,
    205, 206, 209
Begbie, Harold 71
Belgian Army 134, 138, 142
Belgian National Day 108
Belgium 3
Bellicourt 134
Bergson, Henri 186
Bergues 44
Berkendael Institute 112
Berlin 92
Bernsdorff, Graf von 154
Bertry 57
Bethmann Hollweg, Chancellor 170
Béthune 75
Betz 47
bilateral military staff talks 177
Binche 6
Bismarck, Chancellor Otto von 115, 170,
    171, 173

Bixschoote   75
Bloem, Captain Walter   29, 208
Boger, Lt Colonel Dudley   112
Bois de Baudour   152
Bois de la Folie   79
Bois d'Havré   20
Bois la Haut   21
Borinage   12, 95, 100
Bosnia and Herzegovina   177
Boulogne   4
Bourlon Wood   122
Boussu   31, 151
Bradbury   67
bread   103
Bridges, Major Tom   8
Brie-Comte-Robert   69
British Army
    Armies:
        First   77–8, 80, 118–9, 122–6,
            130–1, 134–6, 139–40,
            142–4, 146, 148, 151, 157–8,
            163
        Second   77–8, 82, 119, 121,
            125–6, 134, 138–9, 142, 161
        Third   84, 118–9, 121–5, 130,
            132, 134–40, 142–4, 147,
            152
        Fourth   84, 86, 125, 128–31,
            134, 138–40
        Fifth/Reserve   84, 86, 118–9,
            121–2, 124, 128
    Corps
        I   4, 6, 13, 33, 34–5, 38, 39–48,
            54.57, 64–5   77, 151, 161–2
        II   4, 6, 13–26, 27–33, 34–5, 38,
            39, 41–2, 44, 46, 48, 49–61,
            62–9   77
        III   48, 65, 68–9, 129, 138
        IV   75   78, 162
        V   119
        VIII   142–3, 148, 151–2, 157
        IX   138–9
        XV   139, 163
        XVII   136–7, 143–5, 147
        XXII   135, 142–8, 150–2, 157
    Divisions
        1st Cavalry   4, 6, 13, 35–6, 49,
            51, 53, 63
        3rd Cavalry   75
        1st   4, 47
        2nd   4, 41, 47, 80, 163
        3rd   4, 13–26, 33, 35, 49, 51–2,
            55, 57–8, 60, 63,

        4th   48–9, 51, 53, 55–7, 59–61,
            63, 65, 68–9   131–3, 143–5,
            147
        5th   4, 17, 27–33, 35–6, 46, 49,
            51–2, 54–5, 57–8, 60, 62–4,
            68
        7th   75
        11th   137–8, 150, 152
        25th   141
        32nd   140
        35th   139
        36th (Ulster)   84, 139
        40th   124–5
        46th (North Midland)   139
        49th (West Riding)   145, 147
        51st (Highland)   131–2, 143–5
        52nd   152
        55th (West Lancs)   124–5
        56th   137–8, 150, 152
        57th   132–3, 136–7
        61st   145
        62nd   134
        63rd (RN)   150, 152, 156
    Brigades
        1st Cavalry   53–4, 65, 67–8
        2nd Cavalry   36, 53
        3rd Cavalry   46–7, 53–4, 206
        4th Cavalry   31, 53, 67
        5th Cavalry   41, 46–7
        1st Guards   33   44
        4th Guards   41, 47–8
        5th   33, 47
        6th   42, 47
        7th   18   21, 35, 49, 53, 55, 59
        8th   18, 26, 33, 35, 53, 55, 59,
            71
        9th   18, 23, 25–6, 35, 52, 55,
            58–9
        10th   53, 56–7
        11th   53, 56–7, 59, 69
        12th   53, 56
        13th   27, 36, 52, 55, 68
        14th   27, 36, 52
        15th   36, 52
        19th   17, 31–2, 36, 48–9, 53–4,
            57, 60, 64–5, 68
        169th   137
    Battalions/Regiments
        2nd Dragoon Guards (Queen's
            Bays)   67–8
        5th Dragoon Guards   67
        6th Dragoon Guards   31
        Household Cavalry   67
        11th Hussars   66–8

15th Hussars   43–5, 208
18th Hussars   36
19th Hussars   28
9th Lancers   36
16th Lancers   8, 152
4th Royal Irish Dragoon
    Guards   8, 36, 157, 160
5th Royal Irish Lancers   153, 160
Royal Scots Greys   8
2nd Argyll & Sutherland
    Highlanders   32, 54–5, 57–8
1st Bedfordshire Regt   36, 52
1st Black Watch   44–5
1st Cameronians   32
1st Cheshire Regt   36, 38, 52
1st Coldstream Guards   44–5
2nd Coldstream Guards   47–8
3rd Coldstream Guards   41–2, 47
2nd Connaught Rangers   208
1st Dorsetshire Regt   36, 52
1st Duke of Cornwall's Light
    Infantry (DCLI)   30, 52, 54
2nd Duke of Wellington's
    Regt   29, 36, 52
1st East Lancashire Regt   53
1st East Surrey Regt   30, 52, 54
2nd Essex Regt   53
1stGordon Highlanders   18, 21,
    53, 59–61
2nd Grenadier Guards   42, 47,
1st Hampshire Regt   53, 57, 60
7th Highland Light Infantry   152
1st Irish Fusiliers   53, 57
1st Irish Guards   47
1st King's (Liverpool) Regt   48
1st King's Own (Royal Lancaster
    Regt)   53, 56–7, 61
2nd King's Own Scottish Borderers
    (KOSB)   29, 52, 58
2nd King's Own Yorkshire Light
    Infantry (KOYLI)   29, 52,
    54, 58
1st King's Royal Rifle Corps
    (KRRC)   43
2nd Lancashire Fusiliers   53, 56
1st Lincolnshire Regt   18, 23, 25,
    35, 52
2nd Manchester Regt   30, 32, 52,
    55, 57–8
1st Middlesex Regt   32–3, 57–8,
    68
4th Middlesex Regt   18–20, 53,
    160, 207

1st Norfolk Regt   36, 38, 52, 60
1st Northumberland Fusiliers   18,
    25–6, 52
2nd Oxford & Bucks Light
    Infantry   75
1st Rifle Brigade   53
1st Royal Berkshire Regt   43–4
2nd Royal Dublin Fusiliers   53,
    61
4th Royal Fusiliers   18–19, 21,
    52, 160–1
2nd Royal Inniskilling
    Fusiliers   53, 56, 59
2nd Royal Irish Regt   18, 20–1,
    53, 55, 60–1, 160–1
2nd Royal Irish Rifles   21, 53,
    55, 59
2nd Royal Munster Fusiliers   44–
    6, 208–9
2nd Royal Scots   18, 21, 53,
    59–61
1st Royal Scots Fusiliers   18,
    23–4, 52, 58
1st Royal Warwickshire Regt   53,
    56–7, 61
2nd Royal Welch Fusiliers   32
1st Royal West Kent Regt   27–9,
    52, 68
1st Scots Guards   44–5
2nd Seaforth Highlanders   53, 57
4th Seaforth Highlanders   144
1st Somerset Light Infantry   53
2nd South Lancashire Regt   35,
    53
2nd Suffolk Regt   30–1, 52,
    54–5, 57–8
1st Wiltshire Regt   53
2nd Worcestershire Regt   75
3rd Worcestershire Regt   53, 55,
    59
Artillery
    VIII (Howitzer) Brigade   57
    XV Brigade RFA   52
    XXIII Brigade RFA   53, 58–9
    XXVII Brigade RFA   36, 52
    XXVIII Brigade RFA   52
    XXXVII (Howitzer) Brigade
        RFA   57
    XL Brigade RFA   53
    XLI Brigade RFA   47
    9 Battery RFA   47
    17 Battery RFA   47

37 (Howitzer) Battery RFA 52, 57
41 Battery RFA 55
48 (Heavy) Battery RFA 53
60 Battery RFA 42
61 (Howitzer) Battery 58
65 (Howitzer) Battery RFA 53
107 Battery RFA 19
108 (Heavy) Battery RFA, 58
109 Battery RFA 35
118 Battery RFA 44
119 Battery RFA 36, 38, 68
120 Battery RFA 28–9
E Battery RHA 58
I Battery RHA 66, 68
L Battery RHA 36, 58, 65–8
Royal Engineers 19–20
   1st Field Coy 33
   17th Field Coy 29
   56th Field Coy 53
   59th Field Coy 31, 58
British Legion 162
Brittain, RSM Ronald 168
Brussels 7, 10
Buissy Switch 133
Bullecourt 118
Bülow, Chancellor Bernhard von 176
Bülow, General Karl 6
Bureau d'Approvisionnement en Pommes de Terre 103
Burgundy, House of 10
Byng, Captain 23
Byng, General Sir Julian 121, 130, 163

C

Café Rubens 94
Cambon, Ambassador Paul 174
Cambrai 107
Cambrai, Battle of 121
Cambrai-Le Cateau road 52
Campaign of 100 Days 130
Campbell-Bannerman, Sir Henry 187
Campbell, Phyllis 71
Canadian Corps 118, 121-2, 129-33, 135-6, 142-8, 150-2, 156-7, 159, 163
  Divisions
    1st 76 78, 132, 136–8, 163
    2nd 132, 150–3
    3rd 132, 137, 139, 148, 150–3, 159–60
    4th 136–7, 145, 147–8, 150

Brigades
  7th 151, 159
  8th 151
  10th 145–6
  12th 146–7
Battalions
  2nd Canadian Mounted Rifles 151
  5th Canadian Mounted Rifles 151
  Princess Patricia's Canadian Light Infantry 151–2
  Royal Canadian Rifles (RCR) 152–3
  Royal Highlanders of Canada 156
  42nd 152–3
  44th 145
  46th 145
  47th 145
  49th 152
  50th 145
  116th 160
  Artillery 146–7
Canadian government 130
Canal de Condé 27–33
Canal de Condé, see Mons-Condé Canal 12
Canal du Centre 13
Canal du Nord 133
Cantaing Line 137
Capiau, Herman 112
Caporetto 98
Carency 79
Casteaux 8
Catillon 140
cattle 96
Caudry 52
Cavell, Nurse Edith 111, 112, 213
Central Powers 118
Cérizy 46
Chalandre, M 209
Chamberlain, Joseph 173
Champagne 77
Chantilly 82
Chapeau Rouge 44
Charleroi 5, 91
Charles, Major General Reginald 141
Charrier, Major P 44
Charteris, Brigadier General John 71
Château de la Haie 13
Château de la Roche 13
Cheltenham Ladies' College 182

Chemin des Dames   74
Chetwode, Brigadier General Sir Philip   46
Chimay   7
Churchill, Rt Hon Winston   190
Ciply   23, 35
Cockpit of Europe   10
Cojeul, River   132
Comité de Secours et d'Alimentation   104
Committee of Imperial Defence   189
Conference of London   179
Congrégation des Filles du Sacré Coeur de
    Jésus   88, 89, 92, 100, 109, 113, 115,
    154, 211, 212, 213, 216
Congress of Vienna   169
Conservatoire de Musique   87
Courtrai, Battle of   139
CRB (Commission for the Relief of
    Belgium)   104
Crépy-en-Valois   68
Crespin   150
crime   107
Croix Verte   106
Cuesmes   152
Curragh Mutiny   4
Currie, Lt General Sir Arthur   130, 132,
    133, 137, 145, 159, 162, 163, 197, 203
Czar Nicholas of Russia   180

D

Dardanelles   177
Day, Lt AF   23
DCM   38
Dease, Lt Maurice   21, 23, 160
Declerq, Monsieur   94
de Croy, Prince Reginald   112
de Croy, Princess Maria   112
Delcassé, Foreign Minister Théophile   174
Delsaut, Joseph   113
Denain   143
Denmark   170
deportations   98
Deutsches Industrieburos   95
Dinant   5
Dogs   96
Dompierre   41
Douai   107, 142
Doullens   123
Dour   31
Dreadnought, HMS   183
Drocourt-Quéant Switch   119
Dubail, General   189

E

Eastern Front   77
East Prussia   189
Ecaillon, River   143
Ecole Supérieure de la Guerre   186, 188
education   114
élan vital   186
Ellison, Private George   153, 160
Elouges   13, 36
English Channel   3
Entente Cordiale   172, 173, 174, 175, 176,
    177, 183, 187
Epéhy, Battle of   134
Equipes volantes   101
Escaufourt   53
Escaut Canal   144
Escaut (Scheldt), River   137
Esnes   53
Etreux   44
European Union   167
Evening News   71

F

Falkenhayn, General Erich von   82
Famars   144
Fergusson, Major General Sir Charles   17,
    57, 58
Fesmy   44
Festubert, Battle of   79
Fitzpatrick, RQMS TW   21
Flanders   70
Flénu   91
Flers-Courcelette, Battle of   86
Fleurus   12
Foch, General Ferdinand   75, 78, 79, 123,
    125, 128, 134, 155, 162, 186, 188,
    195, 196
Fontaine-au-Pire   49
Fontaine-Notre Dame   137
Forêt de Raismes   143
Fort Douaumont   83
Frameries   25, 33
France   3
Franco-Russian Military Convention   173
francs-tireurs   90
Franz-Ferdinand, Archduke   180
French Army
    Armies
        First   129–30, 134, 138–9
        Fourth   5, 34

Fifth   5–7, 9, 33, 34, 39–40, 46,
    48, 64-5, 74, 163
Sixth   39, 46-8, 65, 74
Ninth   48, 74
Tenth   79, 127
Corps
    Cavalry (Sordet)   56, 59-60
    III   7
    X   7
    XXXIII   79
Divisions
    28th   126
    45th Algerian   78
    84th Territorial   36
    87th Territorial   78
French, FM Sir John   4, 5, 6, 7, 8, 9, 13,
    32, 34, 39, 46, 47, 48, 51, 62, 63, 64,
    65, 69, 75, 77, 79, 80, 81, 161, 162,
    164, 194, 206
French Revolution   12
Fresnes-Rouvroy Line   132
Fricourt   84

G

Galliéni, General Joseph   74
Garde Civique   87
Gendarmerie   96
Genly   35
Georgette, Operation   124
German Army   147, 184
    Armies
        First   5-6, 16, 21, 39, 47-8, 65,
            74, 163-4, 184
        Second   5, 16, 34, 65, 74, 163-4
        Third   9, 34
        Fourth   125
        Fifth   83
        Sixth   125
        Seventh   74
        Seventeenth   123, 133
    Corps
        II   17
        III   17, 28-9
        IV   17, 66
        IX   17, 19, 21, 24
        XII Saxon   9
    Divisions
        4th Cavalry   66-8
        5th   28, 43
        6th   24
        18th   19

    Brigades
        3rd Cavalry   67
        18th (Hussar)   67
    Regiments
        12th Brandenburg
            Grenadiers   28-9
        52nd Infantry   29
        84th Infantry   21
        Uhlans   66

German Crown Prince   83
German Naval Programme   177
Germany   3
Gheluvelt   75
Gheluvelt Plateau   121
Ghent   10
Ghlin bridge   19
Ghlin-Jemappes bridge (Gas Poste)   24
Givenchy   75
Givet   5
Givry-lez-Mons   156
God   71
Godley, Private Sidney   23, 161
Gommecourt   84
Gough, General Sir Hubert   46, 121
Government General   92
GQG (Grand Quartier Général)   5
Grande Honnelle River   150
Grandmaison, Colonel Louis Loyseau
    de   186
Grand Morin, River   48
Great Britain   3
Greenland Hill   132
Grenay   81
Grey, Sir Edward   176
Grierson, Lt General Sir James   4
Guise   46
Guise, Battle of   39

H

Haig, FM Sir Douglas   4, 7, 13, 33, 35, 39,
    40, 41, 42, 43, 44, 46, 48, 52, 63, 64,
    71, 78, 80, 81, 82, 83, 84, 117, 119,
    121, 122, 123, 124, 125, 126, 127,
    128, 129, 130, 131, 134, 138, 140,
    144, 147, 161, 162, 164, 196, 206,
    208, 210, 211, 214, 216, 217
Hainaut   94
Hainaut, Province of   12
Haine, River   31
Haldane, Richard   177
Ham   46

Hamel, Battle of   128
Hamilton, Major General Hubert   17, 51
Hapsburgs   169
Harmignies   18
Harveng   152
Haspres   143
Haucourt   49, 52
Hautrage   31
Havay   152
Hazebrouck   75
Hensies   33
Hindenburg, FM Paul von   92
Hindenburg Line   100, 118, 119, 121,
   134, 139
Hitler, Adolf   167
Holt, Second Lt HW   20, 160
Honnechy   58
Hoover, Herbert   104
Hopkinson, Lieutenant   156
Hornby, Captain CB   8
Horne, General Sir Henry   35, 46, 118,
   125, 130, 131, 132, 134, 135, 136,
   137, 142, 143, 144, 145, 146, 147,
   148, 150, 151, 157, 158, 162, 163,
   197, 203, 211, 214, 216
Hornu   27
horses   96
Houzeau de la Haye, M Jean   106
Hughes, Sir Sam   163
Huguet, Major   188
Huy   5
Hyon   21

I

Inchy   53
Indian Army   76
inter-Allied Conference   82
Inter-Allied Supreme War Council   122
Iron   209
Isvolsky, Alexander   177

J

Jameson Raid   172
Japan   174
Jard canal   147
Jarvis, Lance Corporal Charles   25
Jemappes   12, 24, 91
Jesuits   114
Joan of Arc   72
Joffre   5

Joffre, General Joseph   46, 65, 75, 77, 79,
   80, 117
Juifs, rue des   43

K

Kaiser Friedrich III   171
Kaiserschlacht   123, 128
Kaiser Wilhelm I   171
Kaiser Wilhelm II   82, 171
King Albert I   108, 138, 167, 181
King Edward VII   172
King George V   82
King Leopold II   185
King Leopold III   167
Kitchener, FM Lord   3, 4, 5, 41, 47, 65,
   69, 76, 77, 81, 82, 117
Kluck, General Alexander von   6, 8, 16, 17,
   39, 47, 48, 74, 164, 165, 195
Kohlencentrale   96
Kommandantur   91
Kruger, President   172

L

La Bascule crossroads   18
La Bassée   75
La Bassée Canal   81
La Boiserette   35
La Fère   41
La Ferté Milon   47
La Flandre Liberale   93
Lagnicourt   119
La Goutte de Lait   105
La Libre Belgique   93
La Longueville   34
Landrecies   41
Landrecies-Guise road   44
Langemarck   78
Lanrezac, General Charles   5, 46
Lansdowne, Marquess of   174
La Province   93
La Sablière   51
La Targette   79
La Voie Sacrée   83
le Camp Perdu   151
Le Cateau   4, 51, 53, 54
Le Cateau, Battle of   39, 44, 53-61, 62-4,
   163
Lee Enfield SMLE rifles   8
Legay, Jules   113
Le Havre   4
Le Lumeçon   72

229

Lens (Belgium)   6
Lens (France)   80
Le Plessis-Châtelain   66
Le Quesnoy   140
Lescarts, Mayor (Bourgmestre) Jean   23,
   87, 98, 154, 165
Les Herbières   29
Les Nouvelles de la Région de Mons   94
Le Tronquoy   55
Liège   5, 35
Ligny   53
Lille   75
Limburg   185
Lister, Captain GD   28
Livre d'Or   156
Lloyd-George, Rt Hon David   86, 117,
   122, 162, 178
Lock 3   135
Lock 4   19
Lock 5   19
Lock No 1   24
Lock No 2   24
Lock No 3   27
Lock No 5   32
Lock No 6   19
Logez, Madame   209
Longsart   53
Loomis, Major General F   159
Loos, Battle of   81
Lorraine   77
Loubet, President Emile   174
Louis XIV   12
Louvain Library   90
Low Countries   169
Ludendorff, Quartermaster General
   Erich   92
Luxembourg   170
Lys, River   117

M

Macdonogh, Colonel George   7, 9
Machen, Arthur   71
Magasins Communaux de la Région de
   Mons   105
Maisières   111
Maison du Sacré-Coeur   88
Mametz   84
Mangin, General Charles   127
Marchipont   150
Maresches   145
Mariette   25
Marly   145

Marne, Battle of the   33, 65, 69, 71, 74,
   164, 165
Marne, River   48
Maroilles   41
Maroilles-Locquignol road   43
Marquion Line   135
Marseillaise   109
Mars North, Operation   123
Mars South, Operation   123
Masson, Fulgence   166
Maubeuge   3
Maurois   53
Mazinghien   53
McNaughton, Major General Andrew   146
Meachin, CSM Frank   112
Mercier, Cardinal   100
Messines Ridge   75
Mesvin   23
Mettet   7
Metz   35
Metz-Thionville   184
Meuse, River   5
Michael, Operation   123
Military Censor   70
Moeuvres   135
Moltke, General Helmut von   179
Monash, Lt General Sir John   138
Monchy-le-Preux   132
Mons
   Administration of   87. 89, 91, 98,
      103–5   107, 110, 154, 165–6
   Air raids   92–3, 154
   Angel of   70–3
   Battle of   9, 13–26, 27–33, 160,
      162–3
   Black market in   106–7
   Casteau show trial in   113
   Confiscations in   95–7, 104
   Deportations from   95, 98–102, 166
   Education in   113–4
   Everyday life in   89
   Fines on   93, 98, 166
   French evacuees to   107
   Human shield in   87–8, 165
   Hunger in   97, 103
   Inflation in   97, 104
   Information dissemination in   87,
      93–4, 115, 153
   Liberation of   1, 116, 130, 148–58,
      163
   Occupation of   87–102, 103–27, 165
   Postwar developments involving   167–
      8

Religious observance in   109, 115
Resistance in   92, 95, 107, 213
Retreat from   1, 34–38, 39–48.49–61,
  62–69, 140, 162
Mons Barracks   168
Mons Communal Cemetery   160
Mons Condé Canal   13
Montauban   84
Mont d'Origny   46
Mont Houy   144
Montigny   57
Mont St Quentin   131
Mormal, Forêt de   41
Morocco Crisis of 1905   173
Mot de Soldat   110
Mount Kemmel   124
Mount Panisel   153
Moy   46
mutiny   119

N

N40   18
Namur   5
Nancy   77
Napoleon Bonaparte   12
Napoleon III   170
Nassau, Louis de   12
NATO   167
naval arms race   172
Naval Laws   183
Néry   65, 68
Nesle   46
Netherlands, the   169
Neuville St Vaast   79
New Zealand   184
Niemeyer, Musketeer Oscar   21
Nieuwe Rotterdamsche Courant   94
Nieuwport   119
Nimy   87
Nimy bridge   19
Nivelle, General Robert   83, 117
Nivelle Plan   117
Nivelles   7
North German Confederation   171
Notre Dame de Lorette   79, 80
Nouvelles   21
Noyelles   41
Noyon   63, 65
Noyon-Roye line   65
Noyon Salient   77

O

Obourg   19
Obourg-Mons   19
Occult Review   71
OHL (Oberste Heeresleitung)   63
Oise, River   41
Oisy   44
Oisy-le-Verger   137
Order of the Day   125
Ors   140
Ostend   121
Owen, Captain Wilfred   141
Ozoir-la-Ferrière   69

P

Palluel   133
Palmerston, Lord   169
Paquet, Monsieur   95
Paris   39
Parr, Private John   18, 160
Passchendaele   121
Passchendaele Ridge   121
Paturages   33
Pax Britannica   182
Payne, Corporal   23
Pensionnat Saint-Joseph   156, 216
Pétain, General Philippe   79, 83, 117, 123,
  211
pigeons, homing   89
Pippine, Mademoiselle   111
Plan XVII   3, 4, 5, 6, 7, 162, 185, 186
Poelcapelle-St Julien road   78
poison gas   78
Pommeroeul   27
Pont d'Hautrage   30
Pont Richebe   24, 25
Poppy Fund   162
Portuguese   124
potatoes   103
Pozières Ridge   84
Préseau   145
Price, Private George   157, 160
Prince Albert   172
Princess Victoria   172
prostitution   108
Province of Hainaut   91
Puiseux-en Retz   47
Pulteney, Lieutenant General Sir
  William   48

Q

Quarégnon 91
Quarry Wood 136
Queen Victoria 172
Quiévrain 33, 36

R

Race to the Sea 74
Raillencourt 137
Rawlinson, General Sir Henry 81, 84, 128, 129, 130, 134, 138, 139
Reichstag 183
Reims 77
Reims-Amiens 65
Reims-Amiens line 46
Reinsurance Treaty 171
Reumont 54
RFC (Royal Flying Corps) 7
Rhodes, Cecil 172
Rhonelle, River 144
Riqueval Bridge 139
Robertson, General Sir William ('Wully') 122, 162
Roeux 132
Rond de la Reine 47
Roubaix 142
Rouen 4
Roulers 119
Royal Navy 70
Roye 65
Rozay 48
Rue des Bragnons bridge 19
Rupprecht of Bavaria, Crown Prince General 92, 93, 98, 159, 196

S

Sadowa, Battle of 170
Sains-lès-Marquion 133
Salisbury, Lord 173
Sambre and Oise Canal 140
Sambre, Battle of the 140
Sambre, River 5
Sarajevo 180
Saultain 49
Scarpe, River 131, 143
Scarpe, Second Battle of the 119
Scheldt Line 144
Schleswig-Holstein 170
Schlieffen, FM Graf Alfred von 184

Schlieffen Plan 3, 16, 33, 61, 74, 164, 184, 185, 186
Schwaben Redoubt 84
Sedan 35
Seeley, Rt Hon Sir Jack 206
Seine, River 39
Selle, River 58
Sensée Canal 142
Serbia 179
SHAPE 168
Shell Scandal 82
show trials 111
Simonet, Charles 112
Smith-Dorrien, General Sir Horace 4, 49, 51, 57, 62, 63, 82
Smith, Sergeant 26
Snow, Major General Thomas 68
Soignies 8
Soissons 46
Solesmes 49, 51
Sommaing 143
Somme 82, 83
Somme, Battle of the 82-6
Somme, River 64
Souchez 79
South African War 4
Spanbroekmoelen 126
Spanish Armada 169
Spanish 'flu 156
Spanish Netherlands 10
Spears, Lt Edward 6, 7, 9, 34
Spiennes 10
splendid isolation 172
St Benin 54
St George 70
St Ghislain 27
St Michael 72
St Quentin 46, 63
St Quentin Canal 134
St Saulve 147
St Souplet 54
St. Symphorien Military Cemetery 160
St Vast 68
St Waast 49
Supreme Allied Commander 123

T

Taillefontaine 47
Tamines 90
Terraine, John 12
Tertre 27
The Times 70

Thomas, Corporal E   8
Thuin   91
Thulin   13, 36
Thulin-Pommeroeul bridge   31
Tirpitz, Grand Admiral Alfred von   179
Torhout   119
Tourcoing   142
Tournan-en-Brie   69
Tournoi   91
Transvaal   172
Treaty of Bucharest   179
Treaty of London   170
Treaty of Madrid   175
Treaty of Utrecht   12, 169
Treaty of Versailles   167
Trith   143
Trith-St Leger   143
Troisvilles   52

U

United States   118

V

Valenciennes   16, 17, 32, 122, 140, 143,
    144, 145, 146, 147, 150, 151, 215
Vauban, Marshal   12
Verberie   68
Verdun   77, 83
Victoria Cross   23, 25, 38, 161
Ville-Pommeroeul   91
Villers Bretonneux   126
Villers-Cotterêts   47
Ville-sur-Haine   160
Vimy Ridge   77, 80, 118
Vis-en-Artois   132
Vitry-le-François   71
Vivières   47
Von Bissing   92
Von Rathenau Plan   94

W

Wambaix   49
War Office   3
War of the Spanish Succession   12
Wasmes   29
Wassigny   44
Waudru   10, 113
Weltpolitik   171

Western Front   70, 74, 75, 76, 78, 82, 85,
    86, 117, 118, 122, 123, 124, 125, 126,
    128, 130, 144, 160, 161, 162, 163,
    169, 209, 216
Wilson, General Sir Henry   3, 5, 6, 7, 16,
    51, 52, 62, 63, 122, 162, 188, 189,
    190, 195, 209, 210, 214, 217
wine   98
Winter Defence Line   133
Wittmer, Captain   154
Wright, Captain T   26
Wytschaete   75, 126

Y

Ypres   75, 119
Ypres-Diksmuide Canal   78
Ypres, First Battle of   75
Ypres Salient   75, 79
Ypres, Second Battle of   64

Z

Zeebrugge   121
Zones d'Etape   91, 92, 102, 111